Walker Percy and the Politics of the Wayfarer

Politics, Literature, and Film

Series Editor: Lee Trepanier, Saginaw Valley State University

The Politics, Literature, & Film series is an interdisciplinary examination of the intersection of politics with literature and/or film. The series is receptive to works that use a variety of methodological approaches, focus on any period from antiquity to the present, and situate their analysis in national, comparative, or global contexts. Politics, Literature, & Film seeks to be truly interdisciplinary by including authors from all the social sciences and humanities, such as political science, sociology, psychology, literature, philosophy, history, religious studies, and law. The series is open to both American and non-American literature and film. By putting forth bold and innovative ideas that appeal to a broad range of interests, the series aims to enrich our conversations about literature, film, and their relationship to politics.

Recent Titles

Walker Percy and the Politics of the Wayfarer by Brian A. Smith
Romanticism and Civilization: Love, Marriage and Family in Rousseau's Julie by Mark Kremer
Aldous Huxley: The Political Thought of a Man of Letters by Alessandro Maurini
Sinclair Lewis and American Democracy by Steven Michels
Liberty, Individuality, and Democracy in Jorge Luis Borges by Alejandra M. Salinas

Walker Percy and the Politics of the Wayfarer

Brian A. Smith

LEXINGTON BOOKS

Lanham • Boulder • New York • London

Published by Lexington Books
An imprint of The Rowman & Littlefield Publishing Group, Inc.
4501 Forbes Boulevard, Suite 200, Lanham, Maryland 20706
www.rowman.com

Unit A, Whitacre Mews, 26-34 Stannary Street, London SE11 4AB

British Library Cataloguing in Publication Information Available

Library of Congress Cataloging-in-Publication Data

Library of Congress Control Number: 2017944829

ISBN 978-1-4985-3754-4 (cloth : alk. paper)
ISBN 978-1-4985-3755-1 (electronic)

♾™ The paper used in this publication meets the minimum requirements of American National Standard for Information Sciences—Permanence of Paper for Printed Library Materials, ANSI/NISO Z39.48-1992.

Printed in the United States of America

Dedicated to Nellie E. Murphy

Contents

Acknowledgments

I first read Walker Percy on a friend's suggestion early in graduate school. I think it was the comic depiction of characters lost and wandering through life that charmed me at first. But Percy's explanation of how we've forgotten what it means to be wayfarers and what that means for America drew me in further. Growing up in a suburb of Los Angeles and then moving from Washington, D.C. to New Jersey has a way of sharpening one's sense of how community shapes our lives or doesn't. Many people inspired the ideas behind this book, and more importantly, made being a member of actual communities possible.

Matthew Sitman and Peter Lawler were the first people to encourage me to pursue writing about Percy, and without them, this book never would have come into being. Similarly, I discussed the book as it developed over the years several times with Elizabeth Amato, and our conversations helped me clarify the direction of the project.

I received crucial early support in the form of a summer research grant from the H.B. Earhart Foundation in 2010. This freed me from teaching for a summer to reread all of Percy's work, and allowed me to conceive of this project as something more than a set of interrelated articles.

Although none of them teach Percy, I've been blessed with many different mentors that have shaped my thinking in more ways than I can count. Brendan, Robert, and Stephanie Purdy introduced me to ideas and what an intellectual life could be. A long list of other teachers invited me into conversations in and out of class: Patrick Geary, Dan O'Neill, and Kirstie McClure at UCLA and Richard Boyd, Patrick Deneen, Bruce Douglass, Josh Mitchell, and Elizabeth Stanley at Georgetown deserve special mention.

As this book slowly progressed, many others read and commented on the drafts. Early on, Aimee Barbeau and Elizabeth Mercurio commented on an essay that became part of chapter 1. Three of my students at Montclair State University—Kate Goldner, Jonathan Maiorano, and Candice Maneri—patiently read and critiqued the individual chapters as I drafted them. They also endured countless hours of anecdotes and analogies from his work. My friend Terry McCord edited the whole manuscript, catching dozens of mistakes and lapses in clarity.

I presented chapters from the book many times, and wish to thank audiences at Berry College, Loyola University of New Orleans, Calvin College, the Conference on Faith and History, and the American, New England, Northeastern, and Southern Political Science Associations. I met Rhoda Faust at Loyola when she worked at the Walker Percy Center, and I am very grateful for the use of one of her photographs of Percy on the cover. In additional to the travel funding for these presentations, I also wish to express thanks to Montclair State University that awarded me a sabbatical leave in Fall 2015, during which time I completed the draft manuscript.

At Lexington Books, Joseph Parry showed enthusiastic interest in the project at a very early stage, and was still excited when I finally submitted a proposal. Emily Roderick ably guided me through the submission and permissions process and ensured things went smoothly. I also want to thank the anonymous peer reviewer for his or her comments, which helped clarify and smooth out the rough edges of the book.

My family has provided a place of rest and different kind of inspiration throughout this project. My children Eleanor, Abigail, and Lincoln were all born as I wrote this book, and they gave me reasons to smile every day and press on. Greg Smith, Linda Smith, Kelly Smith, Allen Morgan, Laura Morgan, and Joshua Morgan have supported my work both morally and materially.

My wife Sarah inspired me to keep going when I thought of moving on, patiently listened to all my ideas about Percy, and read the final draft with care—all while finishing her dissertation. She makes our home a place of rest.

This book is dedicated to my grandmother, Nellie Murphy, who taught me how to read.

Key to In-text Citations of Books and Interviews by Walker Percy and William Alexander Percy

LL	*Lanterns on the Levee: Reflections of a Planter's Son*
MG	*The Moviegoer*
LG	*The Last Gentleman*
LR	*Love in the Ruins*
MB	*The Message in the Bottle: How Queer Man Is, How Queer Language Is, and What One Has To Do with the Other*
L	*Lancelot*
SC	*The Second Coming*
LC	*Lost in the Cosmos: The Last Self-Help Book*
CWP	*Conversations with Walker Percy*
TS	*The Thanatos Syndrome*
SSL	*Signposts in a Strange Land*
MCWP	*More Conversations with Walker Percy*

Introduction

On the Importance of Being a Wayfarer

Walker Percy's various writings contain several puzzles: How did his philosophical essays relate to his novels? What did he intend to accomplish with his theory of language? What does it mean for us to be wayfarers, never fully at home? Percy's novels, just as much as his essays, grappled profoundly with themes of Western decadence and decline, the persistence of alienation, the allure of war, and the effects of science on human happiness. These facets of Percy's thought make him a profound and unrecognized resource for those hoping to understand the fault lines in contemporary culture.

Perhaps more than any thinker since Alexis de Tocqueville, Percy investigated the temptation to seek complete solutions to life's persistent dilemmas, and traces the moral, political, and theological consequences of these challenges. This book explores the ways Percy deploys his understanding of the human person as a wayfarer with particular attention to its effects on our understanding of society and politics. His focus on man as a wayfarer both captures the restlessness of the human heart and allows us to comprehend our desire to leave this predicament behind.

The hope for escape comes in many forms, and over the course of his life, Percy explored many of these through a variety of stories and essays that together form a coherent account of how modern Americans so often go wrong in describing our own condition. Our attempts to eliminate alienation—which Percy defined as the simple phenomenon of a person feeling anxious and out of place despite living in circumstances that objectively fulfill all of the bodily and social needs modern science prescribes—stood at the center of his account (*CWP* 27–28). Today's best scientific approaches still cannot easily explain why a person can be well-fed, comfortable, have many friends, a romantic partner, and a good job but still feel unhappy.

Alienation opens a door to understanding this state of affairs in some unlikely ways. The feeling of being anxious and misplaced that is so central to alienation actually fades away in what we normally consider the most unpleasant of situations. A persecuted writer facing down the agents of a repressive regime is as unlikely to be alienated as the soldier in battle. Both these individuals know who they are and where they stand in the world—knowledge that most denizens of today's society do not possess (*SSL* 171). But regardless of our position, we are always to some degree out of place, homeless, and not entirely at peace with ourselves. We never fully adjust to our varied environments and fields of activity. Politically, this is important because we constantly long for an answer or remedy to our distress. Instead of cultivating a range of partially successful bulwarks that simply mitigate the worst aspects of alienation and give us ways of coping with it, man constantly attempts to discover permanent solutions to his feeling of placelessness.

Accepting the 1961 National Book Award for his first major work, *The Moviegoer*, Walker Percy ended his brief remarks of thanks with a comment concerning his intentions in writing the novel, which he compared to the medical discipline of pathology. In his writing, Percy adopted the "posture of the pathologist with his suspicion that something is wrong," and added that

> the pathology in this case has to do with the loss of individuality and the loss of identity at the very time when words like the "dignity of the individual" and "self-realization" are being heard more frequently than ever. . . . In short, the book attempts a modest restatement of the Judeo-Christian notion that man is more than an organism in an environment, more than an integrated personality, more even than a mature and creative individual, as the phrase goes. He is a wayfarer and a pilgrim (*SSL* 246).

All of Percy's novels emphasize these concerns of self-understanding, but in his fictional explorations of these anxieties, he devotes particular attention to this idea that man's confusion about his purpose in living, his alienation from other people and places, and loneliness all find their roots in his nature as a perpetually homeless creature passing through his world. The mingling of philosophy and art here is the key: by shifting between description, argument, and dramatization, Percy hoped to compel his audience to see the alienated human condition for what it is. This revelation might unsettle his readers, a change in perspective that he believed they desperately needed to see their situation anew.

In his essay "Why Are You a Catholic?," Percy reminded his readers that the wayfaring view rests at least in part upon Christian or Jewish faith, but that this faces certain challenges in the present day. He wrote that in "the old Christendom, everyone was a Christian and hardly anyone thought twice about it. But in the present age the survivor of theory and consumption becomes a wayfarer in the desert, like St. Anthony; which is to say, open to signs" (*SSL* 314). Percy feared that with the fading of our religious inheritance and the rise of secular worldviews, we also lost the language and conceptual framework that allowed us to see ourselves as wayfarers and subsequently, to accept our lack of a complete home in this world.[1] As such, Percy has adopted a somewhat ambivalent attitude toward spreading his faith, one grounded in his conviction that something has profoundly changed in our culture: "I do not feel obliged to set forth the particular religious reasons for my choosing among the Jewish-Christian religions. There are times when it is better not to name God. One reason is that most of the denizens of the present age are too intoxicated by the theories and goods of the age to be aware of the catastrophe already upon us" (*SSL* 314). Instead, Percy adopted a somewhat different approach, one that often concealed his faith in favor of depicting men and women in crisis, and then only providing them an ambivalent ending in their stories.

We can understand Percy's arguments without direct reference to religion in part because the signs of our time's anxiety and depression remain all too clear but the conventional remedies seem unattainable. Indeed, the very words that people used to use to grapple with the human condition—words like soul, sin, good, and evil—do not seem to apply in a scientific age (*SSL* 306). Percy took it as axiomatic that with the end of the "old modern age" and the rise of "a post-modern as well as post-Christian age," our ability to explain our condition had virtually disappeared without anyone quite realizing this had come to pass:

> The present age is demented. It is possessed by a sense of dislocation, a loss of personal identity, an alternating sentimentality and rage which, in an individual patient, could be characterized as dementia . . . It is the most scientifically advanced, savage, democratic, inhuman, sentimental, murderous century in human history. (*SSL* 309)

In this condition, Percy believed that arguments directly aiming at persuading people to accept their alienation and embrace a faith that can address it could have little effect. Only an *indirect* approach to the dilemmas of our age might suffice to awaken a wayfaring sensibility once more. Percy suspected that people raised in the wake of this linguistic confusion would not immediately find a way to recognize and understand their predicament. Revealing these ideas to today's society requires something more than visceral than argumentative, and this explains Percy's indirect and multifaceted approach.

Percy rarely proceeded in a manner that directly admitted his own position. Even in those interviews and essays aimed at an explicitly religious audience, Percy only indirectly explored his reasons for becoming and remaining a Catholic.[2] Indeed, in most of his writings, he merely outlined some fundamental elements of the human condition that ought to lead human beings to see themselves in light of either Jewish or Christian belief. Central to this is his depiction of man as a wayfarer between destinations, never truly at home in his world. Percy suggested that this concealed and indirect approach to revealing the fault lines in the modern mind might provide the only path back to consciousness of our condition, lost in the ruins of the older forms of politics, psychology, and faith that linger in our culture. Given his belief that a direct approach to persuasion would bear little fruit (and perhaps just give offense), he consistently developed a minimal picture of the human person based in readily noticeable elements of life—one which any of us might accept, regardless of our political, moral, or theological outlook.

We might liken Percy's conceptual starting point to a state of nature in at least two senses: first, in that he hoped to persuade his readers to accept it on the basis of empirical observation and reasoned deduction from self-evidently human traits. When we deploy "worn out" words that trigger direct associations with beliefs modern people have rejected (think here of "sin" or "evil"), people who might be persuaded to rethink their perspective instead immediately close their minds and hearts. This means that the art of moral and political persuasion must be both indirect and covert. Effective writing only very subtly introduces new or repackaged concepts into our language. Under those conditions, Percy believed that he might have a chance of "sneaking" past our intellectual defenses. Secondly, Percy's account of language bears a direct relationship to the ways thinkers like Hobbes, Locke, and Rousseau framed their own starting points, although Percy's rests upon a much less speculative set of conjectures about human history. In looking to language as the distinctively human capacity—a faculty antecedent to the full use of reason—Percy provided a starting point with which he believed no modern objective-materialist partisan of science could disagree.[3]

Thus, Percy's state of nature begins with a simple anthropology: the human person distinguishes himself not by the use of environmentally conditioned signals, but rather through complex symbols and signs. At a young age, all normally developing human beings discover the capacity to use signs—words—to name objects, people, and even concepts. Percy believed that an outside observer cannot legitimately understand the process to be reducible to environmental stimuli. Moreover, if an observing scientist tried to reduce language in this way, they would have to deny something fundamental about the human condition. In *Lost in the Cosmos*, Percy likened this to the Fall:

> If the sign-user first enters into an Edenic state by virtue of his discovery and constitution of the world by signs, like Helen Keller or any normal two-year-old, and if aboriginal sign-use is a joyful concelebration[4] [*sic*] of the world through an utterance in which the ancient environment of the Cosmos is transformed and beheld in common through the magic prism of the sign, it is also, semiotically speaking, an Eden which harbors its own semiotic snake in the grass. (*LC* 106)

This capacity to encounter and label our reality with words, and the reasoning ability that develops in its wake emerges once early childhood ends and we become truly self-aware.

However, the appearance of language causes a lapse from this Edenic state. The moment the human being breaks into consciousness, confusion and difficulty suddenly reign. For all their utility as referents to *external* realities, symbols fall short when we apply them to our *internal* selves. The "snake" is this: "The fateful flaw of human semiotics is this: that of all the objects in the entire Cosmos which the sign-user can apprehend through the conjoining of signifier and signified (word uttered and thing beheld), there is one which forever escapes his comprehension—and that is the sign-user himself" (*LC* 106). This inability forms one persistent element of our alienation: as powerful as language is, we can never perfectly bridge the gap between our consciousness and that of others.

The world of language we inhabit does not seem to give us words sufficient to explain ourselves, nor can the words that serve as abstractions of reality fully capture that reality in all its particulars. This is one of the root causes of Percy's sense of alienation. On this point, Percy bears some resemblance to Rousseau, who made a similar point in his *Discourse on Inequality*. For Rousseau, the emergence of language serves as the springboard for invidious comparison, competition, and inequality.[5] Percy and Rousseau agree to a great degree that the limitations inherent in our language and consciousness become the first clue that the human being cannot ever fully be at home in their world. But unlike Rousseau, Percy believed that there was no complete remedy to this feeling, social, political, or biological.

Today, people aspire to explain the human condition exclusively through natural science. But this form of explanation requires that we ignore some of the most salient elements of personhood. Percy deployed this as a second clue to our status as wayfarers. He admitted that scientists can describe the biological function of specific organs, but their account of man's evolutionary origins cannot actually serve as a satisfying answer to the simplest of questions: why are we here? Percy's difficulty with the evolutionary biologist's answer to this question is that it is unsatisfying in a way that literally offends the human being's consciousness by claiming it is nothing more than the byproduct of its environment (*LC* 165). The nature of consciousness seems to reach beyond what an explanation from "within" might provide. This not only deprives human life of a sense of mystery, but Percy contended that it also provides too weak an explanation of how language and culture function.

Scientific humanism metaphorically places human beings in an environment the same way it does other creatures, and Percy's point is that this intellectual move only *appears* to dispose of our nagging questions about the meaning of life. Such answers must use the chemical and biological interactions of the physical world to explain the higher functions of language and consciousness. Of course, many people accept such an answer, but science cannot guide us in morality. Moreover, Percy contended that accepting answers like this leaves human beings as unsettled and out of place as ever—such theory cannot aid us in actually living from day to day.

In a 1977 self-interview that originally appeared in *Esquire* magazine, Percy argued caustically that, "life is much too much trouble, far too strange, to arrive at the end of it and then be asked what you make of it and have to answer, 'Scientific humanism.' That won't do. A poor show. Life is a mystery, love is a delight" (*SSL* 416–7). This intuition led Percy to embrace Christian faith, but in his novels and other nonfiction, he usually depicted this "strangeness" of life in a much more ambiguous way, presenting it as a hint at our status as alienated creatures without a home.

Percy led his readers to a third clue that appears amid the sheer unnamable mystery of life: despite our lack of certainty about our origins and the confusions about our purpose this generates, human beings curiously develop persistent intuitions about our moral life, about right and wrong, and an attendant sense that our actions matter.[6] Percy suggested that it is difficult to understand how this could be true of an organism merely responding to an environment. Moreover, he observed there is a deep irony that the scientific humanist frequently and inexplicably is a moralist (*LC* 161–163). Percy never directly invoked the language of natural law, but his novels' protagonists usually talk as if one exists, and feel increasingly alienated from their friends and neighbors who use the language of amoral utilitarianism to justify their conduct.[7]

Another clue might be found in man's persistent restlessness and dissatisfaction with his surroundings. Logically, if human beings merely adapt to their environments, Percy suggested that it would make a great deal more sense if the process of adaptation eventually ended in contentment with objectively pleasant or satisfying surroundings. But this never seems to happen. Indeed, Percy repeatedly returned to the peculiar fact that people often feel happiest in difficult, painful, or otherwise materially "bad" circumstances, and fall into depression amid a life of physical plenty, comfort, and pleasure (*MB* 3–5). The fact that nothing quite seems able to satisfy our longings in this world suggested to Percy that our consciousness cannot be fulfilled by material things any more than it can be mollified by the materialist explanations of our lives I discussed above.

Percy's "clues" ought to trouble us, but he suggested that because of the loss of a coherent theory of the self, people rarely see such challenges as more than temporary distractions. What Percy would consider permanent signs of distress, contemporary Americans often evaluate quite differently. Instead of seeing our alienation as a permanent condition, we tend to view a sense of alienation or anxiety as a symptom to be diagnosed and treated. To the adherent of this viewpoint, any disorder in our psyches, our politics, our religion, and our culture can, in principle, be cured. Percy found this position dangerously incorrect.

Consider the simplest notions of the American Dream: the pursuit of a fine home, a well-paying career, and the accumulation of toys with which to divert our attention in "free" time. While securing these goals may provide comfort, after a certain point, *things* cannot satisfy us. Therapy and anti-depression drugs provide help for some, but seem only to relieve the worst suffering and leave the ordinary malaise of an ordinary afternoon in a place. The partisans of deep community or various political movements offer their members a kind of newfound meaning in life, but these all too often threaten to subsume the individual into the cause or group. A flight into drugs, sex, or other experiments in anesthesia might provide a temporary "cure," but more often leads the participant down a worse path. Against these antidotes, Percy constantly turned to the idea that our efforts to escape our alienation and anxiety are misguided—indeed, doomed to failure—and his attempts to develop a theory of the human person capable of remembering this make his writing uncommonly insightful for understanding contemporary politics and social life.

READING PERCY

Born in 1916 and educated at the University of North Carolina, Chapel Hill and Columbia University, Walker Percy came of age in the Great Depression and narrowly missed both service in World War II and a career in the medical profession. Training as a pathologist in New York City, he contracted tuberculosis in 1942, and turned to great works of philosophy and literature to pass the time during his enforced bed rest.[8] Because Percy inherited enough money to live comfortably without working, his illness provided an opportunity to escape medicine—a profession he joined only out of the urging of his adopted guardian William Alexander Percy ("Uncle Will"). After recovering from his illness, he settled in Louisiana, married, and made his career as a writer. His first major publications were essays, mostly focused on the philosophy of language, but with the publication of *The Moviegoer* in 1961, he achieved commercial success as well as intellectual satisfaction. Eventually moving to Covington, Louisiana, a suburb of New Orleans, Percy lived there until his death in 1990.[9]

Over the course of his career, Percy published six novels, two substantial collections of essays, and a genre-defying "self-help" book combining fiction with the fruits of his inquiry into many scholarly disciplines. The differences between these genres and styles of writing present challenges to any reader attempting to develop a comprehensive understanding of Percy as a thinker. Percy wrote his philosophical essays in the theoretically dense language of existentialism and semiotics, and his early novels in particular are masterpieces of indirectness and comedy. His later novels steadily develop a more direct approach, retaining the comedic tone while adding an increasingly obvious critical edge in relation to American society's political and cultural trends.

Though Percy's tone and approach changed over his career, certain themes recur in his work. Most scholars of literature focus on themes of existentialism, love, Christian faith, and human nature in Percy's writings, and assume a certain degree of unity exists within his work.[10] With a few exceptions, these authors tend to adopt a method which considers each of Percy's novels or a subset of his nonfiction essays in isolation.[11] These books tend to demonstrate the development of themes or ideas within each genre of Percy's writings, and stress the harmonies present among them.

By contrast, other authors argue that Percy's novels and essays contain a radical contradiction and divide. Patricia Lewis Poteat argues that while Percy's essays operate from what she sees as Western philosophy's characteristic pose of objective detachment—which she associates most heavily with Descartes—his novels, by contrast, allow us to see the human condition in its fullness and particularity.[12] This conclusion draws significant inspiration from the work of Hannah Arendt, and I think Poteat errs by over-identifying Percy with the detachment of what she calls "Cartesianism," and misses a good deal of the satirical and rhetorical importance of Percy's nonfiction. Percy himself referred to her argument (and her husband William Poteat's similar claims) as the "Poteat position," and expressed a good deal of impatience with this line of thinking.[13] But the Poteats' example suggests both the difficulty and peril of evaluating Percy's stories and philosophical works together.

My goal differs from most interpretations of Percy's work by scholars of literature or theology. This book uses Percy's essays alongside his novels to explore his distinctive political teaching, with particular focus on man's nature as a wayfarer, and what this means for how we understand ourselves. A few others have attempted to assess Percy's political importance. Most prominently, Peter Augustine Lawler sees Percy's work as an attempt to revitalize Thomism for a jaded world.[14] Only a handful of scholars have made the attempt to grapple with Percy's potential contributions to political philosophy or social theory, much less the lessons his essays might teach to social scientists.[15]

By structuring a reading of Walker Percy's works around the idea of the wayfarer, I demonstrate the ways that an approach to political philosophy incorporating literature can explore not just the broad social consequences of political ideas, but also the psychological and moral effects of different ways humans live and conceive of themselves. Using Percy's stories, editorial essays, and philosophical work together, I draw out various themes that resonate among them, demonstrating how the permanent temptations to escape the life of the wayfarer create recurring perils in social and political life.

The first and perhaps most important of these themes flows from Percy's claim that modern Americans live lives oriented around "theory and consumption" (*SSL* 309–10). Very few of the choices modern Americans make help them navigate around this peril. They often alternate between trying to explain their lives with various kinds of theory and pursuing satisfaction through material goods. Our age's most widely accepted theories of the human person all suggest that a dislocated, alienated person—a person who cannot feel at home even in his or her favorite place—needs some form of adjustment in chemistry or thinking. None of these theories quite knows what to do with the persistence of alienation amid comfort and plenty. No surprise then, that our attitudes toward our material goods and environment so often assume that the right combination of quantity and quality of items naturally equate to the good life. Indeed, Percy at times suggests that the stereotypical capitalist-hedonist antagonist so often portrayed in 1980s and 1990s films potentially faces as great a challenge as the modern rebel who hopes to find happiness in a flight from the world of striving after wealth. Neither theory nor consumption allows us to accept the plight of the wayfarer.

My second theme centers on Percy's account of the ways human beings sometimes attempt to escape from their alienation by turning to various forms of community. Percy helps us understand the persistent appeal of immersing oneself in a community—and the ideologies that so often accompany such unity.[16] He also shows the various ways that the bonds in relation to a place and the social creeds linking people over long periods of time can grow deranged. By doing this, Percy helps us confront the deadliest political projects of the twentieth century and gives insight into the motives of those that perpetuated such evil.[17] He also provides a serious critique of what he sees as the noblest alternative to the life of the wayfarer: the stoical honor culture of his native South. Throughout, Percy's emphasis remains on the ways that we evade our own predicament by over-identifying with a community of belief.

A third recurring theme relates to Percy's explanation for the violence of the twentieth century. Percy devoted considerable attention to the idea that comfort might engender a longing for violent crisis, war, and destruction as a way of escaping alienation. Not only does Percy's analysis provide us with a compelling way of interpreting thinkers like Ernst Jünger, who glorified the "front experience" of World War I, but it also sheds light on why violence in television and film has acquired such popularity.[18] Dangerous circumstances jar alienated men and women out of their anxiety and depression, and for Percy, even the contemplation of this serves as a temporary departure from alienation. This makes violence a particularly appealing form of escape from the ordinary life of the wayfarer and might help us unravel the puzzle of what motivates comfortable, prosperous young men to contemplate engaging in acts of terrorism and war.

A final theme I draw out of Percy's work rests in the permanent possibility of hope. Percy challenged various forms of literary rhetoric and philosophical argument that insist we cannot successfully struggle against our world's most destructive forces. The greatest advantage of seeing human beings as wayfarers rests in the acceptance of one's finitude—that death and corruption come to all of us—but also in a kind of liberation from determinism and rejoicing in the mystery of life. By rejecting objective-materialist approaches to the human sciences, Percy argued that human beings can then turn to new forms of social inquiry that might measure and trace our capacity to affect the world rather than old ones that merely depict an iron cage. Moreover, life as a wayfarer also leads human beings toward seeing the incompleteness of all our remedies to alienation. For Percy, accepting this fact is the first step toward a decent life together in communities.

In addressing these four themes, this book focuses squarely on Percy as a thinker responding to various crises related man's meaning and purpose in contemporary thought. While at times, I reference events in Percy's life, I make no effort to explain his thinking in terms of his biography or through any psychological disposition. I use him to explore some broad trends in twentieth-century thought and history, but usually only where Percy makes implicit or explicit reference to them. In this vein, while I make several comparisons between Percy and other thinkers that I think highlight his contribution, I avoid attempting to trace out specific influences upon Percy's thinking.[19] An extended effort to trace those influences would distract from my attempt to explore the notion of the wayfarer. Moreover, Percy himself made pointed reference to his idiosyncratic use of texts. In interviews and letters, he emphasized the ways he borrowed from other thinkers as a way of sharpening his own insight, and he was very clear that his uses of these ideas and terms bear little resemblance to the way they appeared in their original form. While he drew inspiration and ideas from C.S. Peirce, Søren Kierkegaard, Gabriel Marcel, and many others, Percy's concern remained focused on using them to shape his ideas for maximum effect.[20]

Working with Percy's stories and essays presents one major difficulty of context. In most chapters, providing an extended summary of each relevant novel's plot would distract attention from my main argument. In most cases where I quote dialogue or recall events from Percy's stories, I provide some brief context rather than a full account of the events. This keeps the focus on the overall picture Percy presents us of the human condition.

AN OVERVIEW

I have structured my account of Percy's political philosophy as an encounter with the successive means by which modern people seek to evade their condition as wayfarers. This follows Percy's approach as a critic and cultural pathologist. I divide the book into three parts spread across seven major chapters. Part I, comprising chapters 1 and 2, centers on Percy's diagnosis of today's reigning theories of the self.

Chapter 1 focuses on Percy's sketch of what he terms the "mishmash" theories of life so prevalent in our time. Operating in a diagnostic mode, Percy presented his readers with accounts of many popular ways of viewing human life, including new-age philosophy and spirituality, existentialism, psychotherapy, neuroscience, and others. The difficulty rests in that all of these efforts reflect only a partial truth about our condition. Some aim at depicting human beings as capable of transcending the limitations of our nature through actions of the mind or soul. Others see human beings as animals with pretentions, and seek liberation from the painful aspects of life through medical or chemical adjustment. Despite their radically differing orientations, both aspire to move "beyond" a notion of the self as ultimately misplaced or lost. They assume that by adjusting man's inner life, alienation might disappear, and the social ills they presume to flow from our psychic disorder would depart as well.

Throughout chapter 1, I explore Percy's suspicion that none of these mishmash theorists provide an adequate account of human life, either from the perspective of explaining our condition to ourselves, or, more importantly, for living by that theory's precepts. By tracing the consequences that result from attempting to live in light of these theories, I show how Percy supports his claim that our theories of the self betray radical gaps and incoherencies, especially when scholars attempt to explain human language-use and consciousness. Here Percy showed that while scientists often succeed in reducing human beings into their environment, this cannot truly explain the way human beings use language. By persisting in this method, Percy's "mishmash" theorists not only destroy our ability to see life as an exercise in wayfaring, but worse, some of them encourage an overreliance on science and its methods to create a worldview that encompasses the whole of human life.

I continue this line of reasoning in chapter 2, which explores the social and political consequences of our mishmash theories and the cult of expertise that emerges alongside those ideas. Here I focus on Percy's account of the materialist and objective vision commonly known as scientism and its effects on our self-understanding. Percy believed that alongside a decline in religious faith, modern people have tended to bestow ever greater authority upon scientific and technical experts. He argued that this overreliance on expertise extends into every corner of human life. Yet once we grant experts this kind of authority—once we cede our sense of sovereignty over our lives—the spiritual element of human life faces great challenges and deprivations. Percy believed that as a consequence of this loss of authority, people would start to see their experience through the preformed theories generated by the experts upon whom they rely. The fact that these ways of seeing the world tend to focus on adjusting us to our existence as material beings further increases alienation, and stands as a deep rejection of man's life as a wayfarer.

This overextension of science and its methods and the resulting exclusive focus on material-objective ways of knowing holds profound consequences for politics as well. Objective-material methods of social inquiry aim at comprehending human action through the environments and structures human beings inhabit. The noble aim to predict human action comes here at the cost of seeing human beings as fully conscious, choosing, and reasoning beings. Percy was at least as concerned here with the practical effects of individuals ceding their sovereignty to social scientific experts as he was with the moral and psychological consequences for accepting this state of affairs. If we live in an iron cage, in what sense do one's actions have meaning? Indeed, why act at all? Living in a society designed to adjust us out of our alienation and discomfort, to manage our depression, and ensure we live happy, productive lives, Percy feared our sense of alienation would only grow amid the contrary hopes and dreams our society encourages.

Part II moves away from the intellectual efforts that attempt to abolish the concept of the wayfarer, and turns toward the sorts of communities within which alienated people seek refuge. Chapter 3 begins this account by looking to the status of American community. Percy agreed with many social critics in his emphasis on the way Americans "ricochet around the United States like billiard balls" (*SSL* 5), but his account is more ambiguous than most about the singular virtues of community. All too often, he argued, alienated people seek to renounce their isolation in favor of an idyllic new community life, and find frustration rather than solace. Ironically, Americans often ask far too little of themselves and their communities, radically detaching themselves from the possibility of bonds beyond their family and close circle of friends and co-workers.

Percy suggested that Americans desire perfect places to live, and all too easily lapse into dissatisfaction and disillusionment when their idea of what community might provide does not come to pass. This leaves us with the necessity of seeing ourselves as wayfarers rather than at home in the world the way Rousseau and other apostles of deep community might hope. Percy believed that the increasing standardization of suburbs and decline of regional distinctness—what he termed "losangelization"—would complicate our capacity to return to wayfaring. The hope of mitigating our isolation through the properly moderate form of community remains. By exploring this theme, I show that for Percy, our social bonds can never fully eradicate our alienation. They can, however, attenuate our longings for perfection if we view them rightly as offering wayfarers a temporary place of rest.

The only serious alternative Percy suggested might compete with the notion of the wayfarer can be found in the peculiar beliefs of the American South. When journalists and public intellectuals discuss the South's dominant moral code today, they often focus upon various strains of Evangelical Christianity. Percy argued that was not the case in the 1930s through 1960s—and perhaps it is not as true today as one might think. In chapter 4, I turn my attention to what Percy saw as the dominant strain of aristocratic Southern thinking: a code of stoical honor that stands in uneasy tension with Christian belief. Percy explains the best and worst in this honor code. In this way of living, magnanimity, a decent code of manners, a sense of responsibility, and solicitude toward the weak exist alongside a great capacity for violence, isolated individualism, and refusal to countenance equality. This account of honor bears particular importance for the ways it helps Percy explain the typical white Southerner's reaction to the American Civil Rights Movement, and why Christianity played such a peculiar role in the moral culture of white Southerners. He argued that many of the most moral Southerners held more to a distorted kind of stoicism than they did to any religious creed—think here of Atticus Finch. As such, Christian faith was allowed only so far into the stoic's heart. In place of a humble submission to truth and renunciation of pride, the stoic raises up their own unassailable kingdom of the self.

Percy used the stoical honor code to show the limitations and dangers of honor as a way of binding community, as well. I devote a lengthy section of chapter 4 to his guardian, William Alexander Percy, whose experiences in World War I and after allow us to see an apostle of the stoical creed in full. Reading the younger and elder Percy together, I show that the ultimate danger of this stoic honor rests in its class-based solipsism. The ultimate frame of reference for any such code rests in the community of honor-lovers that enforce its dictates and their own reputations. Offenses to honor are always mediated through the individual honor-lovers' judgment of how the dishonoring affects them. This stands in stark contrast to a theory of justice such as that Percy saw in the Christianity of the Civil Rights Movement. But this problem also suggests a deep flaw at the heart of any effort to escape alienation by rooting oneself in a community of honor-lovers. In a society that for the most part rejects honor as deeply as our own, such communities might only appear through violence and rebellion. This is a particularly important danger for alienated peoples who cannot name their condition.

In chapter 5, therefore, I focus on the interrelationships Percy noted between boredom, violence, and apocalypse, and their role as escapes from our everyday life. Boredom in particular struck Percy as a clue to understanding ourselves as wayfarers. He argued that our dissatisfaction with materially pleasant circumstances such as those enjoyed in American suburbs presents a puzzle to the popular ways of understanding the self and society. Americans constantly fight boredom, he argued, and they do so in part through the covert love of malice, conflict, and violence. Percy explored this phenomenon on several levels, describing our love for these escapes both in fiction and in reality. Percy suspected our imagination may not be so harmless. He claimed that the constant pull of disaster should be a clue that we need to reconsider our relations to one another and to places—that it might lead us back to being wayfarers. These thoughts all too often lead the most fragile human beings into suicide and other acts of destruction.

As a directly political matter, Percy used the desire for violent renewal as way of explaining the terrors of the twentieth century, and he devoted considerable attention to understanding what drove Germany into the hands of the Nazi Party. Mixing revulsion and sympathetic analysis, Percy suggested that a combination of disgust with the bourgeois materialism of the West alongside a desire to escape alienation-created conditions in which that monstrous ideology might flourish. His explanation bears particular importance for us today because of the many ways objective-materialist social science tends to ignore "fuzzy" ideas like alienation as an explanation for this sort of political revolution. He suggested that boredom might lead the young to accept—or aggressively seek—a new order. But these are precisely the sorts of explanations modern social science marginalizes or ignores.

Part III of the book emphasizes Percy's contributions to renewing society. In chapter 6, I turn to Percy's account of how a renewed social science might better address the concerns of human beings understood as wayfarers. Percy argued that the primary difficulty with social science flowed from its unwillingness to abandon the causal assumptions upon which natural and physical science rests. Treating human beings the same way as other animals, as creatures that merely respond to environmental stimuli in the broadest possible sense, defies some of our deepest assumptions about what it means to be human. In particular, social science must take the products of human thought and feeling and reduce them to their imputed causes. This undercuts our ability to understand politics as human beings shape and live it, and also fosters a kind of hopelessness and despair because of the determinism implicit in such analyses.

In place of this, Percy proposed the creation of a social science that takes the products of human language and thought seriously. He would place ontology at the center of any new social science: in the development of a minimum working model of the human person that recognizes the distinctive function of language, and perhaps identifies certain other elements important for the development of an explanatory theory about some aspect of social life. This approach, as I will show, would foster greater descriptive depth and clarity about how and why human beings act, but could not aim at predicting such behavior in advance. This mode of inquiry would refocus attention on choices and attitudes that create habits and character, and show how these serve as more fundamental causes of social trends and events in our world. Abandoning the pursuit of root causes, social science might speak to a wider audience precisely because it would depict human beings acting in recognizable ways. Such an approach might be eclectic, exciting, and ultimately remind human beings of the limitations of grand social theories and orient us away from seeking cures to our alienation. Instead, it might serve as a reminder of the limits of any form of theory to address human needs, and would point us back toward lived experience.

My last major chapter (chapter 7) turns toward the stabilizing elements in human life that Percy emphasized in his novels and essays: family, community, and the church. Despite the real dangers of taking any of these to excess, Percy suggests all three bonds can help mitigate alienation and remind men of their place as wayfarers. In his novels, most of his protagonists ultimately recognize the ways their behavior and thoughts denied or simply ignored that moderation. In this chapter, I show the ways that the ambiguity of Percy's stories underscores his insistence that we have no perfect place of rest. His fictions always remind the reader of the harsh realities of death and loss, but also the promise of love.

Without love, Percy's characters could not bear the more sorrowful aspects of their realities. Percy dismissed the romantic temptation to view family as everything, however, and endorsed Alexis de Tocqueville's suspicion that modern Americans might use their family as a respite from the world, retreating into a cold privatization of life. Thus, Percy insisted that we need political communities and civil society to come alongside the family to help jar us out of our isolation. Percy returned time and again to notions of care and responsibility, placing them alongside humor and irony as central elements of a decent political life. He suggested we ought to see politics as the messy but necessary business of accepting responsibility for our past, present, and future without disregarding human dignity. This acceptance of responsibility also mitigates against man's recurring desire for exit: as uncommitted individuals, we find it easier to entertain fantasies of escape from ordinary life; people rooted in a civic order that offers them a reason for their labors are far less likely to indulge in such flights of fancy.

As alienated creatures lost in a complex world, human beings require multiple places of rest. In homes we achieve relational love and dependence, which remind us that our fantasies of individualism cannot stand. If we join the works of our society, it will give us purpose in return. Yet, interestingly for a committed Catholic, Percy's account of his church is somewhat muted. He focuses attention on the ways that faith completes his characters' varied searches for meaning and truth in life. He also does not hesitate to show all the ways that religious faith can fall prey to extremes that reflect the broken nature of our souls.

Percy sought to understand and explain the deepest dilemmas of modern life. In this book, I sketch his outlook on the human person as a wayfarer and the political outlook this demands. I believe his voice is a valuable one precisely because he defies easy categorization as a political and social thinker, and throughout his career, he drew attention to some of the most vexing difficulties Americans face. As a prophet in reverse, he hoped to mitigate the worst symptoms of our malaise, and unlike so many remained alert to the possibility that we cannot blame the most fundamental elements of our condition on politics or economics or education, but rather on the permanent facts of our existence as wayfarers destined for another home.

NOTES

1. Charles Taylor's *A Secular Age* (Cambridge: Belknap/Harvard, 2007) is perhaps the most synoptic recent work dealing with the nature of secularism in modern times.

2. In Percy's most explicit essay on this point—"Why are You a Catholic?"—he dispensed with any direct apologetics, and after sketching the condition of the age which I quote above, merely affirms his belief in the truth of Christianity before moving onto an account of the present state as he understands it: confusing, deranged, and explicable only through the miraculous, that is, God (*SSL* 304–15).

3. Percy's account of language bears some resemblance to what Augustine describes in the *Confessions*, trans. Henry Chadwick (Oxford: Oxford University Press, 1998), 10–11.

4. A Percy neologism: to celebrate with another.

5. See *Discourse on Arts and Sciences* in Rousseau, *Basic Political Writings*, trans. Donald A. Cress (Indianapolis: Hackett Publishing, 1987), 61.

6. C.S. Lewis's *Abolition of Man* (New York: HarperCollins, 2001) dwells upon this point in terms that resonate with Percy. Also, for a more extended analysis of

these intuitions, see Hadley Arkes, *First Things: An Inquiry Into the First Principles of Morals and Justice* (Princeton: Princeton University Press, 1986), especially 51–84.

7. Consider Ellen Oglethorpe's insistence in *Love in the Ruins* that euthanasia is "not right" without advancing any particular argument to defend this point (158).

8. For an account of Percy's disease and course of sanatorium treatment, see Jay Tolson, *Pilgrim in the Ruins: A Life of Walker Percy* (Chapel Hill: University of North Carolina Press, 1994), 160–183.

9. For a brief but comprehensive treatment of Percy's life, see Ralph C. Wood, "Walker Percy: A Brief Biography," in *A Political Companion to Walker Percy*, eds. Peter Augustine Lawler and Brian A. Smith (Lexington: University Press of Kentucky, 2013), 11–28. I reference three other longer accounts of Percy's life and family in this work: Jay Tolson's *Pilgrim in the Ruins*, cited above; Patrick Samway, S.J., *Walker Percy: A Life* (Chicago: Loyola Press, 1997); and Bertram Wyatt-Brown, *The House of Percy: Honor, Melancholy, and Imagination in a Southern Family* (New York and Oxford: Oxford University Press, 1994). For an illuminating series of interviews with Percy's family and friends, see David Horace Harwell, *Walker Percy Remembered: A Portrait in the Words of Those Who Knew Him* (Chapel Hill: University of North Carolina Press, 2006).

10. For some examples, see Martin Luschei, *The Sovereign Wayfarer: Walker Percy's Diagnosis of the Malaise* (Baton Rouge: Louisiana State University Press, 1972); Jac Tharpe, *Walker Percy* (Boston: Twayne Publishers, 1983); Linda Whitney Hobson, *Understanding Walker Percy* (Columbia: University of South Carolina Press, 1988); Gary M. Ciuba, *Walker Percy: Books of Revelations* (Athens and London: University of Georgia Press, 1991); Edward J. Dupuy, *Autobiography in Walker Percy: Repetition, Recovery, and Redemption* (Baton Rouge: Louisiana State University Press, 1996); and Allen Prigden, *Walker Percy's Sacramental Landscapes: The Search in the Desert* (Selinsgrove: Susquehanna University Press, 2000).

11. Examples of explicitly comparative work utilizing many of Percy's writings include Peter S. Hankins, *The Language of Grace: Flannery O'Connor, Walker Percy, and Iris Murdoch* (New York: Seabury Classics, 2004); Mary K. Sweeny, *Walker Percy and the Postmodern World* (Chicago: Loyola University Press, 1987); and Marion Montgomery, *Eudora Welty & Walker Percy: The Concept of Home in their Lives and Literature* (Jefferson, NC: McFarland & Company, 2004).

12. Patricia Lewis, Poteat, *Walker Percy and the Old Modern Age: Reflections on Language, Argument, and the Telling of Stories* (Baton Rouge: Louisiana State University Press, 1985).

13. William Poteat's essay on this, "Reflections on Walker Percy's Theory of Language: Or, It Is Better to Stay with Hellen Keller at the Well-House in Tuscumbia, Alabama, Than to Venture to Mars and be Devoured by the Ravening Particles," appears in *The Art of Walker Percy: Stratagems for Being*, ed. Panthea Reid Broughton (Baton Rouge: Louisiana State University Press, 1979), 192–218. For brief accounts of Percy's response to the "Poteat position," see Tolson, *Pilgrim in the Ruins*, 459–60 and Samway, *Walker Percy*, 377–8 and 387. A related criticism of Percy's theory of language may be found in Nathan P. Carson, "Walker Percy's 'Theory of Man' and

the Elimination of Virtue" (in *A Political Companion to Walker Percy*, 87–118), which argues that while Percy's novels strongly suggest the importance of virtue and its cultivation, his theory of language rules out the very possibility of virtue. Carson claims that if we take Percy's position to its logical conclusion, we cannot describe our own virtues, and therefore Percy's theory denies the moral category of virtue.

14. On Percy's Thomism, see Peter Augustine Lawler, *Postmodernism Rightly Understood: The Return to Realism in American Thought* (Lanham, MD: Rowman and Littlefield, 1999), 77–81, and *Aliens in America: The Strange Truth about Our Souls* (Wilmington: ISI Books, 2002), esp. 51–74.

15. For the other major accounts of Percy's contributions to understanding politics and society, see the essays in *A Political Companion to Walker Percy*; Elizabeth Amato, "The Pursuit of Happiness in the American Regime," Ph.D. Dissertation, Department of Political Science, Baylor University, 2011; John F. Desmond, *Walker Percy's Search for Community* (Athens and London: University of Georgia Press, 2004); Matthew Sitman and Brian A. Smith, "The Rift in the Modern Mind: Tocqueville and Percy on the Rise of the Cartesian Self," *Perspectives on Political Science*, Vol. 36, No. 1 (Winter 2007), pp. 15–22; and Brian A. Smith, "Losing Sight of Man: Percy and Tocqueville on the Fate of the Human Sciences," *Perspectives on Political Science*, Vol. 40, No. 3 (July–September 2011), 140–46.

16. In some ways, Percy's account here serves as a critique of Rousseau, whose aspiration in various works—especially *The Social Contract* and *Government of Poland*—seems to have revolved around creating a community capable of eliminating alienation entirely.

17. Some scholars compare Percy's work in this respect to that Eric Voegelin. For examples, see Cleanth Brooks, "Walker Percy and Modern Gnosticism," in *Southern Review*, Vol. 13 (1977), 677–87, James V. Schall, S.J., "On Dealing with Man," in *A Political Companion to Walker Percy*, 80–1, Desmond, *Walker Percy's Search for Community*, 88–89, and Ciuba, *Walker Percy: Books of Revelations*, esp. 4–7 and 274–5.

18. See Ernst Jünger, *Storm of Steel*, trans. Michael Hofmann (New York: Penguin, 2004) and chapter 4 of Jeffrey Herf, *Reactionary Modernism: Technology, Culture, and Politics in Weimar and the Third Reich* (Cambridge: Cambridge University Press, 1984), 70–108.

19. Other authors do this admirably, however. For two examples, see Ch. 2 in Luschei, *The Sovereign Wayfarer*, 19–63, and Mary Deems Howland, *The Gift of the Other: Gabriel Marcel's Concept of Intersubjectivity in Walker Percy's Novels* (Pittsburgh: Dusquene University Press, 1990).

20. Relatively late in his life, Percy exchanged a series of letters with Kenneth Laine Ketner primarily focused on the philosophy of Charles Sanders Peirce, and in one of these he referred to himself as a "thief" rather than a student of Peirce, and claimed interest in his philosophy "insofar as I understand his attack on nominalism and his rehabilitation of Scholastic realism." Percy observed that "what would set CSP spinning in his grave is the use I intend to put him to . . . to use CSP as one of the pillars of a Christian apologetic." See letter from Walker Percy to Kenneth Laine Ketner, February 27, 1989, in *A Thief of Peirce: The Letters of Kenneth Laine*

Ketner and Walker Percy, ed. Patrick H. Samway, S.J. (Jackson: University Press of Mississippi, 1995), 130. A second example of Percy's attitude can be found in a 1974 interview with Bradley R. Dewey, where he expressed a similarly cavalier approach to the interpretation of Kierkegaard's writings (*CWP* 110–12).

Part I

DIAGNOSING THE MALAISE

Percy commonly said that he carried the disposition of a pathologist into his work as a writer. Chapters 1 and 2 explore this premise systematically by looking at the varied worldviews Americans commonly accept as remedies for their alienation and the perils of trusting blindly in any one of the numerous authorities competing to guide our lives. The spiritual illnesses that Percy identified all share a central element: the hope for completeness in this life.

"Mishmash theories of the self" in chapter 1 all do this in different ways. Some notions, which I term the "immanent" theories of the self, attempt to explain alienation as a curable symptom of bodily distress. They assume that like all the other animals, human beings have needs that must be fulfilled if we are to find happiness and rest. "Transcendent" theories, on the other hand, aim to help man escape his alienation by rising above their past experiences or moral conflicts. Whether through psychotherapy or new-age philosophy, adherents of this position believe that we can progressively unlock our creative potential to become who we are meant to be. Percy held that both views, and the faith in expertise they generate, require us to abandon moderation.

A wayfarer must look upon therapy or neuroscience or fulfillment-through-consumption as nothing more than distractions from the fundamental truth that no human theory or tool can satisfy our longings for completeness. Indeed, by holding out the possibility of temporal fulfillment, all of them contribute to the unhappy human condition.

Chapter 1

The Mishmash Theory of Man

This chapter sets the foundation for exploring Percy's conception of the wayfarer by beginning where he did: with his diagnosis concerning humanity's sense of self. Throughout his works, Percy evoked human beings' confusion about themselves. Percy put it this way, as rhetorical questions at the outset of his essay, "The Delta Factor":

> Why does man feel so sad in the twentieth century?
>
> Why does man feel so bad in the very age when, more than in any other age, he has succeeded in satisfying his needs and making over the world for his own use?
>
> Why do people often feel bad in good environments and good in bad environments? (*MB* 3–4)

To these opposites, we might add more: we want to be left alone, but desperately need community; we think we desire comfort, but often feel quite ill at ease in the best of material circumstances. For Percy, what made these desires so difficult is that we no longer retain that many useful concepts with which to name our situation. Perhaps because of this deficit, Americans rarely confront our self-contradictions directly.

Human beings possess consciousness, but often deny their capacity to will and choose, along with their moral responsibility for their actions. We believe we have a self that deserves certain protections and rights, but by rooting our explanations for human life in biology, we deny ourselves a theory of the human person adequate enough to justify human dignity (*SSL* 273–4). Modern Americans' most commonly accepted theories of the self cannot do justice to our experience or easily guide us in understanding the place of human beings in the cosmos.

In the past, religious belief often attenuated this confusion, or at least provided a coherent story about the nature of the human person that allowed human beings to recognize their alienation as a natural fact of life. For Percy, any adequate theory of the human person must do this and thus explain our condition as wayfarers. In some ways this is mostly a dilemma of the modern age. Before the emergence of a widely accepted philosophical or scientific materialism, seeing oneself as a wayfarer was a much simpler proposition. But Percy argued that as scientific materialism spread in the twentieth century, even religious people increasingly adopted theories of the self that undermine the wayfaring sensibility. This poses political dangers because a thoroughgoing materialism undermines our ability to state what is uniquely human and defend it.

Percy believed we must recognize the nature of our age in order to begin to see where our self-understanding fails us, and how that failure contributes to our alienation. No available label seemed to fit our time, as we are both "post-modern" and "post-Christian," and "possessed by a sense of dislocation, a loss of personal identity, an alternating sentimentality and rage, which in an individual patient, could be described as dementia" (*SSL* 309). In his understanding, the twentieth century was the "most scientifically advanced, savage, democratic, inhuman, sentimental, murderous century in human history," which he labeled "the age of the theorist-consumer."

This label, "theorist-consumer" deserves some explanation: Percy argued that people often oscillate between the acceptance of relatively one-dimensional theories to explain the world and consuming the many goods and services that our world has to offer. They oscillate because neither is particularly satisfactory for living, but having lost other options, most people keep looking for happiness where they can find it (*SSL* 309–310). The incompleteness of our theorizing and the impossibility of fully satisfying our soul through "consuming" material reality provides clues to how we ought to think instead.

Percy maintained that alienation is simply part of human life. Misguided theorist-consumers tend to forget this reality. Percy lamented the absence of a science with which we might meld these divergent narratives. To diagnose our situation, he analyzed and dramatized how our confusions give birth to increasingly one-sided and partial attempts to define the value of a good human life. His approaches to explaining this differed by genre: in his essays, Percy sketched the logical and moral dilemmas our divergent views create; in the novels, he depicted human beings undone by their embrace of one slapdash position or another. Throughout both, he suggested that the danger our predicament creates remains lost on us and that most Americans retain no language conceptually rich enough to name our alienation and reconcile ourselves to its role in our life.

Without a theory or worldview that places and accepts our alienation as a given, this experience is an initially "unspeakable" phenomenon. Most people stand in this position of deprivation because of our society's largely materialist and utilitarian worldview, and because of the relative failure of religious and philosophical education as a counterweight in our culture. Since they cannot capture the feeling with an adequate label, they also cannot articulate their natural discomfort with it. The alienated layman relies in part on others—artists, philosophers, theologians, and the like—to *name* their condition and articulate aspects of it. Thus, Percy claimed:

> There is a great deal of difference between an alienated commuter riding a train and this same commuter reading a book about an alienated commuter riding a train. . . . The nonreading commuter exists in true alienation, which is unspeakable; the reading commuter rejoices in the speakability of his alienation and in the new triple alliance of himself, the alienated character, and the author. His mood is affirmatory and glad: Yes! that is how it is! (*MB* 83)

The "truly" alienated commuter experiences nameless sufferings and longings. They sense that something is missing from their life but cannot articulate either the experience or the missing element. Having the situation insightfully depicted in a story or an essay serves as a relief, perhaps even a revelation. However, the person who has this momentary experience still faces a challenge. An author that labels a circumstance may not provide a language adequate to the whole of life, and is even less likely to have offered his reader a compelling theory of the self that helps him see alienation as an inescapable part of life. "Yes, that's the way it is!" does not readily yield to, "I'm sorry . . . you can't fix it."

Percy did not deny that traditional theological remedies for alienation remain. The difficulty he noted was that the very words and meanings associated with Jewish and Christian orthodoxy, words that once stirred consciences and moved people to conversion, have lost much of their power to persuade. He argued that "it's almost impossible for a novelist" to talk about important matters directly "because you have to use the standard words like 'God' and 'salvation' and 'baptism,' 'faith,' and the words are pretty well used up" (*CWP* 41). The phrase "used up" here bears some thought: Percy suggested here that in a scientific age, what were once seen as eternal concepts seem not only deprived of relevance to ordinary life, but also deprived of their claim to truth. It is not just old technology that progress undermines, but also the old certitudes of religious language. Percy identified words here that no one but a believer is usually comfortable hearing, to say nothing of their ability to relate them to everyday experience. When the words directly associated with ideas become used up, Percy argued that writers hoping to demonstrate to modern people that their alienation has no cure need to become more indirect and clever than before. A successful approach would expose the failures of the theories of the age to adequately account for our experience. Ideally, it would also show the reader a pathway to rediscovering their status as a wayfarer.

Percy believed that too few avenues remain in our culture that allowed us to simultaneously comprehend both our biological natures and the complexities of our souls. Most approaches emphasize one side of the human person at the expense of the other, he argued, rendering human beings into either angels or beasts and leaving the Aristotelian mean behind. For the inhabitants of "a post-religious age," it is all too easy to think that "the only recourses of the self are self as transcendent and self as immanent" (*LC* 122). The self either transcends the body like an angel, or alternatively, we attempt to explain the self entirely through our immanent experience within our body as if we were an animal. Both of these general modes of thinking omit something about human life. At the same time, the philosophies of immanence and transcendence appeal to a wide audience in contemporary America because each purports to offer us a nontraditional, usually nondogmatic cure for the malaise in which we live. Even when they stem from ancient philosophies like Buddhism, these theories of life seem new to Western audiences. Moreover, these cures claim to allow us an escape from the alienation, depression, and boredom that persists amid material wealth. Percy believed they only offered false hope.

To better see why Percy adopted this view, consider his closest contemporary rival in existentialism. The existentialist reminder that man has no home in this world remains a potent one—but it only moves us partway back to seeing human beings as wayfarers.[1] We can learn something from the existentialists (as Percy did in the sanitorium), but his emphasis on coping with alienation demonstrates some of the limits of their philosophy.[2] As a rebellion against the apparent meaninglessness of so many human projects in the last century and the catalyst for at least part of Percy's own turn to writing, the movement clearly held his attention; as a method of diagnosing and describing human life, Percy embraced many existentialist themes and arguments. Percy interpreted the existentialist as a kind of person whose artistic or philosophical recognition of the piercing truths of life gives him a moment of fullness and joy, followed inevitably by the logical—if demoralizing—question, "what next?" The existentialist view therefore presents profound dangers to those that hold to it.[3] The existentialist obsession with suicide and death may naturally follow from the absence of hope in this philosophy. If life is meaningless, suicide becomes a viable—perhaps even a reasonable—option.[4]

Percy suggested, though, that existentialism provides a useful starting point to guide people back to a reasonable theory of the self because this view at least *names* the maladies of our age, our alienation, confused longings, and despair amid plenty, and calls it absurd.[5]

In *Lost in the Cosmos*, Percy stated that while "[e]xhilaration comes from naming the unnamable and hearing it named," this insight holds the thinker transfixed for a moment and then passes, for "both the artist and the self which receives the sign are back in the same fix or worse—because both have had a taste of transcendence and community," and then lose it as that sense of unity fades (*LC* 121). This is a difficult situation within which to live, and as proof, Percy pointed his readers to the spectacular ways that artists and existentialist dreamers fail. They *need* to name or understand their condition, but rooted as each "naming" and recognition is in each individual's irreducible perspective, the philosophy in itself cannot provide a way out. The paths forward must be found outside the belief: in action, not in thought.

Percy's protagonists face this dilemma constantly, and only survive by moving beyond the existentialist insight to something more: they usually attempt some form of "meaningful" action, and then despair of "making" meaning at all.[6] This stands as a backhanded critique of Victor Frankl and others who embark upon a search without end, or those who within a church tradition do the work of secularization by turning to modern psychology for answers rather than the doctrines of faith.[7] Consider the example of Jack "Binx" Bolling, from *The Moviegoer*. Set in the early 1960s, the novel presents a series of episodes in Binx's life. He is a thirty-year-old Korean War veteran living in New Orleans who feels profound dissatisfaction with his life as a successful stockbroker. He finds everyone and everything essentially meaningless. Binx decides he must embark upon a search for meaning and authentic life. He is joined in his quest by his lifelong friend Kate Cutrer, and together, they navigate their anxieties and inability to find comfort in the kind of life their family and friends expect them to live. Binx provides a concrete example of the sort of person who aims at a complete, transcending solution to his problems.

Having stumbled onto the possibility of his "search," Binx sees the everyday resolution of life's dilemmas—or at least the way Hollywood resolves them—as a form of death:

> The movies are on to the search, but they screw it up. The search always ends in despair. They like to show a fellow coming to himself in a strange place—but what does he do? He takes up with the local librarian, sets about proving to the local children what a nice fellow he is, and settles down with a vengeance. In two weeks time he is so sunk in everydayness that he might just as well be dead. (*MG* 13)

If we take this passage at face value, it seems that human beings are just miserable. With or without the awareness that something is wrong with our lives, we end up in despair. Hollywood does nothing to help this impression. But Binx articulates a greater challenge than a simple critique of the artificial happiness of film. He associates everyday boredom and alienation with conventional American sources of fulfillment. Films end in this despair because they imagine happiness to be bound up entirely with the protagonist adjusting to an environment while fulfilling the usual goals of "self-realization." They secure a job, home, husband or wife, and suddenly the cares of their soul disappear. But life goes on after the credits roll, and this is part of Binx's difficulty: he wants the kind of closure that comes at the end of a film but nevertheless knows something is wrong with finding happiness in this manner and cannot quite capture this with words.

Binx's conviction that everydayness is equivalent to meaninglessness requires a radical response. At the outset of the novel when Binx shares this observation, he desires to transcend everydayness so badly that he fails to see the extreme nature of the existentialist refusal of ordinary life. As a misguided and unselfconscious existentialist for most of the book, Binx consistently fails to see the ways that ordinary relationships might attenuate his despair and reduce his alienation from others. He finds no comfort until the end of the novel, when he accepts marriage, embarks upon a new profession in medical school, and embraces his ties to his extended family and community. Only then does he begin to cope with the fact his alienation would never fully leave him.[8]

Introducing a second character from Percy's novels helps explore other dimensions of this problem. Both the younger and older Will Barrett also faced the same forms of alienation. When introduced in Percy's second novel *The Last Gentleman*, Will is a young man adrift who suffers from a host of psychological difficulties, and like Binx, feels lost in the modern world. This persists, as Will cannot find rest in ordinary life either as a young man or as the fifty-year-old widower he appears as in *The Second Coming*. In both stories, Will begins his journey by being jarred out of his everydayness and casual despair by a seemingly random encounter.

In *The Second Coming*, the older Will Barrett finds himself under rifle fire in his garage. Rather than finding terror in the threat to his life, the moment of hitting the ground and finding himself staring into the eyes of a cat brings him a revelation—human beings are never fully "themselves" and cannot ever be in the way the cat coincides with its own body (*SC* 16). That is to say, human consciousness comes with a near-constant sense of being ill at ease, alleviated only in moments of fullness, where a cat only loses that sense of well-being when he or she experiences pain or fear. Animals are not alienated, and humans only can become like them in moments of immanence, where their bodily life fully coincides with their mental states. For Percy, this fact helped explain the many ways people turn to sex and drugs as escapes; it also provides a clue into the allure of materialist theories of the self.

In relation to politics, Percy used our attempts to eliminate alienation as a way to explain twentieth-century man's periodic love of violence and desire to have a purpose, an enemy.[9] Hiding under cover in his garage and contemplating his situation, Will Barrett

> smiled and nodded: I know why it is better to be shot at on a Sunday afternoon than not be shot at. Because it means maybe there *is* an enemy after all. If there is no enemy, then I am either mad or living in a madhouse.
>
> Peace is only better than war if peace is not hell too. War being hell makes sense. (SC 21)

Percy recognized that some nihilists and existentialists are tempted to violence and especially war as an escape from ordinariness, and that they do so because such momentous events invest day to day activities with vitality and meaning.[10] He suggested that this was particularly true because as deep relational bonds to person and places fade, the need to define ourselves shifts outward—to the need for comrades and enemies. By exploring the various facets of existentialism, Percy attempted to remind his readers that simply living with the belief that existence is both meaningless and absurd often leads to dangerous alternatives: nihilism, suicide, or a restless engagement with projects that we invest with meaning in the world.[11] Existentialism in this sense may not be a stable theory of the self through which to view life, but rather only a path toward death.

Perhaps this realization explains the appeal of spiritual theories and practices that aim at transcending our bodily existence. These neither embrace the detailed dogmas of orthodox religion nor if sincerely held do they require us to concede to existential despair. It might also explain the appeal of psychoanalysis as a way of accommodating oneself to the terrors of existence. Furthermore, our inability to reconcile ourselves to existence through an adequate form of belief might also explain our tendency to medicalize disorders of the soul.

Percy identified several inadequate theories of the self. I categorize them in terms of their relationship to human consciousness: Percy described "transcending" modes as those efforts to escape the flaws of the human condition through an intellectual or spiritual discipline. He contrasted these to "immanent" modes, which attempt to explain the human being's profound difficulties navigating the world through material-objective methods of science, and prescribe cures for these issues through medicine. I discuss the transcending modes first, and then turn to the attempt to place human life in an immanent frame.

THERAPY, SPIRITUALISM, AND THE TRANSCENDING SELF

Percy identifies two major paths transcendence takes: psychoanalysis and various forms of spiritualism. Both recognize the idea of a self, soul, or mind that navigates our world and has the immutable yearning to transcend the body and its ordinary experiences. Percy attempted to show how these two methods fail to generate an adequate account of life as we actually live it, either for the purpose of dealing with crisis, or more importantly, for how one goes about finding a way to live with the boredom of an ordinary Thursday afternoon.

Percy spoke with a certain amount of authority about psychoanalysis on two levels: first, he seriously considered psychiatry as his medical specialization and kept current with both biological and psychoanalytic approaches to the field over the course of his career; and second, his own extensive experience undergoing therapy, which he perceived to be valuable, but ultimately incapable of helping him determine the cause of his anxiety and depression.[12] While Percy noted that therapists widely discarded many of Freud's specific theories as the 1950s wore on, the warring schools of psychology and psychiatry remain extremely popular in America (*SSL* 251).[13]

Percy believed one reason doctrinaire Freudianism failed to take hold lay in Freud's attempt at making his new science an analogue to the physical sciences. The specific problem he observed is that "Freud made a mistake only a twentieth-century professor would have been capable of: trying to explain the human psyche by a mechanical-energy model," a model that forced us to understand hidden "drives" and base "impulses" so mechanistically that only comedy could result (*CWP* 166). This critique may not extend to all post-Freudian approaches, but it does suggest a difficulty with oversimplifying how we understand human motivation. Percy began to convey this at the start of *The Last Gentleman* when he depicts Will Barrett's last session with his longtime therapist, Dr. Gamow. Looking for hidden meanings and little slips of the tongue, Gamow believes he hears anger rather than Barrett's agreeable response to a question:

> "No, it's not bad at all."
> Dr. Gamow pricked up his ears. "Did you say mad?"
> "No, I believe I said bad; it's not bad at all."
> "It seemed to me that at first you said mad."
> "It's possible," said the agreeable patient.
> "I can't help wondering," said Dr. Gamow shyly, "who is mad at who." (*LG* 34)

Having seized upon the idea, Gamow cannot believe Barrett bears no anger toward him. He refuses to believe that Barrett means what he says, and given the tenets of his theory, must explore Barrett's supposed deceptions to find the truth.[14] Obviously, this scene has a comic element and a literal one. Percy never denied that the exploration of hidden meanings may help some individuals, but the practice of psychoanalysis may conceal a deeper difficulty. An integrated personality by definition is one that has accommodated itself to the world, and if we accept the premise that our nature is wayfaring, this cannot ever happen.

After attempting the therapeutic project himself, Percy retained little faith in the psychoanalytic project as usually practiced. The analyst's quest for uncovering the hidden or repressed meanings implicit in a patient's speech reveals something more elusive: the hope that the subject achieves a kind of normal function in their society. Percy pointed us to the banality of the terms that psychoanalysis suggests: we describe an integrated personality or a "functional" life, and indeed, "what most of us seem to be seeking are such familiar goals as maturity, creativity, autonomy, rewarding interpersonal relations, and so forth" (*SSL* 208). These are terms without a moral measure or clear end beyond seeing the means we use to get by in life as ultimately fulfilling ends.

Similarly, the loss of language adequate to describe ourselves as wayfarers makes it difficult to see guilt, anxiety, or depression as anything other than curable medical or psychiatric symptoms (*SSL* 208).[15] Percy drew attention to the notion that even if psychologists can help their patients achieve the ends mentioned above, they also quite often proceed on the assumption that our common alienation, discomfort, and anxiety all stem from some form of psychic *disorder* rather than interpret these conditions as a constituent element of human life. Cure the disease, and the malaise may pass—so the therapist and their patients hope. As a result of such a process, human life might transcend the normal limits our previous psychological dysfunctions impose upon us.

If we expect that psychology can help us cope with ordinary life, this still leaves the problem of how living by its precepts will ready us for disaster and death. In *The Last Gentleman*, Rita Vaught embodies this position by highlighting the ideals of self-actualization and satisfaction. Hoping to persuade the family that her plan to take their dying brother Jamie to New Mexico offers the boy the best possible environment, Rita expressed her "desire for Jamie that he achieve as much self-fulfillment as he can in the little time he has. I desire for him beauty and joy, not death" (*LG* 244). The therapeutic notion seems to focus on man expressing himself in the best possible way, experiencing the greatest quantity of enjoyable things and minimizing the amount of pain in life. But is this a crusade for impossible perfection? Can it ever cope with the ultimate failures of human life—especially death?

Rita refuses to see what her ex-husband Sutter Vaught and the novel's protagonist Will Barrett both do: Jamie refuses to settle for therapeutic fulfillment. He hopes for something more—truth. Sutter assaults her way of life, confessing that the desire to manage one's "self-actualization" proved too much for him (and presumably will fail Jamie, too), for a perfect relationship and a perfectly ordered, prosperous life struck him as "far more demanding than Calvinism" (*LG* 246). Using this story, Percy implied strongly that the desire to be "well-adjusted" is not so much difficult as it is impossible, as the adjustment would presumably have to overcome the human condition itself. By this account, at least Calvinism succeeds where therapy fails precisely because such faith recognizes that Christianity is a religion for failures, not those who aspire to perfect self-creation. Consider the contrast between such faith and what Rita Vaught proposes: her path is that of willful self-creation. If this fails the patient, what then?[16]

Therapeutic analysis aims at helping us master the vicissitudes of our condition, but leaves us helpless against our failures to progress in our adjustment. If a patient cannot "make progress," what does this say about them? One might conclude that their life itself is a failure, and barring a miraculous change in their personality, psychological theory can do little but describe their ongoing dysfunctions. Therapy fails for Percy because it explicitly rejects the notion that we must live with our alienation and the pain it can bring. For this reason, in a lecture on the future of treating mental health disorders, he expressed some deep reservations with the American psychological profession as a whole:

> American psychiatry has almost nothing to say about the great themes that have engaged the existential critics of modern society from Søren Kierkegaard to Gabriel Marcel. The very men whose business is mental health have been silent about the sickness of modern man, his emotional impoverishment, his sense of homelessness in the midst of the very world which he, more than the men of any other time, has made over for his own happiness. (*SSL* 252)

Freud, his followers, and even those that explicitly set out on a different path in therapy all too often fail to account for the most pressing disasters of human life. Percy believed this flowed from their assumption that "existential" concerns are curable symptoms of man's disorder, rather than as more or less permanent aspects of our lives.

This leaves the theory inadequate to the task of living life. In a lecture on psychology, Percy went on to write that the "suspicion is beginning to arise that American psychiatry with its predominantly functional orientation—its root concepts of drives and counterdrives, field forces, cultural criteria—is silent, given its basic concept of man, it is *unable* to take account of the predicament of modern man" (*SSL* 252). Our predicament is at least partially a moral one. Considered as a scientific endeavor that describes emotional needs and drives, psychological theory of this sort cannot provide any clear moral imperatives about how people should live. Percy believed this inability to reckon with the impoverishment of the self should lead us back to the notion of living as wayfarers. However, all too often, Percy thought that those who fail to change their lives in therapy turn to other "transcending" modes of spiritualism rather than accept the permanence of alienation.

Percy recognized his debt to Alexis de Tocqueville in understanding elements of the modern spirit as tied into "pop Cartesianism," and for seeing the ways this would alter our relationship with religious belief. Percy argued that Tocqueville recognized the likely path of this "spiritual" phenomenon when he argued that pantheism would increasingly hold sway in democratic times: obsessed with the ideas of equality and unity, man

> is embarrassed by this primary division of things and seeks to expand and simplify his conception by including God and the universe in one great whole. If one finds a philosophical system which teaches that all things material and immaterial, visible and invisible, which the world contains are only to be considered as the several parts of an immense Being who alone remains eternal in the midst of the continual flux and transformation of all that composes Him, one may be sure that such a system, although it destroys human individuality, or rather just because it destroys it, will have secret charms for men living under democracies.[17]

This remains a compelling depiction of our situation and the reasons why new-age spiritualism and its innumerable imitators retain their appeal.[18] Percy dramatized this sort of belief system in *Love in the Ruins*.

In the wake of her daughter's death, Doris More turns to what her husband Tom More calls "mournful spirituality" (*LR* 66). She read widely, searching for a source of meaning beyond the "loving God" that allowed their daughter to die from a neuroblastoma (*LR* 72). For Tom, Doris's mind "was ruined by books, by books and a heathen Englishman, not by dirty books but by clean books, not by depraved books but by spiritual books" (*LR* 64). The search for "higher" values often leads people into denying their previous beliefs; moreover, Percy suggested that it also leads to hubris. Doris denies that alienation is natural, and in so doing, denies herself a vital defense against nihilist self-creation. Her search leads to what strikes Tom as a peculiar conclusion: "Transcendental religion could rescue Western materialism. How? by making-and-meditation, meditating and making things with one's hands, simple good things like clay pots" (*LR* 67). By pursuing the self through meditation and the expression of one's artistic longings, the self could transcend the limits of ordinary life, it could "find" or "discover" the authentic meaning of its strivings. The fact that this search cost Doris her life in the novel does nothing to diminish the appeal of coping with the human predicament.[19]

Doris's story blends a mix of two phenomena Percy identifies in *Lost in the Cosmos*: Eastern Pantheism and the transcendence of the self through art. He notes that in such beliefs, the "self is identified with God, the God which is everywhere in the world, including one's self, yet behind the illusory appearances of world-signs. Therefore, God is to be found in the true depths of the self" (*LC* 111). But aside from encouraging self-indulgent solipsism, Percy implied that this way of living leaves its adherents claiming they become one with God giving them no real guidance with which might navigate our world. As a result, "[b]oth the world and the self are problematical," and the human person must forever attempt to subsume one into the other (*LC* 111). If for most people what Percy termed the "traditional resources of the self" such as those found in religion and deep cultural traditions "are no longer available," frustrated seekers like Doris who reject religious orthodoxy and refuse to turn to science retain few options but to blend their ideas more or less incoherently together. Often this becomes something like Doris's ideal, mixing artistic expression, consciousness-raising group discussion, and meditation (*LC* 113).

Percy defended the notion that any spiritual or intellectual attempt to transcend the self will result in ultimate disaster. He suggested that the dilemma that follows from any attempt to do so emerges as a byproduct of the more or less catastrophic difficulties we face "reentering" that ordinary life. Psychoanalysis aims at explaining our malformed longings and then hopes to transmute them through discussion, leaving us an integrated whole amid a community of "normal" selves. Pantheistic transcendence grants life a kind of meaning only by unifying it with the world as whole, but this comes at the cost of losing any perspective from which we might see the human person as a distinctive kind of creature. The temporary relief these philosophies provide by seeming to name and label our condition fades as a direct result of their inability to accommodate our persistent alienation. As such, neither of these presents a satisfying account of life. The progress of science suggests a different approach, however. Percy argued that even more than transcendence, this path proves the most alluring to modern peoples.

LIFE AS IMMANENT: BEHAVIORISM AND ITS SUCCESSORS

In their focus on exploring the objective-material basis on which human life operates, efforts to explain human behavior through rigorous scientific inquiry bear some kinship with the goals of Freudian psychology and the other efforts I describe above. These methods all share the desire to define and shape human life through kinds of special or technical knowledge. Modern science departs from psychoanalytic practice and more philosophical or spiritual efforts in its focus upon tracing and predicting material relationships. While materialist in its method and thereby seeing all life in an immanent frame, this practice of knowing also sometimes allows its adherents a kind of escape from ordinary life. After all, the world and work of pure science can be absorbing and diverting.

Percy argued that genuine science can open the path to a life of excitement and intellectual depth open to no layman. This allows a few members of the knowing elect to "orbit" the rest of us in the ordinary world for a time. Perhaps real greatness as a scientist requires a level of "absentmindedness" or distance from others; nevertheless, Percy suggested that for most who attempt this path, "reentering" the ordinary world poses severe difficulties. The tragicomic antics of Tom More in *Love in the Ruins* allow us to explore one way Percy thinks a scientist abstracted from ordinary concerns can fail to live well in the world.

The novel's central events are triggered by government interest in More's invention: the "ontological lapsometer," a device that can measure the correlations between a person's neuro-chemical makeup and their emotional state. Over the course of the novel, More learns how to use his device to treat people as well, and really believes that his invention "could save the world or destroy it" (*LR* 7). More's opinion is that salvation might come from using the lapsometer to diagnose the source of man's malaise; national destruction might flow from the ways the device can push individuals toward murderous extremes. Ultimately, More's dreams lead him to disaster. While paying lip service to the quaint idea of human dignity and the idea of a soul, More consistently attempts to reduce all the difficulties of the human condition to the quantifiable readings of his lapsometer. He treats the ordinary ups and downs of his own emotional life with doses of heavy sodium ions, just as any psychiatrist might treat a depressed patient, only more effectively.[20] More's alternating elation in science and depression flowing from the ordinary failures in his life provide a picture of the dangers Percy saw in investing too much of one's life into scientific projects.

Nevertheless, Percy described the true, practicing scientist as "the prince and sovereign of the age," a member of an "elect community of other scientists" with whom he can share an objective view of the universe, bypassing some or all of the difficulties of ordinary life (*LC* 115). A scientist's mastery comes from their unique perspective: like the convinced existentialist or practicing psychoanalyst, such a person knows they comprehend reality, and "stands in a posture of objectivity over against the world, a world which he sees a series of specimens or exemplars, and interactions, energy exchanges, secondary causes" (*LC* 115). The scientist gains another advantage from his research: at least a temporary joy that comes from escaping boredom and its cousin in alienation (*LC* 70–1).

Percy had no qualms about endorsing the value of science as a vocation, nor did he see a real conflict between true scientific inquiry and religious faith. In a 1984 interview with Linda Whitney Hobson, Percy argued that the danger in modern life is not science, as

> science is the most beautiful, the most elegant, the most satisfying discipline. As a matter of fact, science makes for far more happiness as a career than just about anything else these days. I'm talking about real scientists, though—not technicians, which is what most "scientists" really are. (*MCWP* 96)

Percy contrasted true science with the idea of "scientism," which "instead of seeing science as one valid way of knowing . . . elevates science to an omniscient way of approaching reality," until the person who thinks this way "denies any serious reality to any other way of knowing" (*MCWP* 96). A real scientist knows the limitations of their theories and applies their methods to fields where they can rightfully be used and does not imagine science can be the basis for understanding all of human life.

Percy argued that this way of turning the general structure of scientific inquiry into a totalizing way of life poses significant dangers because an objective-material approach cannot serve as a source of meaning. The attempt to elevate science into a worldview leaves its adherents with a significant difficulty: "the scientist, in practicing the scientific method, cannot utter a single word about an individual thing or creature insofar as it is an individual but only insofar as it resembles other individuals" (*SSL* 211). Such a method gives us a point of reference for understanding others, but leaves very little room for guiding one's own life, or the specific choices of individuals that depart from whatever the psychological theory in question categorizes as normal behavior. Percy asked a pointed question in this regard:

> How can the Harvard behaviorist, living in the best of all scientific worlds, begin to understand the behavior of the Harvard undergraduate who comes from the best of all lay worlds, the affluent, informed, democratic and ethical East (let the professor specify this world, make it as good as he chooses), who nevertheless turns his back on both worlds and prefers to live like Dostoevsky's underground man? (*MB* 23)

The best material environment, Percy suggested, may serve as a surprisingly poor context within which to discover a sense of purpose or meaning in life. Even if we grant that the behaviorist *could* explain his student's choice in the narrow scientific terms that such a scholar might wish to use (i.e., reducing the student's choice to a form of insanity or irrationality), such an approach must understand each individual human choice to its relative fit with whatever typology the scientist employs. It cannot take reasons outside the scientist's preformed typology for human action seriously. Understandably, then, adherents of scientism cannot comprehend behavior that falls outside a narrow kind of utilitarian rationality.[21] Percy posed a difficulty for scientism: On what grounds would this pretention to science provide a worldview that can sustain a moral life?

Natural science in all its forms can describe and at least sometimes its practitioners purport to predict human behavior, at least in generalities. This stance places human beings in a theory as an "organism in an environment, a sociological unit, an encultured creature, a psychological dynamism endowed genetically like other organisms with needs and drives, who through evolution has developed strategies for learning and surviving by means of certain adaptive transactions with the environment" (*MB* 20). Morally speaking, most people who accept this theory do not discard the idea that human beings also somehow possess "certain other unique properties" they do not share with other creatures, such as "inalienable rights, reason, freedom, and an intrinsic dignity." Indeed, Percy suggested that "most educated denizens of the Western world would subscribe in some sense or another to both propositions" (*MB* 20). Yet to self-consciously maintain this position requires any individual to overcome some difficulties.[22]

If we view human consciousness as determined entirely by its constituent environment, it becomes very difficult to see human choice and reason as anything but illusions. Creatures whose mental capacities are determined by their environments cannot truly be free. Taken together, these concepts cast doubt on the moral importance of rights and about the idea of dignity. On the matter of rights, even if we only think of them as socially granted conventions about which human beings agree, or as the consequence of discoverable rational rules of human life, they require a concept of the human person that retains reason and choice as central attributes. By contrast, an entirely evolutionary understanding of rights makes it almost impossible to use them as a fixed measure of any society's politics or morals. Consider dignity in this vein as well: If our moral measures are scientific and utilitarian and the human person adapts poorly to its environment, would not the concept of dignity come under assault? Would not dignity simply have to be understood as a social response to our (false) sense of specialness as reasoning beings? For Percy, these simple quandaries suggested that many adherents of science as a way of life refused to look squarely at the limitations of their ideal.

Percy argued that the moment we represent ourselves simply as adapted organisms with evolved values, and specifically, when we begin to see "individuality and freedom as 'values,' a certain devaluation sets in" (*MB* 21). Consider the "devaluation" implied in the shift from morality to values in the first place: as a historical concept, morality carries with it assumptions about the reality of human reason and judgment's powers in determining the right course of action. In the context of morals, individuality and freedom have an obvious weight and power—a choosing and reasoning being deserves to have both traits respected. By contrast, thinking in the realm of values suggests that both concepts only ever have relative importance. It is worth noting in this respect that "values" is Nietzsche's word, invoked with the intention to do away with morality entirely.

The person who attempts to reconcile their faith in rigorously scientific and epistemologically skeptical methods of arriving at their beliefs with a notion of rights must quickly realize that the merely scientific inquiry into the nature of our material world cannot so easily secure for themselves a specifically moral theory from that inquiry. Put another way, we cannot so easily derive *is* from *ought*.[23] This means that whatever moral code those that embrace scientism might utilize must come from "outside" the supposedly scientific methods they might use—from their preferences, sentiments, or simply attributed to the wider culture they inhabit.

Percy frequently returned to the notion that those who might wish to live out a scientific ethos constantly return to utilitarian standards as their measure of morality, presumably because such a calculation places ethics on the most physically measurable grounds available. Any attempt to create a genuinely scientific set of values requires a point of reference—a measure by which to judge human action. In science, Percy reminds his readers, we cannot really claim to know anything if we cannot measure and verify that knowledge. This means that for this kind of scientist any reasonable ethical life cannot rest in abstract assertions about the relation between an act and a moral claim, but rather, *must* find their root in more tangible outcomes.[24] Sickness and health, happiness and sadness: these must become the real moral measures of the scientific utilitarian.[25] This is the point from which Percy's idea of moral "devaluation" sets in, and one that Percy dramatized most effectively through the misadventures of Dr. Tom More in *Love in the Ruins* and *The Thanatos Syndrome*, who in two stories set years apart, faces down a variety of moral challenges related to scientific materialism.

In the stories, Percy implied that the idea of natural rights necessitates an understanding of human nature that transcends our merely biological traits. If scientism requires the presumption that human beings bear no truly special characteristics that set them apart from other species, from whence do our rights come? (*MB* 20) Using measures of bodily "wellness," the apostles of science in Percy's stories assert that the only rational way to view human life is as a good contingent upon happiness and health.[26] Dr. More describes the situation in the "near-future":

> Here's the hottest political issue of the day: euthanasia. Say the euthanasists [*sic*] not unreasonably: let's be honest, why should people suffer and cause suffering to other people? It is the quality of life that counts, not longevity, etcetera. Every man is entitled to live his life with freedom and to end it with dignity. (*LR* 122)

For a scientific utilitarian, dignity can only be a property that inheres in a life that maintains its proper biological functions and that fades when a person loses their health or mental acuity. Under the aegis of scientism's morals, one cannot speak much beyond a presumption in favor of life. Percy suggested that the natural logic of this position leads to something far more disturbing—that this stance authorizes not just the adult choice to end life on one's own terms, but rather that it allows (or even makes into a moral imperative) the elimination of unwanted persons.

In *The Thanatos Syndrome*, Percy imagined a future state where unwanted children up to eighteen months old would face the possibility of euthanasia, as their right to life hinged on their attainment of language and a minimal level of individuality (*TS* 199–200). Bob Comeaux, a cheerful representative of this position, explains his position to More:

> What we're doing, as you well know, is following the laws of the Supreme Court, respecting the rights of the family, the consensus of child psychologists, the rights of the unwanted child not to have to suffer a life of suffering and abuse, the right of the unwanted aged to a life with dignity and a death with dignity. Toward this end we—to use your word—dispose of those neonates and euthanates who are entitled to the Right to Death provision in the recent court decisions. (*TS* 199)

This seems to retain a very thin presumption in favor of life, but Percy feared that the ideal it represents would not just lead to individuals *choosing* death for themselves or another, but also a distinctly illiberal outlook on all matters of human life.[27]

A lack of tolerance and charity in argument with profound political consequences flows from this extreme materialist method: if scientism logically reduces human experience to its biological bases, those that embrace this position lose the logical ground for understanding why someone might disagree with them. All arguments would either flow logically from sound scientific premises, or not. Under such circumstances, the apostle of scientism demands agreement and often imagines only "unreasonable" people will disagree with them (*LR* 197–8).[28] We cannot underestimate the tremendous appeal of definitively "right" answers that settle political dilemmas for all time—part of the appeal of a scientific approach to political questions is that the answers aim at ending conversation entirely.[29] Percy suggested that so long as people look to an overextended vision of science for these answers, tolerant political life cannot exist in safety.

Percy's various lines of critique against scientism all returned to the idea that in disrespecting the limits to genuine scientific inquiry, one denies an Aristotelian insight about theorizing the human condition:

> a well-schooled man is one who searches for that degree of precision in each kind of study which the nature of the subject at hand admits: it is obviously just as foolish to accept arguments of probability from a mathematician as to demand strict demonstrations from an orator.[30]

We should only ask of any given science what such an inquiry can legitimately comprehend. Biological and physical science can reliably tell us much about the processes related to objects in the material world. A general, predictive theory of human emotion based on neurology can say nothing to a particular human being about how they *should* or *should not* feel. But human matters require a distinctively human approach, one that might actually provide moral direction to our lives.

Speaking to psychologists in particular, Percy argued that when we turn our attention to human questions, especially those that require some criteria for human well-being or happiness, we require "a value scale of rightness, authenticity; in short, a concept of human nature and what is proper to it." Where in natural science, the measures of inquiry exist in nature, with human things, Percy suggested that the relevant measures are moral. If Percy is correct that "there are certain human needs quite impervious to the biological approach," some significant correction in our thinking must occur before we regain an honest theory of the self (*SSL* 257). To address this more fully, I look to Percy's efforts to show the ways that the incomplete theories of man discussed above fail in practice, creating a condition we might call the "Cartesian self."

INCOMPLETE VISIONS AND THE DREAD CHASM OF THE MODERN MIND

Instead of attempting to live consistently within one of the positions I discussed above, Percy argued that most people either consciously ignore or fail to realize the tension between their various beliefs. They develop their own implicit theory of human nature, for "it is hard to imagine how one can live one's life and work with other people day in and day out unless one has already made certain assumptions about one's own nature as well as other people's." The difficult question Percy asked is whether "the theories we more or less unconsciously profess make any sense," and most importantly whether they aid us in recapturing a sense of self capable of coping with our alienation (*SSL* 111). This is especially true when we attempt to think about some of the obvious but painful facts about our world.

Percy suggested we should measure the adequacy of our implicit ideas of human nature by using them to address the serious and inescapable difficulties of life—illness, pain, death, anxiety, or doubt. Time and again, Percy called attention to "the remarkable fact that contemporary man feels strangely out of place in the very world he, more than any other man in history, has most successfully transformed for his own use" (*SSL* 127). Think for a moment about each of the "partial" theories I discussed above: How might they address this point?

The pantheist or apostle of new-age philosophy would likely tell us that our discomfort rests not in our poor adaptation to a world transformed by modern technology, but rather, in our unwillingness to find the authentic self and disclose it to the world (*LC* 111). Such a person might also assail the conveniences of the modern world as a distraction from that internal search. In their emphasis on making and sharing, the claim of such people is that by acts of artistic and craft-like self-expression and the honest disclosure of the self to others, we can leave alienation behind. Psychoanalysts and biological scientists alike must return to the idea that the problem rests not with the society, but with the maladapted person. For the former, the act of therapy moves our neuroses into full consciousness and allows us to integrate them into our personality. For the latter, adjustment to our environment requires the remedy of various neurological imbalances. The difficulty with both of these is that they encourage the person under treatment to believe that full relief of alienation is possible. Neither therapy nor transcendence gives individuals much comfort in the face of pain or tragedy; Percy suggested that they engaged in something like a diversion from the essential tasks of life.

The existentialist might be the closest to Percy's position by identifying what he calls the fact of alienation, but has no answer other than to demand man rebel against this circumstance.[31] As I note above, though, while Percy agreed that we need to look squarely upon our alienation and mortality, an adequate theory of the self would give us a vocabulary with which to discuss our situation, and a way of helping attenuate it. Instead of embracing these ideas, Percy wanted to direct our attention to the promise of constructing a coherent anthropology (*MCWP* 136–137) and use it as the basis of a new science that understands the human condition through the uniquely human actions we undertake (*MB* 11).

Percy directed us to reconsider the way we usually understand the relationship between mind and body. He claimed that those who spend their lives investigating questions about human nature ought to see the logical difficulties in their positions, especially because their failures inevitably carry over into the wider society. Against the popular culture's understanding of these matters, he argued that "the main error . . . of both the armchair behaviorist and the armchair psychologist is not the quick extrapolation from the simple hypothesis to complex human reality but rather the willingness of both to accept the age-old split of the human creature into this strange Janus monster comprising body and mind" (*SSL* 114). Psychoanalysts look at the psyche or mind and attempt to render an account of human life internal to that element of the person; the purely biological or neurological analysis of behaviorists and their successors in cognitive science hope for a similar explanation of human behavior from material relations alone. But rather than actually confront the limitations of each of these schools, the leaders of various human sciences and many of their popularizers ignore the Cartesian split of these two elements and attempt to unite them without seeing the bizarre mismatch of ideas and terms this can create.

Percy invented an analogy to show this: he invited his readers to contemplate the approach often taken in an undergraduate introduction to psychology class. There, one hears about "neurons, signals, synapses, transmitter substance, central nervous system, brain, mind, personality, self, consciousness, and later such items as ego, superego, archetypes," a list of terms that encompasses two very different sorts of ideas or phenomena (*SSL* 273). He further notes that when scholars do recognize or discuss this tension, they trivialize it with analogies (brain : mind :: computer : software) and assume a reductionist posture that puts nothing beyond the realm of materialist explanation (*SSL* 275). Percy argued that these categories and concepts are incoherent, in the literal sense "from the Latin *in-cohaerere*, a not-sticking-together," and he believes that no amount of effort from one side (brain) to another (mind) could possibly close the gap in our understanding because language and our consciousness in no way follow from the standard models of natural science (*SSL* 275–276). Using a reductive theory of consciousness merely "disposes" of the problem—it does not advance our understanding of the human condition at all (*MB* 62–63).

Percy found some hope in looking closely at the fragments that the sundered self leaves behind, and asked that we see them "not as disparate parts, body and mind, which never seem to have fit together, but at least as parts of the same creature" (*SSL* 117). He suggested that no effort in this vein ought to deny true science's explanatory power. In his 1989 NEH Jefferson Lecture in the Humanities, Percy reiterated his argument about the incoherence of the human sciences, but immediately noted that his purpose was not "to attack the social sciences in the name of the humanities," but rather to assail the current practice of "science in the name of science" (*SSL* 272–273). Having surveyed the failures of so much contemporary work, Percy turned to what he saw as the most logical starting point for a new kind of inquiry:

> Where does one start with a theory of man if the theory of man as an organism in an environment doesn't work and all the attributes of man which were accepted in the old modern age are now called into question: his soul, mind, freedom, will, Godlikeness?
>
> There is only one place to start: the place where man's singularity is there for all to see and cannot be called into question, even in a new age in which everything else is in dispute.
>
> That singularity is language. (*MB* 7)

In the first instance, Percy defended this claim by noting the relative failures of all attempts to teach nonhumans language. He drew upon the example of chimpanzees, and noted that only after "the most rigorous training, months and years of input, a chimpanzee can be taught perhaps seventy-five hand signals by means of which he can communicate this or that need, where by contrast, over the same time a human child "will learn to utter and understand an infinite number of new sentences in his language" (*SSL* 118). For Percy, looking at the phenomenon of language allows us to see the uniqueness of humanity, and helps bring us closer to a new starting point for a coherent theory of the human person that might satisfy both the most empirical scientist and the humanist critic.

Percy's inspiration for undertaking this project came from the writings of American philosopher Charles S. Peirce, whose work on problems of language and human perception arrived at what Percy found a vitally important insight: the recognition that there are two kinds of natural events in the world, dyadic and triadic, each of which corresponds to very different sorts of phenomena.[32] Utilizing Peirce's ideas, Percy argued that the first kind, dyadic relationships, treads on the understood ground of physical and biological science. Such sciences trace cause and effect ("A interacting with B; A, B, C, D interacting with each other"), and always have the character of "mutual action between two things" (*SSL* 279). Percy explains more fully in "A Triadic Theory of Meaning":

> Dyadic events are . . . those energy exchanges conventionally studied by the natural sciences: subatomic particles colliding, chemical reactions, actions of force-fields on bodies, physical and chemical transactions across biological membranes, neuron discharges, etc. (*MB* 162)

No matter how complex the interrelations between these sorts of phenomena, Percy argued that these never grow into anything beyond a "complexus of dyads," with the whole comprehensible as a "sequence of dyadic events" that "can be represented quite adequately by a simple drawing which shows structures . . . and arrows connecting them" (*SSL* 279–280). Both Peirce and Percy strenuously denied the idea that one could explain human behavior this way, and particularly looked to language as the place where this method of thinking fell apart.

By contrast, Percy termed a "triadic" event a "non-linear, non-energetic" phenomena of a much greater order of complexity than that present in dyadic interaction. Once a person moves from analyzing simpler interactions to the use of symbols and the minds of symbol-users, no direct analysis of cause and effect avails because while the use of language requires the use of body parts that one can understand through a dyadic analysis ("sound waves in air, excitation of sensory end-organ, afferent nerve impulse, electro colloidal synaptic event" and so on), the whole is not merely the sum of the parts (*MB* 162). His favorite descriptions of this phenomenon involve the ways that children learn language:

> The simplest example I can think of—and it is anything but simple—is the child's early acquisition of language, an eighteen-month-old suddenly learning that things have names. . . . What happens when the child suddenly grasps that the strange little sound "cat," an explosion of air between tongue and palate followed by a bleat of the larynx followed by a stop of tongue against teeth, *means* this cat, not only this cat but all cats? Naming is a new event. (*SSL* 280)

Percy argued that the crucial element in this analysis is the fact that from the moment a child learns words, she acquires the potential to use and combine them in ways unseen and unheard—ways that a rigorously behaviorist cause-effect analysis could not legitimately explain. A child's language activity can only be understood as a different order of complexity than the way a chimpanzee uses sign language.

Animals respond to signals and stimuli; children use symbols together with a system of grammar that flows in no predicable way from their environment's stimuli, combining three distinct elements (the speaker, the cat, and the *idea* of cat represented by the word). Percy's concern here ran in two major directions. The first rests with the failures of the purely scientific inquiry, and the ways in which projects aimed at understanding human life in this key will always remain incoherent. This failure follows from the fact that efforts to reduce our language and culture to some prior or "deeper" set of causes places triadic events under the auspices of a set of dyadic cause-effect chains that cannot explain the functions of consciousness. The second issue bears directly on the ways the failed self-understanding that flows from these projects spills over into everyday life. Is it possible that the person who sees their thoughts merely as a response to their environment will feel a kind of devaluation of their personhood? Percy saw modern social and behavioral science as a threat to our ability to recovering an awareness of our confusions about the self because these sciences encourage us to "go from biology (dyadic science) to grammar (triadic science) without anybody seeming to notice anything strange. Such *belle indifférence* can only have come to pass either because the scientist has not noticed that he has jumped the chasm or because he is at a loss for words" (*SSL* 282). Without a theoretical language that lets people start to explore how their previous theories fail them, we remain enmeshed in the tragic mishmash of our old understandings instead of engaging in the work of rethinking how to explain the real complexity of human life (*SSL* 218).

In these efforts, Percy provided a starting point and moral measure of the ways we understand relationships and political community. The first point one might make using Percy's analysis is a simple one: putting language at the center of our theory of the human person means reaffirming the idea that human beings really are *social* animals, made for company though not always escaping grief from the experience. Percy argued that the very etymology of the word "consciousness" should orient us to thinking about the social implications of language:

> "Conscious" means "knowing with." And "knowing with" is not a state of affairs but rather a relation, or rather two relations, the relation of knowing and the relation of with. . . . They [the phenomenologists] say that consciousness is not simply a state—we are never simply conscious—rather we are always, when we are conscious, conscious of something. (*SSL* 124)

What makes this consciousness possible is the reality of language as a medium through which human beings live their lives in common. The key moral element here to observe is the relational one: acts of speech can affirm or undermine our sense of being. Words can fall far short of their potential to name the realities of life or treat human beings with dignity. As a consequence, Percy suggested that this provides us a novel way to assess how adequately a theory or worldview accounts for human life.

Borrowing the concept of authentically human "I-Thou" and devalued "I-It" relationships from Martin Buber, Percy used these ideas to show that treating human beings as merely organisms in an environment *always* implies a failure to treat them as moral beings. Percy suggested that even most biological reductionists would agree upon the need to see human beings as deserving of legal protection. As individuals, they would demand to be treated with some level of dignity as well. Percy argued that this becomes a problem when the reductionist of whatever stripe fails to treat their subjects or interlocutors (or themselves) as complex beings with creativity. In Percy's terms, a genuine interpersonal relation cannot fail to do this, because such a bond is "not merely a desirable state of affairs, as Buber would say, but is rather the very condition of being and knowing and feeling in a human way" (*SSL* 127). Human beings cannot live well without being a "thou" in some facet of their lives; living as an "it" can only exacerbate our alienation.

Percy explained that while the inability to truly dispose of the social world with theory may create the anxiety that "of all the things in the world, oneself is the only being that cannot be symbolized," we also know we are not nothing (as the existentialist might have it): "I am rather a person, a namer and a hearer of names. Nor are you formulable under the auspices of a symbol. If I do conceive of you as *something* in the world rather than as a co-celebrant of the world, I fall from the I-thou to the I-it" (*SSL* 136–137, emphasis added). Failing to recognize the relative emptiness of labels and categories in dealing with human beings leaves us with little basis upon which to see others as more than matter in motion or means to ends.

The "I-it" relationship degrades and alienates the human being by turning a thinking person into an object to be manipulated.[33] Percy argued that a failure to conceive of human consciousness in terms that respect our creativity and personhood represent a moral affront that undermines decent political community. Percy's most pointed imagery of this appears in *Love in the Ruins*, where he imagined a "Love Clinic" based at a massive federal scientific research center in Louisiana that focuses on understanding the nature of human sexuality purely as a set of biological rather than relational acts. In the Love Clinic, doctors observe and record the neurological impulses of individuals and couples engaging in various sexual acts. The entire process removes any emotional or personal component from these performances; the scientists only seek to understand the precise mechanisms of orgasm to maximize the bodily pleasure of those participating. At no point do the doctors or volunteers link their sexual lives to emotion, much less procreation. Percy implied that this way of arranging our relationships is defective in that it effaces love as a generative force that binds people together over a full life. Instead, the doctors in the clinic and many of the characters in the novel embrace ephemeral connections, a way of living that strongly undermines community (*LR* 121–32).

The Love Clinic strips sexual acts of their interpersonal components because no actual communication occurs there. The doctors dictate how and when various acts should be undertaken, measuring and recording the sexual activities without speaking with the subjects, only *at* them. They actively discourage the participants from doing anything but directly engaging in the acts directed. When the couples find performing difficult, the doctors treat the issue as nothing more than a technical problem they must overcome. Because of its frankly authoritarian character, the entire procedure bears little relation to love. In treating human beings as little more than lab rats, the clinic's doctors break the natural bond sex generally reinforces between couples, and instead makes the sexual act alone the object of their relationship.[34]

Percy argued that treating thinking human beings as objects undermines the moral fabric of life. While an example like sexuality might serve as a personal reminder of this, he also criticized the way social sciences often objectify human choice and reduce triadic relationships to simple cause-effect dyads. These analyses treat human choice as a predetermined, environmentally conditioned necessity rather than as a means of explaining events. Here Percy's account echoes Tocqueville's fears concerning the way historians would increasingly deny human agency and dignity in democratic times:

> Most of them attribute hardly any influence over the destinies of mankind to individuals, or over the fate of a people to the citizens. But they make great general causes responsible for the smallest particular events. . . . Historians who live in democratic ages are not only prone to attribute each happening to a great cause but are also led to link facts together to make a system. . . . Once the trace of the influence of individuals . . . has been lost, we are often left with the sight of the world moving without anyone moving it.[35]

Tocqueville's account of history foreshadows what social scientists in general do at their worst: they reduce human relationships to determined causes, and the person and their capacity to choose disappears in the process. Like Tocqueville, Percy recognized that all scientific theory must simplify the reality that it purports to study, but feared that this particular inability to see the difference between dyadic and triadic relationships will forever leave human beings without a way to recover an understanding of themselves.

Percy's peculiar approach to the crisis he observed in the social sciences seems to fall short of bringing about the genuine revolution in understanding for which he hoped. As with his efforts to dissect the other approaches to the self, Percy's critical edge strikes most deeply in his philosophical essays, and by comparison, some argue his constructive efforts seem rather weak.[36] Even if a behaviorist accepts Percy's arguments against her discipline as true, she nonetheless retains little recourse within her discipline, other than to slightly change the emphasis of research or its tools of inquiry. It might be more accurate to say that her discipline allows her no conceptual language with which to reformulate questions into a triadic framework. Percy could only speculate at the sort of general social science research he thought might fulfill the promise of seeing human beings as distinctive because of their symbol-using nature. I will return to this problem later in the book at greater length. By pointing toward a new theory of semiotics, he hoped he could revitalize that discipline and make it the basis of a new anthropology. Even if it fails, the critique alone opens up some interesting lines of inquiry and suggests that at the very least, social scientists ought to be more eclectic in their methods and open to a wider variety of questions.[37]

GRAND THEORY FOR THE SELF

Percy's critique of our self-understanding remains a powerful one, and although we can read it simply as an artifact of the upheavals of postwar America, this misses the depth and prescience of his analysis. He presented his vision of an America torn asunder, with citizens lost in the ruins of theories that never fully account for the distinctiveness of the human person. The curiously unsatisfying blends of popular science and new-age philosophy that so often appear in the self-help section of bookstores may be the most obvious example of the incoherence Percy observed in the world. Percy exposed the weakness of these theories and pointed his audience toward a better way of understanding.

Percy wrote amid the death of "grand theory" that purports to explain the whole of human existence.[38] Even if it has returned to some extent, very little of what has arisen in place of the older theories of human life can evade Percy's criticisms. Contemporary neuroscience continues the behaviorist project in different terms; modern methods of therapy and self-help all rest on many of the same assumptions as the old Freudian model. Existentialists still suffer from despair and tend to launch themselves into peculiar, terrifying projects in the world. The theories we use to depict the world in social scientific terms all too often rest heavily on dyadic modeling instead of building upon language-rich triads. Percy insisted these visions remain little more than "mishmash" theories of the person.

Chapter 2 continues this focus on the perils of scientism and its incompleteness as a way of life. Building upon Percy's characterization of the mishmash theories of the self, it devotes particular attention upon the role experts plays in everyday life, and the effects their influence has upon politics and society. Percy suggested that the loss of self-awareness that mishmash theory creates in human beings opens them to a radical loss of sovereignty, and makes them ever more distant from the concept of the wayfarer.

NOTES

1. Early work on Percy's novels focused heavily on the themes of existentialism in his writings. See especially chapter 1 in Martin Luschei, *The Sovereign*

Wayfarer: Walker Percy's Diagnosis of the Malaise (Baton Rouge: Louisiana State University Press, 1972). For a more balanced account of Percy's recognition of the "limited truth" of existentialism, see Peter Augustine Lawler, *Postmodernism Rightly Understood: The Return to Realism in American Thought* (Lanham: Rowman and Littlefield, 1999), 83–84.

2. On Percy's time in the sanitorium, see Jay Tolson, *Pilgrim in the Ruins* (Chapel Hill and London: University of North Carolina Press, 1992), 160–183; and Patrick Samway, S.J., *Walker Percy: A Life* (Chicago: Loyola Press, 1997), 118–142.

3. For a scholarly discussion of the idea of fullness, see Charles Taylor, *A Secular Age* (Cambridge and London: Harvard/Belknap, 2007), 4–8 and C.S. Lewis, *Surprised By Joy: The Shape of My Early Life* (New York: Harcourt Brace, 1955), esp. 15–21.

4. John F. Desmond, "Walker Percy and Suicide," *Modern Age*, Vol. 47, No. 1 (Winter 2005), 58–63.

5. On Camus's existentialism and the nature of absurdity, see Taylor, *A Secular Age*, 582–586.

6. Patricia Lewis Poteat, *Walker Percy and the Old Modern Age: Reflections on Language, Argument, and the Telling of Stories* (Baton Rouge: Louisiana State University Press, 1985), 62–63.

7. See for example, Victor Frankl, *Man's Search for Meaning* (New York: Beacon Press, 2006) and *The Feeling of Meaninglessness: A Challenge to Psychotherapy and Philosophy* (Milwaukee: Marquette University Press, 2010). On the rise of therapeutic secular themes of this sort and the rise of "searching" within American religion, see Alan C. Petigny, *The Permissive Society: America, 1941–1965* (Cambridge: Cambridge University Press, 2009), 76–82 and 92–97.

8. For some analyses of Binx's search, see Allan Prigden, *Walker Percy's Sacramental Landscapes: The Search in the Desert* (Selinsgrove: Susquehanna University Press, 2009), 50–1; Sweeney, *Walker Percy and the Postmodern World*, 31; and John M. Desmond, *Walker Percy's Search for Community* (Athens: University of Georgia Press, 2010), 62–63.

9. This idea seems especially prominent in modern German thought from Friedrich Nietzsche to Carl Schmitt. On this, see Jeffrey Herf, *Reactionary Modernism: Technology, Culture, and Politics in Weimar and the Third Reich* (Cambridge: Cambridge University Press, 1984), esp. Ch. 1, 1–17, and William E. Scheureman, *Carl Schmitt: The End of Law* (Lanham: Rowman and Littlefield, 1999), esp. 15–37.

10. On the existential appeal of war, see Ernst Jünger, *Storm of Steel*, trans. Michael Hofmann (New York: Penguin, 2003); J. Glenn Gray, *The Warriors: Reflections on Men in Battle* (Lincoln: University of Nebraska Press, 1998); Roland N. Stromberg, *Redemption by War: The Intellectuals and 1914* (Lawrence: The Regent's Press of Kansas, 1982); and James Hillman, *A Terrible Love of War* (New York: Penguin, 2004).

11. Percy's analysis of this point compares interestingly with Eric Voegelin's idea that mass politics becomes a kind of religion substitute. See Voegelin, "Ersatz Religion: The Gnostic Mass Movements of Our Time," in *Science, Politics & Gnosticism* (Wilmington: ISI Books, 2004), 61–87.

12. Samway, *Walker Percy*, 104–8, Tolson, *Pilgrim in the Ruins*, 138–142.

13. On the importance of Freudian and other psychological thought to America in the period, see Wilfred McClay, *The Masterless: Self and Society in America* (Chapel Hill: University of North Carolina Press, 1994), 226–268; and Petigny, *The Permissive Society*, 15–52.

14. For two analyses of the dangers this method poses, see Richard Webster, *Why Freud Was Wrong: Sin, Science, and Psychoanalysis* (New York: Basic Books, 1995) and Frederick Crews, et al., *The Memory Wars: Freud's Legacy in Dispute* (New York: New York Review of Books, 1995). For a discussion of Dr. Gamow and Will's last session, see Mary K. Sweeney, *Walker Percy and the Postmodern World* (Chicago: Loyola University Press, 1987), 19–20.

15. Petigny, *The Permissive Society*, 24–25.

16. On the overman and self-creation, see Friedrich Nietzsche, *Thus Spoke Zarathurstra*, trans. Walter Kaufmann (New York: Penguin, 1978), 86–88.

17. Percy discusses Tocqueville approvingly in a 1989 interview with Scott Walter (*MCWP* 232–233). The Tocqueville quote can be found in *Democracy in America*, George Lawrence, trans., J.P. Mayer, ed. (New York: Harper, 1969), 451–452

18. The scholarly literature on Tocqueville treats his account of religion quite unevenly. For two accounts that place faith, alienation, and the despair of the democratic soul at the heart of their analysis, see Peter Augustine Lawler, *The Restless Mind: Alexis de Tocqueville on the Origin and Perpetuation of Human Liberty* (Lanham: Roman and Littlefield, 1993), esp. 141–158 and Joshua Mitchell, *The Fragility of Freedom: Tocqueville on Religion, Democracy, and the Human Future* (Chicago: University of Chicago Press, 1995), 78–87.

19. On Doris's role in *Love in the Ruins*, see Jerome Taylor, *In Search of the Self: Life, Death and Walker Percy* (Cambridge: Cowley Publications, 1986), 58; and Gary M. Ciuba, *Walker Percy: Books of Revelations* (Athens: University of Georgia Press, 1991), 149–150.

20. On More's distorted vision, see Desmond, *Walker Percy's Search for Community*, 122–125.

21. On the degree to which natural scientific (or at least scientistic) efforts to explain human choice must always engage in a kind of reductionism, see Peter Augustine Lawler, *Postmodernism Rightly Understood*, 84–87.

22. Think here of the example of Larry Arnhart. In *Darwinian Natural Right* (Albany: SUNY Press, 1998), he attempts to develop a defense of natural rights from an evolutionary perspective alone. At best, Percy would have to argue these rights form little more than agreed-upon-norms. Other libertarian thinkers like F.A. Hayek face a similar dilemma in desiring to defend a basically materialist conception of the human person alongside a robust theory of rights. See, for example, Hayek, *The Constitution of Liberty*, ed. Ronald Hamowy (Chicago: University of Chicago Press, 2011), esp. Ch. 1, 57–72.

23. Here Percy echoes Leo Strauss's discussion of Weberian social science and its pretentions to objectivity. See *Natural Right and History* (Chicago: University of Chicago Press, 1953), ch. 2, 35–80.

24. My account of the difference between morality and values owes a great deal to Hadley Arkes's *First Things: An Inquiry Into the First Principles of Morals and Justice* (Princeton: Princeton University Press, 1986), esp. 69–74.

25. On this, see Elizabeth Amato, "Walker Percy's Critique of the Pursuit of Happiness" in *The Moviegoer*, *Lost in the Cosmos: The Last Self-Help Book*, and *The Thanatos Syndrome*, in *A Political Companion to Walker Percy*, eds. Peter Augustine Lawler and Brian A. Smith (Lexington, University Press of Kentucky, 2013), 47–68.

26. Percy's writings on the nature of life largely predate the major work of Peter Singer, who presents the clearest example of the trend in thinking that Percy opposed. See Singer's *Rethinking Life and Death: The Collapse of Our Traditional Ethics* (New York: St. Martin's, 1994). Singer's appeals to quality of life dominate the book's reasoning, and it aligns very well with Percy's predictions of where this reasoning leads.

27. C.S. Lewis also argued that the pursuit of biological improvement will lead to man's diminishing liberty. See *Abolition of Man*, 57–58.

28. See also Desmond, *Walker Percy's Search for Community*, 123–124.

29. On the link between scientism, utilitarianism, and illiberal rhetoric, see Kenneth Minogue, *The Servile Mind: How Democracy Erodes the Moral Life* (New York: Encounter Books, 2010), 59–66.

30. Aristotle, *Nicomachean Ethics*, trans. Martin Ostwald (Upper Saddle River: Prentice Hall, 1999), 1094b25, 5.

31. Recall, though, Albert Camus seems to have eventually understood that this ethos untampered by other forces can only destroy. See *The Rebel: An Essay on Man in Revolt*, trans. Anthony Bower (New York: Vintage, 1991), esp. Part V, 279–306.

32. Percy called himself a "thief of Peirce," and adopted elements of the latter's idea without endorsing either his whole system or his abstract mode of explaining the ideas. For a representative sample, see Charles S. Peirce, *Selected Writings (Values in a Universe of Chance)*, ed. Philip P. Wiener (New York: Dover, 1958), esp. Ch. 3, "Some Consequences of the Four Incapacities," 39–72. Also see the collection of letters between Percy and the C.S. Peirce scholar Kenneth Laine Ketner, *A Thief of Peirce: The Letters of Kenneth Laine Ketner and Walker Percy*, ed. Patrick H. Samway, S.J. (Jackson: University Press of Mississippi, 1995).

33. Consider here the example psychiatrist Theodore Dalrymple presents in his essay collection *Life at the Bottom: The Worldview of the Underclass* (Chicago: Ivan R. Dee, 2001). He recounts the tendency among violent offenders to depersonalize their crimes. Even while admitting the act of stabbing another person, Dalrymple notes they often use the passive voice: "the knife went in", 5–14.

34. I have adapted this discussion of the Love Clinic from my "Walker Percy's Last Men: *Love in the Ruins* as a Fable of American Decline," in *A Political Companion to Walker Percy*, 196–198. On the authoritarian nature of the Love Clinic's procedures, see Desmond, *Walker Percy's Search for Community*, 123–4.

35. Tocqueville, *Democracy in America*, 494–495.

36. Percy's staunchest critic in this regard, Patricia Lewis Poteat, argues that his forays into science actually undermine his very effort to escape the almost hardwired Cartesian paradigm of American thought. In particular, she claims that in order to address scientists in his essays, Percy corrupts the distinctive elements of his literary message so thoroughly that the Percy of the essay bears little resemblance to that in his novels. Poteat asserts that because Percy's philosophical analysis trades in universals (and therefore, the "Cartesian" tradition) rather than the concrete

particulars presented in each of the novels (a "storytelling" tradition), he places his work radically at odds with itself (*Walker Percy and the Old Modern Age*, 58–59). The idea that philosophical universals cannot be made compatible with particular events of stories strikes me as self-evidently wrong. Percy often blended the philosophical arguments of the essays into the speech and action of his novel's characters.

37. On this point, see James W. Ceaser, *Liberal Democracy and Political Science* (Baltimore and London: Johns Hopkins University Press, 1990), esp. Ch. 3, 41–69.

38. Percy wrote roughly contemporaneously with others who sought a return to "grand theory" of this sort. On this, see Quentin Skinner (ed.), *The Return of Grand Theory in the Human Sciences* (Cambridge: Cambridge University Press, 1985).

Chapter 2

On the Cult of the Expert and the Dangers of Scientism

The idea that science might form the basis for an entire worldview has many adherents in modern American life. Given John Dewey's influence on the American education establishment, we should not be surprised by this.[1] Dewey argued that widespread adoption of (or acculturation to) a kind of scientific attitude might chasten democracy's excesses, defend against superstition, and focus society's progress. The irony of Dewey's approach rests in his belief that an attitude embracing the critical methods of science would serve as the public's "sole guarantee against wholesale misleading by propaganda," and the "only assurance of the possibility of a public opinion intelligent enough to meet present social problems."[2] This sets a bold mandate for education and provides a good backdrop to understand Percy's account of how the public's faith in scientific expertise goes so wrong in American life.

The traits Dewey believed necessary for democracy to flourish include the embrace of uncertainty and doubt. Because of this, he listed several ways that his ideal conflicts with Americans instincts; a more pragmatic, less dogmatic democracy would develop to cut against some deep longings in the human heart:

> Uncertainty is disagreeable to most persons; suspense is so hard to endure that assured expectation of an unfortunate outcome is usually preferred to a long-contained state of doubt. . . . Fear of the unknown, fear of change and novelty, tended, at all times before the rise of the scientific attitude, to drive men into rigidity of beliefs and habits.[3]

This triumphal progressivism associates "rigidity" with feared and this view turns doubt into a high civic virtue. While Dewey fears this scientific attitude would not spread far enough throughout society to restrain the foolishness of the mob or what he saw as the systematic exploitation that flows from the private sector, he did not question whether the raising up of science as the ideal was wise. If Percy is right, science is a mode of inquiry that no one applies to their entire lives, and it may create a society intellectually subordinate to experts.

Chapter 1 discussed Percy's notion of the "mishmash theory of man," and the peculiar ways Americans rely on theories of the self that remain inadequate for explaining alienation and coping with this condition. Percy argued that many people who think relatively seriously about human nature want to embrace their understanding of man as an "organism in an environment" that merely adapts to circumstance. Man is thus much like other creatures, a being "who through evolution has developed strategies for learning and surviving by means of certain adaptive transactions with the environment." At the same time they proclaim their similarity to other members of the animal kingdom, those who hold this view also see themselves as endowed with "certain inalienable rights, reason, freedom, and an intrinsic dignity" (*MB* 20). Percy argued that this was not just self-contradiction, but a kind of cognitive dissonance. Certainly he would have argued that Dewey's position fits this description. The belief in science as the only path to understanding human life comes at a price, however.

Percy's argument in "The Delta Factor," provided a direct challenge to Dewey's prescription:

> Science cannot utter a single word about an individual molecule, thing, or creature insofar as it is an individual but only so far as it is like other individuals. The layman thinks that only science can utter the true word about anything. But the layman is an individual. So science cannot say a single word to him or about him except as he resembles others. It comes to pass then that the denizen of a scientific-technological society find himself in the strangest of predicaments: he lives in a cocoon of dead silence, in which no one can speak to him nor can he reply. (*MB* 22)

The layman's position of relative ignorance regarding what science actually does explains his willingness to grant such enormous authority to scientists. But the very weakness of the layman's position in relation to her better-trained counterpart encourages a half-blind faith not just in the products of truly scientific inquiry, but also in virtually all of the statements that come from an expert source or authority in the culture. Moreover, both the expert and layman find themselves in an unenviable position with only two options: first, they can subsume themselves under the theories they claim can explain the world—theories that neatly dispose of not just the complexity of the world, but also the uniqueness of their own character. In the second option, individuals can exempt themselves from the theory they hold about politics, human nature, and other things, insisting on their special character (think here for example in Marxism of the intelligentsia's role as the vanguard of the proletariat and the nature of their escape from ignorance). Alternatively, they can simply refuse to notice their theory's implications for themselves as a human being while applying the model to the world at large. Thus a person who accepts a deterministic model of some aspect of human life but also wishes to see humanity (or at least himself) as bearing some form of dignity and deserving of special protection finds themselves in the position of a remainder in long division: left-over and cast aside without place in the order of things.

Whatever we imagine ourselves to be, Percy insisted we cannot explain our consciousness on the basis of those models that reduce us to a function of simple cause-effect stimuli. Percy's argument that the human creature's language alone sets him apart bears important consequences for how man views himself in the world. This carries particularly problematic consequences for a people that embrace scientific expertise as their guide to life:

> Once the symbol-mongering organism has a world, he must place himself in this world. He has no choice. He cannot not do it. If he refuses to make a choice, then he will experience himself placed in this world as one who has not made a choice. He is not like a dog or cat who, when deprived of all stimuli, goes to sleep. Unlike an organism in an environment, a man in the world has the unique capacity for being delighted with the world and himself and his place in the world, or being bored with it, anxious about it, or depressed about it. . . . He, of all creatures, is capable of feeling good during hurricanes and sad on ordinary Wednesday afternoons. (*SSL* 127)

If the human person comprehends their place in the world incorrectly, they will suffer for that mistake. Consider the fact that our world, more formed and harnessed for our use than during any other era—and becoming ever more so with time's passing—still leaves us sad, bitter, and out of place. For Percy, that this alienation remained was a clue to how scientism goes terribly wrong.

The Deweyan wager that a scientific attitude will save democracy from itself may grant Americans material prosperity, deeper equality in education, and ever-greater control of their environment. But what science cannot do is prevent an increasing dependence on the part of laymen on experts in all fields. Indeed, such a vision *relies* on the sovereignty of expertise in managing a democratic community's progress.[4] Dewey hoped (without explaining how such a state might come to pass) that this dependence on socially beneficial expertise would make democracy stronger and more moral by making it more equal and rational.

Despite the constant growth in our material capacities, Percy believed that the turn to expertise undermines the moral capacities of citizens. Percy identified the layman's essential surrender of his capacity to know and decide fundamental matters in his life to the expert as one contributing factor to this decline (*SSL* 210–11). This is not merely a problem where one class loses sovereignty against another: whatever their pretentions to knowledge, every expert remains nothing more than a layman outside their field. All suffer a deprivation that Percy thought people today could hardly name. While Percy gave enormous credit to the proper role of science, he argued that the very method of turning science toward attempts to "solve" perennial human dilemmas comes at a cost.

In this chapter, I consider the ways that the expert's relentless pursuit of improvement erodes the layman's individual capacity for choice, and thus, adds to his anxiety and displacement in an ever-changing world. Percy returned again and again to the peril of engineering improvements in human life through scientific manipulation, which I explore to help understand this danger. From there, I turn to how this creates a temptation to embrace deeply illiberal and authoritarian politics, and conclude with an account of how even in a world convinced of the superiority of science, we constantly find ourselves confronted with jarring reminders of how much our theories of the self cannot explain. But first, I turn to Percy's idea that humanity loses something in its subjection to expertise.

LOSING SOVEREIGNTY IN A WORLD OF EXPERTISE AND AUTHORITY

Percy claimed that Americans all too often place themselves in a subservient role before experts. Believing in the authority of science in its rightful sphere, Percy did not wish to deny that we *ought* to listen to our physicians or auto mechanics. Instead, he pointed to the way a misapplied faith in scientism and expertise can deprive human beings of their sense of sovereignty over their lives. Examples of the deprivation caused by this cult of expertise abound in Percy's fiction, and by exploring the characters Percy imagined, we can better understand the dangers this poses.

Early in *The Last Gentleman*, Will Barrett embarks on a quest to plan and order his life along scientific principles. Coming from a manic depressive with bouts of temporary dislocation and amnesia, this is no small irony. As he puts it: "I shall engineer the future of my life according to the scientific principles and the self-knowledge I have so arduously gained from five years of analysis" (*LG* 41). Even if he were a scientist, Barrett's effort would have led him into a deep dependence on others for a plan or a technique for improvement. Unsurprisingly, just after committing to the plan, he turns to his therapist Dr. Gamow for guidance about what he was "*really* supposed to do" with his life (*LG* 38). As the novel unfolds, Barrett's constant search for authorities that might guide him leads to greater and greater confusion.

In his wanderings around New York City, Barrett encounters and befriends a Southern family, the Vaughts, and later returns to the South with them as something like a family assistant. He develops a particular fascination with the family's elder son, a failed physician-turned-coroner named Sutter. Sutter does not scorn Barrett's company, but also seems to view him more as a clinical experiment than as a friend:

> Barrett: His trouble is that he wants to know what his trouble is. His "trouble," he thinks, is a disorder of such a character that if only he can locate the right expert with the right psychology, the disorder can be set right and he can go about his business. (*LG* 353)

Looking to live by the myth of science forces Barrett into an attitude of subservience and leads to the rejection of his sovereignty as a man. This is a logical consequence of seeing human life as a matter of finding the objectively correct mode of adjusting one's life to environmental conditions, which automatically lead to living well.

As an expert of sorts at navigating the complexity of the world and sharing some understanding of its disorders, Sutter appears to Barrett as the perfect role model, but Sutter thinks that Barrett follows him and seeks his wisdom for all the wrong reasons:

> That is to say: he wishes to cling to his transcendence and to locate a fellow transcender (e.g., me) who will tell him how to traffic with immanence (e.g., "environment," "groups," "experience," etc.) in such a way that he will be happy. Therefore I will tell him nothing. For even if I were "right," his posture is self-defeating. (*LG* 353)

Barrett depends upon authorities for his salvation and happiness; throughout the story, he willingly subordinates himself to each new idea and person, hoping that it might "solve" his disorders once and for all. This is what makes the quest fruitless: as a kind of demonic existentialist, Sutter knows what Barrett does not, that alienation is here to stay, and while he does not really adjust himself to this fact, he revels in the release from morality that seeing existence as a meaningless endeavor allows him.

Barrett's desire for certainty and guidance remains unfulfilled in part because Sutter's "answer," such as it might be, remains his alone. Barrett wants a theory of health and fulfillment, but such an abstraction cannot tell him how to live. It can only provide general rules that an anonymous person who faces no actual challenges might follow. Percy argued our world is filled with individuals like Barrett in that they find it hard to live without the sanction and certification of authority—here recall Binx Bolling's love of membership cards that "prove" his existence as a man and good citizen. Paradoxically, most people also desire some sort of fulfillment and autonomy (*MG* 6–7).

In a series of essays that thematically parallel these stories, Percy attempted to explain this phenomenon more directly. By devaluing the common sense ordinary people used to take for granted—and totally dismissing the notion of man as a specifically reasoning being under the auspices of a natural law—most people find themselves allowing others to define their experiences of reality.[5] As a consequence of our subordination to expert theorists and loss of previous senses of meaning (our loss of a clear theory of the person, our failing attachments to a defined creed or place), Percy suggested the whole of human experience now "is staked out by 'them,' the experts." What is left to us is a more or less passive consumption of the experts' preformed notions and theories of reality, an "eager surrender of sovereignty." A surrender is understandable given the exhausting nature of a search for answers in a world where the older sources of truth and meaning have died (*MB* 54).

Percy did not limit his account of this phenomenon to the relationship between scientists and laymen, but between all people who come to a situation with vastly different levels of knowledge and experience:

> I refer to the general situation in which sovereignty is surrendered to a class of privileged knowers, whether these be theorists or artists. A reader may surrender sovereignty over that which has been written about, just as a consumer may surrender sovereignty over a thing which has been theorized about. The reader may also be content to judge life by whether it has or has not been formulated by those who know and write about life. (*MB* 55)

The surrender Percy described here presents itself not just as a choice on an individual's part to accept the wisdom of those more knowledgeable in some field, but rather a systematic attitude of subservience and incapacity. Thus, highly accomplished individuals in whatever field might place themselves in the position of ordering their lives around theories of the self and surrender their judgment about any number of matters to others.

Percy used a variety of examples to make this more concrete: in one anecdote, he wrote of a psychiatric patient finding joy in recounting "a symptom or dream which fits the prevailing theory," not because it might help him or her improve, but so that he or she might achieve recognition as a "real" neurotic (*SSL* 211). In another, a vacationing couple observe a native ritual and yearn to recount it to their ethnologist friend, not out of any genuine curiosity about the culture itself, but merely to gain his approval that this is an "authentic" ritual (*MB* 53–4). To cite one other example: early in *Love in the Ruins* before he learns how to use the lapsometer to treat patients, Dr. Tom More's patients felt better simply because More's "very act of locating the site" of their malaise "touching the sore spot, so to speak," improves their condition (*LR* 31–32). In these cases, the individuals Percy described yearn to get the "right" answer, to fit their experiences or their very character into a preformed typology. This ought to trouble us, politically, if only for what it says about the condition of citizens who live with this mentality.

Consider the matter of education, which Percy touched on repeatedly in relation to this attitude of subservience. If students cannot encounter texts or natural phenomena without the aid of a preformed notion of how to interpret them, and much less without the crutch of knowing that a comforting, unambiguous answer awaits discovery in a text or lecture, passivity becomes the norm in learning. Percy lampooned this point in both *Love in the Ruins* and *The Last Gentleman*. In the former, Tom More observes that students are "a shaky dogmatic lot. And the 'freer' they are, the more dogmatic. At heart, they're totalitarians: they want either total dogmatic freedom or total dogmatic unfreedom, and the one thing that makes them unhappy is something in between" (*LR* 233). This "something" in between would require leaving dogma behind—thinking critically about subject matter for themselves. In a similar moment, Will Barrett notes his and his friends' comfort with textbooks, in "the orderly march of chapter and subheading," which presented the truth about their subject matter with disarming clarity that tells the students exactly what to think and how to proceed in doing so (*LG* 200–1).

This set of learning attitudes brings other consequences: Percy argued that introductory biology course laboratories now might be the last place one could critically encounter nature, just as a college literature class is probably not an ideal space in which one might be moved by Shakespeare (*MB* 58–61). The student's position in either case is not an enviable one, because not only are these subject areas "owned" by the experts, but also they are all too often "*disposed of* by theory" (*MB* 62). Students fit biological specimens into a typology and do not discover on their own; they are taught to interpret texts through a literary theory that dictates how to determine the works' meaning. Many call both of these good learning outcomes, but to the degree Percy is correct, the students remain subjects, not active, discovering minds that might contemplate learning in isolation. In these cases the student is deprived of experiencing the act of discovering knowledge on their own, and Percy argued that it establishes habits of subservience throughout our lives.

The passivity Percy identified as a consequence of the layman's subservience cannot remain a matter merely for educational concern. This passivity might well generate a similar attitude toward citizenship. Politically, this form of character poses two interrelated dangers to the life of a commercial republic. First, the denizen of a passive culture like Percy described would become unlikely to grow alert to new possibilities, or see on their own the implications of the ideas they or others hold true. Think here of the necessity of a kind of intellectual alertness: as a source of new scientific achievement, technical improvement, or entrepreneurship, this remains an invaluable character trait. So too must it matter politically: How else might a citizen know which direction their society may soon go, or moreover, where it ought to go?[6] Secondly, the passive minds that Percy described possess traits that make them extremely well suited for conversion to a totalizing ideology. Such people express a willingness and desire to submit themselves to a preformed theory of the world. They also seem to have a need to dispose of that world via a clear-cut explanation of causes that render all things comprehensible under the auspices of that theory. They betray a deep desire to retain a semblance of autonomy, which adherents of ideology so often claim through their affiliation with a movement.

In *Lost in the Cosmos*, Percy provided an example of how preformed theories and ideological movements like this operate. In a depiction of a diverse set of characters attending a Native American Corn Dance festival in Taos, New Mexico during World War II, Percy included the story of a Soviet spy working as a technician on the Manhattan Project. For this man, reading Marx served as a revelation:

> All at once, he saw how it all worked, saw the very mechanism of his sadness and therefore the means of rising above it. Above it he was and above all this, the people whom now he understood, the Indians, the tourists, even the scientist whom he knew by reputation. They, not he, were puppets worked by strings they could not see. But he knew, could see the strings and, best of all, work them himself—for the good of the Soviet Union and therefore for world peace. (*LC* 133–134)

The manner in which the Soviet agent uses ideology to dispose of himself and the world bears notice. Adherents of ideologies often see themselves as exempt from the normal rules of their theory. The theory becomes a possible path to power.

But what Percy intimated through his depiction of ideology is the relationship between the adherent of a theory like this and the world they inhabit. Theory of this kind imposes an artificial order onto the world, and it cannot help but obscure the understanding of those that believe in it by forcing them to see other people's beliefs and choices as illusions driven by deeper causes. The difficulty today rests in that not science, but *scientism* has become the reigning ideology of many of the residents of modern technological society.

Having surrendered themselves to this view of the world, some invest science and technology with almost magical power and authority.

SCIENTISM, MATERIALISM, AND THE DYADIC APPROACH TO LIFE

As an undergraduate, and especially as a medical student, Percy found himself drawn to the clarity of science. It was the very "elegance and precision" of science that drew him away from psychiatry—which he seriously considered—and into pathology as a discipline (*CWP* 11).[7] After his illness, however, Percy broadened his perspective somewhat. Always preoccupied with questions of life's meaning, he naturally turned to existentialism and other philosophical arguments as a way of understanding reality:

> If the first great intellectual discovery of my life was the beauty of the scientific method, surely the second was the discovery of the singular predicament of man in the very world which has been transformed by this science. An extraordinary paradox became clear: the more science progressed, and even as it benefited man, the less it said about what it is like to be a man living in the world. Every advance in science seemed to take us further from the concrete here-and-now in which we live. (*SSL* 188)

Science as a method cannot speak to the distinctive traits of any particular event, person, or phenomenon as an individual unit, but only insofar as the object of study fits in with its class or category. This explains the peculiarity of a people who, because they rely so heavily on science, become less and less able to see their own status as language-using, choosing, creative beings not wholly subject to their environment. At the same time, such creatures find themselves less and less able to explain their predicament as unique creatures without reducing their experience to the contours of the general theory.

Percy argued that this condition poses political dangers because a considerable number of people turn to scientism and attempt to make it into something like a coherent worldview. This relates directly to the surrender of personal sovereignty because scientism "is a certain cast of mind characteristic of laymen and consumers of popular science and scientific technology, laymen who may be educated but who are at a remove from the method and practice of science" (*SSL* 297). People begin to view what they think of as science and the scientific method not merely as a parsimonious, clear way of knowing narrowly applicable to certain sorts of questions. Rather, he argued that the adherents of this position see it as "an omniscient way of approaching reality" that rules out the validity of "any other way of knowing" (*MCWP* 96).

In defining the subject this way, Percy followed many other thinkers. F.A. Hayek differentiated science from scientism by noting the latter's "mechanical and uncritical application of habits of thought to fields different from those in which they have been formed."[8] Since scientism extends the distinctive traits of science far beyond their normal limits of explanation and marries this to a thoroughgoing materialism, Percy argued it makes for a peculiarly dangerous creed.

Science requires objective measurements focused on the material world. For narrowly empirical questions, this makes logical sense. Scientism fails to respect this limit, and indeed, because they rule out all "unscientific" explanations in any area of life, its adherents tend to "misplace" the reality of things. Their primary failure rests in the obsession with finding reality in the measurable, tangible, and quantifiable (*SSL* 214–15). Thus, for the follower of scientism, the "real" relations between human beings occur at a level one might consider above or below that of the symbols and words we use to represent such relationships. For instance, the "vulgar" forms of Marxism state that all artifacts of culture are merely the superstructure resting upon the basis provided by the economic mode of production. Similarly, the neuroscientist may root the causes of culture "beneath" rational analysis in our brain chemistry and biological need. In every case, the goal is to obliterate Percy's distinction between dyadic and triadic relations: the scientific method, which classifies and seeks to understand relationships between predictable units of analysis fits the study of dyadic cause-effect relationships perfectly. Triadic relations involving language, by contrast, cannot be fully understood as the product of any straightforward chain of causal relations—the grammar they require to function is both creative and untethered to specific causes (*LC* 94–100).

This bears the practical consequence that scientism's adherents tend to view the products of language and culture as reducible to some other set of simple causal relations. Indeed, by so disposing of cultural artifacts as more or less "unreal" or unimportant, they devalue the means by which human beings come to grips with their lived experience. In one of his more technical philosophical essays, Percy described this: "Culture, in its most characteristic moments, is not a catalogue of artifacts or responses to an environment but is rather the ensemble of all the modes of assertory activity," and as such, it is "all human inheritance, material as well as spiritual" (*MB* 222). Think of the mishmash theories of the self that all too often people embrace: when we combine these with an attitude toward the world that subsumes words and meanings into material relationships alone, Percy argued human beings lose a valuable means of grappling with their alienation.

This allergy toward grappling with the nonmaterial on its own terms, or "ontophobia," as Percy labeled it following Gabriel Marcel, leaves human beings without a vocabulary to describe their feelings and beliefs except as functions of something else—moving them further away from a view that makes it possible to come to grips with alienation. Thus, to take the example of myth, Percy noted that when it "is studied as an empirical phenomenon, it is evaluated not according as it is true or false or nonsensical but according to the degree to which it serves a social or cultural function" (*MB* 224–225).[9] If we extend this mode of analysis to any norm or belief, sacred or profane, some peculiar consequences result. Consider the effect viewing the world this way must have on an individual scientist's attitudes:

> If the scientist believes theoretically in the indispensability of myth for an integrated culture, it becomes difficult for him to make a coherent objection to the Nazi or Soviet ethos. The upshot is the anomalous situation, so familiar in academic circles today, of the professor who in the field and classroom recognizes only functional relationships and refuses to recognize norms, and who in private and public life is a passionate defender of the freedom and rights and sacredness of the individual. (*MB* 226)

The relative weakness of the scientist's position here can only be magnified when replaced by the much less considered perspective of the adherent of scientism. How might they live their lives?

In practice, Percy suspected that the adherent of scientism usually becomes a dogmatic believer in the magical possibilities of science to transcend the limits of human life—perhaps not the limits of his life—but certainly those of future generations. One memorable example of this can be found in C.S. Lewis's *Abolition of Man*, where he recounts the following:

> "Man has nature whacked," said someone to a friend of mine long ago. In their context the words had a certain tragic beauty, for the speaker was dying of tuberculosis. "No matter," he said, "I know I'm one of the casualties. Of course there are casualties on the winning as well as the losing side. But that doesn't alter the fact that it is winning."[10]

That scientism's believers misunderstand or at least overexaggerate what science can do for them and the world on one level seems harmless. When taken as an exclusive dogma that rules out all other forms of wisdom, peculiar arguments emerge.

Percy observed that such people find it difficult to accept the very possibility that human beings bear special characteristics worth defending, particularly when we discuss issues on the supposed margins of human life, such as abortion and euthanasia. If we begin with an ideology that insists on reducing human beings to the sum of their environmental stimuli, "what is more natural than to think of man's peculiar gifts of language, culture, and technology as but yet another evolutionary stratagem not only for adapting to an environment but also for conquering it?" (*SSL* 112) As we have seen, Percy believed this view undermines our capacity for taking our rhetoric and ideas seriously as causes for human action. But worse still, this dogma develops a sense of indignation at all suggestions contrary to its conclusions. As Percy put it, "[d]oes it not, in fact, offend one's sense of the continuity of science if somebody suggests that man is truly unique—unique in a sense not allowed by the organismic view of man?" (*SSL* 113) Part of the danger of scientism rests in its adherents' unwillingness to accept discontinuities or gaps in their worldview. In this view, the mysteries of human life become a scandal that must be purged from our consciousness. Everything worth knowing *must* be explained through the objective-material method. A view of this sort rules out all alternative explanations not merely as false but also as *unreasonable*—for the canons of reason itself become linked to our ability to justify our actions in terms of strictly materialistic theory.

Percy argued that the scandal of man's uniqueness—what he considered an inescapable fact, but one which adherents to the dogma of scientism cannot accept—leads to a constant effort on the dogmatists' part to negate our pretentions to being distinctive. Think for a moment of efforts in behavioral psychology, evolutionary biology, and particularly neuroscience in the last thirty years: many scholars in these fields devote their lives to tracing out the "root" causes of what we might see as the nobler human capacities and emotions (reason, love, if not truly free will, then at least the capacity for bounded choice), and destroying them. Usually this effort moves toward two linked outcomes: fatalistic determinism and the denial of moral responsibility.

Determinism results from the genuinely scientific but overextended desire to predict and understand natural phenomena, which scientism transmutes into an obsession. This casts doubt on several facets of ordinary life: If we are really only an organism responding to circumstances well beyond our control, how can choice matter? Once we accept the premise that we must see all our hopes and dreams as a delusion, how can we believe in any one individual's ability to change anything? And if we cannot, then why bother with any of the trappings of democratic life at all?

Some ideas carry within them the hope of liberation from nature's constraints, but this view seems more likely to cause despair in the hearts of its adherents. In a 1968 interview, Percy explained this by referencing the Southern dilemmas of race, and his fear that writers and intellectuals might approach this via sociological categories, rather than moral ones:

> Perhaps the danger here is greater than that of becoming embroiled, or getting caught up in an issue, or getting embittered. Young writers, even young Negro writers, tend too often to understand themselves in terms of what the sociologists say: that they are victims of slavery, of broken homes, of a matriarchal

> society, and of various other things. They begin to feel themselves as exemplars of this or that sociological theory, forgetting many of the riches of their own lives. (*CWP* 19)

One consequence of this self-deprivation through theory is that individuals lose faith in themselves as creative or moral people to act in the world, and instead dispose of their own lives through the categories their theory provides them. People may theorize themselves into a kind of existential paralysis and never recover a sense of self untainted by the shadow of futility.

Worse still, this scientism may lead to attitudes that undercut our ability to see human beings as truly worthy of love or respect. In an account of his period as a materialist, atheist, and skeptic of morality, philosopher J. Budziszewski explained his own agony in dealing with the consequences of his position:

> I ended up doing a doctoral dissertation to prove that we make up the difference between good and evil and that we aren't responsible for what we do. . . . I resisted the temptation to believe in good with as much energy as some saints resist the temptation to neglect doing good. For instance, I loved my wife and children, but I was determined to regard this love as merely a subjective preference with no real and objective value. Think what this did to the very capacity to love them. After all, love is a commitment of the will to the true good of another person, and how can one's will be committed to the true good of another person if he denies the reality of good, denies the reality of persons, and denies that his commitments are in his control?[11]

This account of the psychological and moral tension involved in trying to live with the moral views an objective-material position fits well with the struggles Percy believed come with scientism. In this case, scientism deprives its adherents of the tools that might let them live a decent life. Despair naturally flows from this position.

Beyond a kind of fatalism, the quest to collapse the human creature together with the rest of the animal kingdom also leads to the denial of the idea that individuals can be held responsible for the actions they take in life, or that human life itself might deserve special protection under the law. Percy traced out this problem chillingly in *Love in the Ruins* and *The Thanatos Syndrome*: in both cases, euthanasia creeps into acceptance, largely on the basis of this shift into seeing human beings as truly human only when they meet certain empirically verifiable standards or thresholds that merit protection. Scientism transmutes a philosophical or theological belief that life is sacred into a mere disposition in favor of life, one subject to certain qualitative standards. Thus, Percy fictionally suggested that someday in the not-too-distant future, human infants would only acquire the legal protections of human beings at the age of eighteen months because most children acquire the ability to speak by that point, and everyone would be subject to euthanasia when their life failed to measure up to standards of health and quality set by medical and political authorities (*TS* 199–200). Percy's concerns about the erosion of a culture protecting life also apply to many other areas of political life.

The entire idea of moral responsibility falls into disregard when the attitude of scientism becomes widely held. Animals respond to environmental stimuli; they are not moral beings in a responsible sense. By disposing of the universe through theory, adherents of scientism do not just theorize away themselves, but the person who follows this through actually removes any mechanism on the basis of which they can really argue a person bears responsibility for their actions.[12] Scientists who follow this mode of thinking look to medicalize and trace the origin of crime, not judge it on its own terms: "Accordingly, it did not strike anyone as peculiar when scientists sought an explanation for man's perversity and upsidedownness in this or that atavism from man's evolutionary past. Man blamed the beasts for his madness" (*MB* 27). After all, if men are but higher animals, we must be able to find analogues or explanations for our worst conduct in that evolutionary past. This conduct must be explicable in terms of that genetic inheritance, or perhaps in the way it interacts with our social conditioning. This line of reasoning implies that individuals cannot be held morally responsible for their actions. Laymen follow this, refusing to exercise their capacities toward reason and prudence in judgment over their fellow citizens. Moreover, they almost disbelieve they have the capacity to do so. This is not surprising given what Percy claimed is true about the passivity our education system cultivates. People trained to look for textbook-correct answers often find themselves paralyzed when forced to make a moral judgment.[13]

Both experts and laymen fall into the perennial temptation of explaining evil actions through the medical category of insanity. Consider the example of the twisted "love community" Tom More encounters in *Love in the Ruins* that commits several brutal murders in the style of the Manson Family. Throughout the novel, More talks to people—both scientists and laymen—who all view this as the "work of a madman" (*LR* 83). No one uses moral language to describe this group's acts. After all, if we view individuals as the sum of their stimuli, and we live in a world of the best of material circumstances, how else would we explain truly savage acts? What vocabulary remains?

Percy believed that in scientism, the only logical modes of addressing human concerns become therapeutic and institutional. Scientism cannot look to individual human will and choice as a possibility for change. Its adherents turn to more "systemic" answers and the conception of politics as a kind of art that tends to people's souls falls away. To an expert with this view, changing the psychological, social, and cultural conditions that determine the life of a people is the only path forward. The broader idea of altering the structure of society as a direct path to improvement raises a different set of challenges. Percy addressed them in his essays on social science, and in his stories, largely through the character of Tom More.

THE SCIENTISTIC WAR FOR IMPROVEMENT

One of the perils of understanding the difficulties inherent in human life "systemically" comes from the ways that the adherents of such theories fall prey to what Percy calls the "besetting sin" of social science: the relentless desire for improvement (*SSL* 261). The adherent of scientism must see any failure to embrace progress as deeply irrational, if not unethical. Percy saw many difficulties for those who embrace this worldview—as either laymen or experts. But several specifically political implications also follow from the obsession with improvement, particularly as a result of the way people who hold to a scientistic view treat dissenting voices.

If there is only one relevant or acceptable path to understand reality, curious things happen to the language people use to describe not just man's struggle with nature (as C.S. Lewis suggested), but also the way they explain social phenomena. In *The Thanatos Syndrome*, Tom More's nemesis John Van Dorn considers his efforts akin to a war, and insists that in "time of war and plague you have to be Draconian" (*TS* 218). Van Dorn labels crime, teenage suicide and drug abuse, and AIDS as "social plagues," and insists that they all require systematic cures rather than limited treatments that alleviate these ills (*TS* 218–19). The systemic impulse here flows directly from the way scientism deprives human beings of agency: if we view everyone as the product of their environment, only changes to the environment as a whole carry a good chance of effecting change. More expresses unease at Van Dorn's way of seeing the world, but as usual, does not actually find words with which to oppose him. Percy's point in leaving More silent here may have something to do with the danger of transmuting social problems into a warlike concern.

A good example of why Percy had cause to worry about this can still be seen in William James's 1910 essay and speech "The Moral Equivalent of War." James united scientism with the militarized pursuit of progress in a few important ways. He accepted an objective-material account of the human person, but refused to believe our warlike impulses are merely a matter of social conditioning. Evolution itself produced our violent tendencies, and only an account of social progress that put these instincts to use stands a chance of allowing humanity to leave war behind. James suggested that the best path to accomplishing this will come through channeling humanity's needs for competition and struggle into various social and economic ills, through the waging of metaphorical wars on poverty, illness, and the like.[14] James also appealed to the clarity of victory and defeat, and the capacity a warlike attitude grants its adherents for dealing with internal conflict. This attitude, however, places disagreements beyond the pale, and this is where scientism of the sort James endorsed relates to Percy's account.

Percy implied that scientism leads to an attitude where we close off the possibility of debate whenever the fugitive perfection of progress might be reached.[15] Under such circumstances, no argument will avail unless we can tie its basis to materialist canons of evidence. Indeed, throughout his novels Percy depicted characters that resist the scientistic attitude toward progress and "improvement" of individual life as exhausted and unable to articulate their own position in ways that their interlocutors can even understand, let alone view as legitimate. Two examples from *Love in the Ruins* illustrate this point.

The first appears in an exchange between Tom More and his "neobehaviorist" friend Max Gottlieb. This conversation reveals a great deal about how the scientistic mind views other forms of thought. The discussion begins with More trying to relay news of potential disaster in their city—news of shootings, planned abductions, and perhaps a localized revolution. More remains aware of how odd it all sounds, and observes it may all be foolishness. But Max sees Tom in a diagnostic mode: "'I didn't say I didn't believe you, Tom,' says Max affectionately. 'Belief. Truth values. These are relative things'" (*LR* 112–3). Max cannot take Tom's words seriously, in part because he views Tom as hopelessly metaphysical and in deep need of various therapies that might recondition his way of seeing the world. In particular, Max focuses on breaking Tom of his "hang-ups" regarding sex and relationships, but cannot understand the very language through which Tom expresses his position. Tom believes his conduct toward women to be sinful but feels little or no guilt; Max tries, but cannot understand Tom's worries at his lack of guilt. Max's medical diagnosis cannot allow him to see Tom's perspective (which, after all, is relative to his feelings and not any claim to material-objective truth), but rather in psychiatric conditioning. More observes:

> "That's what worries me: not feeling guilty."
> "Why does that worry you?"
> "Because if I felt guilty, I could get rid of it."
> "How?"
> "By the sacrament of penance."
> "I'm trying to see it as you see it. . . . If you would come back and get in the Skinner box, we could straighten it out."
> "The Skinner box wouldn't help."
> "We could condition away the contradiction. You'd never feel guilt."
> "Then I'd really be up the creek." (*LR* 117–118)

Percy suggested that even the most well-disposed and sympathetic friend will fail to comprehend a different approach to human life if that friend lives by scientism. But throughout these exchanges, Tom cannot actually articulate an alternative.[16] In this first example, he does not give an explanation of his attachment to the Catholic Church. To the degree he provides reasons, they follow the perfunctory report of feelings as in the passage above. The difficulty rests not just with Max's incomprehension, but also in the ways that More's own ability to speak seems undermined by the scientistic attitude.

A second example of this from *Love in the Ruins* presents an even more unnerving issue in the scientistic attitude toward life and death. More confronts a fellow doctor, Buddy Brown, over whether an uncooperative senior citizen, Mr. Ives, should be sent to a euthanasia facility called Happy Isles, where elderly people were implanted with a device called a "euphoric switch," allowing them to feel pleasure at will. Percy imagined a form of euthanasia to which he imagined few could possibly object: one initiated by throwing a euphoric "switch that stays on, inducing a permanent joy—no meals, no sleep, and a happy death in a week or so" (*LR* 121–122). Unsurprisingly, Brown insists More has no rational grounds for saving Ives, and Tom cannot articulate any basis for his disagreement:

> "This time you're wide open."
> "How do you figure?"
> "Because you have allowed nonscientific considerations to affect your judgment."
> "Nonscientific considerations?"
> "Religious considerations."
> "I? Religious? How's that?"
> "Tell the truth. You oppose in principle Happy Isles and the Euphoric Switch."
> "Yes."
> "And you don't want Mr. Ives to be sent there."
> "That's true."
> "Why?"
> "Why what?"
> "Why do you disapprove?"
> I fall silent. (*LR* 197)

This continues throughout the book: More and others who wish to oppose this sort of materialism fail to defend their beliefs in speech, and only occasionally succeed when they represent themselves in deed. Their opponents constantly assume that religion automatically is irrational and reasoning from such beliefs is inadmissible as a proper kind of public argument. Only statements issued in a scientific key can defend Mr. Ives and all the others threatened by this worldview, and the novel's resolution leaves Tom More and those that might oppose euthanasia or similar measures without any hope of a renewed language or belief. The difficulty here flows from the fact that while Tom has principles, he either cannot articulate them as more than intuitions, alternatively, and worse still for society, Tom has good arguments but knows they will be dismissed, and so does not bother.

Scientism abets the disposing of human life both in theory and in practice. The theory does not allow for even gentle dissent, and forecloses real conversation by denying any reality to other visions. As a result, scientism's opponents begin their struggle at a significant disadvantage, and these attitudes that scientism cultivates toward public life inevitably undermine the liberalism in which the apostles of scientism so often claim to put their political faith.

Without the possibility of public conversation that allows for varied perspectives, one carried on with some spirit of charity, liberal notions of toleration lose a great deal of their power. Percy implied that the real danger here comes not in direct assaults on free speech so much as the pressure that a scientistic public life places upon individuals to turn away from ways of living and thinking that defy strictly materialist justification. Indeed, Percy saw a significant problem in that even moderate consistency when applying a scientistic approach to society leads to a set of attitudes toward politics and social life that deny religion, culture, or morality an independent role in shaping our understanding. Instead, scientism's apostles view all of these as products of deeper material or biological forces acting upon human life. In particular, Percy suggested these attitudes result in a kind of abstract approach to dealing with human beings, one that treats their individual cares and needs with suspicion or contempt.

Percy repeatedly returned to examples from psychology and neuroscience to help his readers understand the high stakes involved in this turn away from a constitutionally oriented liberalism. Think for a moment about anxiety and depression, perhaps the most universally treated mental disorders of our era. Few people completely escape their grasp, but one distinctive change we confront in our scientistic era rests in the belief that we need not live with these feelings, and indeed, all the reigning theory of the age insists that we view these mental states simply as disorders. Despite their different emphases, both psychoanalytic thought and students of the brain's inner workings come to a similar conclusion about this. Whether we view mental distress from the former position, where "guilt and anxiety were regarded as overt signs of a covert psychic disorder, signs whose meanings could be fathomed only by the use of special techniques, such as psychoanalysis" (*SSL* 254), or the neuroscientific position, in which we treat the bad feelings solely as symptoms of a chemical imbalance, both must view our disorders as materially reducible to the patient, the environment, or as a mix from both sources (*LC* 75–76).

Under the auspices of these theories, an alternative assumption about depression like that Percy developed in *Lost in the Cosmos* cannot stand. In place of a therapeutic method that treats depression as a symptom of a disease we might cure, Percy asked his readers to accept the fact of their depression and invert the usual claims people make about this:

> Now, call into question the unspoken assumption: something is wrong with you. Like Copernicus and Einstein, turn the universe upside down and begin with a new assumption.
>
> Assume that you are quite right. You are depressed because you have every reason to be depressed. No member of the other two million species which inhabit the earth—and who are luckily exempt from depression—would fail to be depressed if it lived the live you lead. You live in a deranged age—more deranged than usual, because despite great scientific and technological advances, man has no the faintest idea of who he is or what he is doing. (*LC* 76)

To the adherent of scientism, this statement must read as dangerous ontological nonsense. But moreover, Percy implored us to consider some of the other consequences of this position.

Having denied the idea that we can identify or name moral or ontological disorders at all, and instead reducing them into solely psychological "issues," other consequences follow. If science can identify no moral reality, how exactly can we see rights as natural in any sense? In their place, we receive constructivist "human" rights and the concrete demand that human beings suffer less and less.[17] If we can defend no objective rights, on what grounds can any humane society justify letting individuals suffer from depression? Peter Augustine Lawler frames this pointedly by questioning whether people in the future will even retain the right to refuse treatment of "preventable" illnesses, such as anxiety or sadness.[18]

Even if for the moment we dismiss Lawler's extension of this argument as hyperbole, when we marry the absence of rights to an obsession with progressively improving our material life, the distinctiveness and oddities of individual human beings bear the strong chance of getting lost in abstraction. Science cannot come to grips with individual cases. Thus, Percy insisted that a true scientist understands this limitation and circumscribes their ambitions accordingly. But those that would overextend science's reach may fall prey to another danger: the willful disrespect of individuals before the abstract social, psychological, and political types their chosen theories advance. Human beings cannot easily live in this manner. If they could do so, more adherents of scientism would follow theory to its logical conclusion and deny themselves any status as rights-bearing creatures. They might follow Budziszewski in his logical but horrifying dismissal of his family bonds as objects of serious moral concern. If we understand Percy's argument here about scientism and expertise, what remains is engaging with the very human remainders that resist being subsumed under the auspices of any theory.

THE HAUNTING REMAINDER

Both the subjects and practitioners of overextended science face an obstacle to living well. To the degree they attempt to live a coherent life around the theories they claim to hold dear, they will suffer a deprivation of their ability to understand the distinctive elements that make up their existence. But the difficulty Percy suggested that even amid his subjection to scientism, modern man cannot escape the sense that something is missing. If scientific materialism does not fully satisfy our longings, but deprives us of any ontological ground to assess our lives, what might ordinary human beings then do? This difficulty explains the appeal of the "mishmash" theories of man. There remains too the possibility that human beings unsatisfied by the obvious options of our age might turn to more radical options as an escape from the facile explanations of sterile theory, the appeal of honor, or the longing for conventional community.

Scientism tends toward a kind of fatalism and denial of moral responsibility. Perhaps the most telling political problem this theory creates for our lives is how we deal with evil. Social theories of this sort have to view violence as a departure from the normal, comfortable world that we all wish to inhabit. They have to understand deviance from the norm not in moral terms, but as a malformation of the human animal that science must strive to understand and prevent in the future. Note the ways that we must evaluate our political life that follow from this: if human beings merely respond to their biology and environment, mass movements can only emerge as a consequence of real needs and legitimate concerns.

If this is true, we cannot see fascism, communism, militant Islamism, or any other possible totalizing view in a qualitatively different way. Such political movements could only emerge as direct reactions to a society's material circumstances and psychological response to those causes. An outsider studying these movements in this way could not, then, argue against them as unjust or criticize them on the basis of their threat to our society's moral beliefs. An adherent of scientism could admit that these movements differed from his or her preferences, but could not in any way logically claim that they had a *moral* reason to defend their society against another's. By restricting their analysis to material causes and their outcomes, scientism deprives its adherents of the intellectual strength to oppose these movements.

But let us consider a variation of Percy's thought experiment about depression and apply it to this situation. Could the very methods we use to "treat" disorder and evil actually exacerbate them? What if the unspoken materialist assumptions are wrong, and that sometimes mass movements address not the material world but our longing to be free from the theoretical prisons we have made ourselves? After all, Percy repeatedly noted that we live in a peculiarly sentimental age that also coincidentally is an age of terror and mass murder. With these arguments, Percy asked his readers to consider the possibility that our conventional ways of viewing politically dangerous movements insufficiently grasp the way they try to satisfy their adherents' longings—and more specifically, their desires for escape from the boring everyday world we inhabit.

NOTES

1. On Dewey's role in American education, see Jay Martin, *The Education of John Dewey* (New York: Columbia University Press, 2002) and Robert B. Westbrook, *John Dewey and American Democracy* (Ithaca: Cornell University Press, 1991). For a critique of Dewey's influence, see Henry T. Edmonson III, *John Dewey and the Decline of American Education* (Wilmington: ISI Books, 2006).

2. John Dewey, *Freedom and Culture* (Amherst, NY: Prometheus Books, 1989), 114.

3. Dewey, *Freedom and Culture*, 112.

4. For two examples, see Dewey, *Culture and Freedom*, 80–81, 105–106. Consider also the ways that Tocqueville believed democratic people place themselves in a kind of intellectual bondage to "general ideas," notions that come from experts. See *Democracy in America* (New York: Harper Collins, 1969), 433–444.

5. On this attitude toward authority, see Alan Petigny, *The Permissive Society: America 1941–1965* (Cambridge: Cambridge University Press, 2009), 12–13

6. On the matter of alertness and its importance for liberty and dignity in a bourgeois order, see Deirdre McCloskey, *Bourgeois Dignity: Why Economics Can't Explain the Modern World* (Chicago: University of Chicago Press, 2010), 20–21, 410–411.

7. On Percy's experiences in medical school and early devotion to science as the basis of a worldview, see chapter 4 in Patrick Samway, S.J., *Walker Percy: A Life* (Chicago: Loyola Press, 1997), 89–117.

8. F. A. Hayek, *The Counter-Revolution of Science: Studies on the Abuse of Reason* (Indianapolis: Liberty Fund, 1979), 24.

9. For a contemporary example analyzing myth in these terms, see Karen Armstrong, *A Short History of Myth* (New York: Canongate, 2005).

10. C.S. Lewis, *The Abolition of Man* (New York: HarperCollins, 2001), 53.

11. J. Budziszewski, *The Revenge of Conscience: Politics and the Fall of Man* (Eugene: Wipf and Stock, 2010), xiv–xv.

12. See, for example, Bruce N. Waller, *Against Moral Responsibility* (Cambridge: MIT Press, 2011).

13. On this phenomenon's influence in the legal system, particularly in jury trials, see Norma Thompson, *Unreasonable Doubt: Circumstantial Evidence and the Art of Judgment* (Philadelphia: Paul Dry Books, 2011).

14. See William James, "The Moral Equivalent of War," in *Writings, 1902–1910* (New York: Literary Classics of the United States, 1988). See also Wilfred B. McClay, "The Moral Equivalent of War?," *National Affairs*, No. 5 (Fall 2010), 134–144.

15. Compare to Tocqueville's account of progress and perfectibility in *Democracy in America*, Vol. II, Part I, Ch. 8.

16. For a provocative account of this passage that situates Percy's writing in broader social trends, see Andrew Delbanco, *The Real American Dream: A Meditation on Hope* (Cambridge: Harvard University Press, 1999), 99–103.

17. Consider here the U.N. Declaration of Human Rights and its turn away from both the idea there is any kind of natural law and its implicit denial of the kinds of metaphysical rights claims one finds in the U.S. Declaration of Independence.

18. For this argument, see Peter Augustine Lawler, *Stuck with Virtue: The American Individual and Our Biotechnological Future* (Wilmington: ISI Books, 2005), 130–133.

Part II

AMERICAN ATTEMPTS AT A CURE

While materialism and science might serve as the most significant background conditions for our social life today, Percy argued that Americans face other temptations as well. Communities and their social life provide for many human needs, but in the absence of a philosophy or animating faith that restrains our longings for complete satisfaction in this world, we engage in social life with intemperate expectations. A wayfaring sensibility might moderate this, but because of the damage our faith in experts and in mishmash theories cause to our sense of self, Percy suggested that we overwhelmingly tend to adopt extreme positions in relation to others.

In chapters 3–5, I explore Percy's arguments concerning how the intellectual dangers I discussed in Part I manifest themselves in our expectations concerning society. Seeking a complete remedy for our alienation, we thrust ourselves into communities, and when they do not satisfy us, we frantically retreat into isolation. Disgusted by the typical American forms of community life, Percy argued that some people will look to join or create alternative communities bound by honor, which may bring with them extremely dangerous political consequences. Others will embrace varieties of envy and malice as a kind of distraction and escape from the limitations of real communities. All of these efforts aim at a complete remedy to our alienation, yet for the attentive soul that despairs of them, Percy suggested that these means present clues that might lead us back to seeing the world as wayfarers.

Chapter 3

Individualism, Community, and the Longing for Place

As early as the 1830s, Tocqueville argued that apart from farming families, each generation of children retains little incentive or ability to hold onto their parents' property, and instead scatters in search of fortune and fame.[1] Indeed, Tocqueville emphasized throughout *Democracy in America* that the restless search for happiness and material prosperity—and our tendency to conflate the two—would do much to threaten the vibrant associational life he believed so important for the maintenance of liberty. At least since Robert Putnam's *Bowling Alone* quantified Tocqueville's philosophical analysis, and ever since, the picture most social scientists paint of the prospects for robust community life in American has been bleak: scholars note with concern the hollowing out of civic bonds, placing the lion's share of the blame on our materialistic pursuits, our relentless individualism, and lack of attachment to particular places.[2] Likewise, Percy observed that something is amiss in our sense of community, and asked his readers to ponder what it is that drives us away from embracing the places in which we live. He also suggested that the political and social implications of this tendency were profound.

This chapter focuses on how Percy understood the dangers and promise of American community. In both his novels and essays, Percy developed a complex account of what we can hope to gain from a well-ordered community; he also paints a stark picture of the perils of community deformed and shattered under the pressures of our politics and culture. Percy echoed many of the common arguments about the unraveling of community, but his account departs significantly from the standard communitarian narrative of decline. Percy's understanding of the politics of the wayfarer sets him apart: community cannot save human beings from alienation, but the right bonds between people can attenuate this feeling. Hoping for a community that feels no alienation is as dangerous as retreating from life in one altogether. Thus,

Percy's critique of the common attitudes toward community in America rested in part on his conviction that too often we ask too much or too little from the places we live, and very rarely live in a mean between extremes of isolation and restless engagement. Americans have an overly romantic notion of what community might be, and because of this search of fugitive perfection, no actual community can quite live up to our expectations.

At first glance, Percy's assault appears to apply most pointedly to suburban life. He feared that the American South in particular would suffer the fate of the Southern California suburb and become what he called "losangelized." Percy abhorred the standardization of places on both aesthetic and moral grounds, for the rise of uniformity and monoculture make distinctive regional identities so essential to real community somewhat harder to create and maintain. For this reason, Percy rendered pointed judgment on the stereotypical American housing tract throughout his novels. At the same time, Percy saw more than a small dose of hypocrisy in elite criticism of how most Americans live:

> We are all familiar with an entire literature about the ennui of life in suburbia and the split-level nightmare. . . . Aside from the worth or lack of it in such novels, I cannot escape the suspicion of a degree of bad faith both in the novelist and in his characters, that, in short, for all their complaints, neither of them would dream of changing places with the nineteenth-century housewife or low-paid nineteenth-century novelist. (*SSL* 209–10)

Percy suggested that the difficulty might not rest with standardized suburbia per se. It is not the American Dream's family life with two children and a pet, nor the restless materialism he particularly associated with our great cities, and not even the friendly oppressiveness of the small town that we have to fear. What endangers the republic flows from man's boredom with himself amid the most perfected comfort and his inability to call any place home for long. For Percy, our disorderly relations to place and community represented a clue into human longings for certainty, love, and fulfillment—clues that we often ignore. Communities may attenuate our alienation, but only if people adopt a moderate relationship to them and take on obligations of duty and care for their neighbors.

Many kinds of American communities, Percy suggested, receive a great deal of dishonest criticism from their enemies. Percy sought to avoid a pose of protest or nostalgic yearning for a life neither he nor any other critics would ever choose: "Witness the writers of the Agrarian Movement in the South, nearly all of whom ended up in Northern universities" (*SSL* 6). Instead, in his essays on community, he aimed at an even-handed account of what we lose in the growing suburbs or the then-resurgent cities of the South; in his novels, we see striking portrayals of characters trying to find fulfillment in the world and in their communities, a satisfaction that always remains deferred. Percy suggested we always need a place to call home and people with which to share our lives, but also noted that this is a need we never fully satisfy: this means that the physical communities we inhabit remain reminders of a deeper need, and of our status as wayfarers with another home.

PLACE AND COMMUNITY IN AMERICA

The real dilemma comes from trying to understand what people need from their communities. The confusions we face about this flow directly from misunderstandings about human nature. Our bonds with others and to specific places matter profoundly, but Percy believed we often rank these needs too high or too low. A great deal of modern unhappiness stands not as a pain we can and should remedy with therapy or anti-depressants, but rather, as a sign of our unrecognized wayfaring character.

Percy examined this phenomenon by recognizing the problematic ways in which we relate to our homes: one can very easily live in a nondescript suburb of Los Angeles that has no immediately observable history or sense of communal identity, spend three hours a day commuting alone to a well-paying job in the city, and bear no meaningful ties to any of these places: suburb, city, or workplace. Such a person is little more than passing through, and Percy suggested this individual might fall entirely between places, existing in a "nonplace." He argued that it is entirely possible that this person could feel as completely alienated on the road as they are at home or work (*SSL* 3–4, *MB* 87). This is the worst-case picture of modern life and provides a great deal of fodder for television melodrama; it nonetheless provides a starting point for discussing Percy's view on our ways of relating to a place.

Modern theorizing and consuming people do not simply abide in their homes and find what happiness they can in their families and communities. Their sense of self does not easily allow for such patience. Percy described how he thought Americans related to their homes in his 1980 essay "Why I Live Where I Live." His focus in this essay was on his own experience, particularly as a writer, but the work provides a window into Percy's thinking about what makes our attachments to places healthy or not. By describing a spectrum of relationships using labels like "placement," "nonplacement," and "misplacement," he helps us comprehend the degree to which communities draw their members in to their particular culture, history, and more.

Some people grow up drenched in the identity of a place. But this is not the norm. Percy argued that the central difficulty we experience actually relates to one of our nation's great blessings, liberty: "Free people have a serious problem with place, being in a place, using up a place, deciding which new place to rotate to. Americans ricochet around the United States like billiard balls" (*SSL* 5). Being totally placed in one's community completely defies the typical American experience of uprooting one's family in pursuit of prosperity. Percy described this "total placement" as being born in the 1920s in a city like Charleston or Mobile or a small town today, a place "where one's family has lived for two hundred years," and the bonds of family history and collective memory weigh on everyone (*SSL* 3). Percy implied that the totally placed person would find it difficult to describe themselves without constant reference to their locale—as opposed, to say, relating the facts about their lives and their experiences in terms of their career, school, or specific people.

In a condition of total placement, where a person is from becomes the center of how they relate themselves to others in the world. This is not entirely bad, since such a community provides its members with a ready-made understanding of what it is to live well, do right by one's neighbors, and all the company one could stand. However, Percy suggested that the oppressiveness of this relationship may rebound to a kind of alienation: it is possible to become so tied to a place and its history and inhabitants that home suffocates rather than nourishes. This makes such communities something of a scandal to a liberal individualist, and if they were the only kind of community bond available to people, Percy implied that most Americans would reasonably stay on the move.

Percy described the opposite phenomenon from total placement as "nonplacement," which he defined as "to do what Descartes did, live anonymously among the burghers of Amsterdam. Or do what Kierkegaard did, live in the business district of Copenhagen, pop out into the street every half hour, and speak to the shopkeepers so one will be thought an idler" (*SSL* 3–4). To return to my example above, today, one might be the stereotype of a lonely, transplanted Southern California commuter. Here, the complete absence of relational bonds and personal history in a place leaves one without the capacity to speak of oneself in terms of any locale. It also stands in the way of relating to those that live there in the way that people from a specific, culturally defined place often do. This person's alienation from other human beings would be nearly complete. Percy argued that for intellectuals—the writers, the scientists, and the philosophers—that might be the point, because they can turn to the peculiar resources of their professions and the methods they allow for "orbiting" ordinary life as I described earlier. Such people share in a series of temporary escapes from the alienation of ordinary life that is unavailable to most people. Consider the modern technological alternative to this in social media, where we can have very distant connections with a wide range of people whom we never meet. It might also be true that today's immersive multiplayer online games and virtual worlds provide a substitute for face-to-face relationships. But for Percy, none of these options satisfy the needs of the heart. Instead, Percy argued that most people at least try out some degree of placement in a community.[3]

Presumably most Americans live somewhere between being drenched in their family's historical memory and ties to a place, and the opposite extreme of ghostly distance from their neighbors and colleagues.[4] The weight of Percy's critique fell on the destructive tendencies that rest in between these extremes, and the lengths that people go to trying to escape the "confinement" of ordinary communities that reflect that middling state. By discussing the degree of placement we feel in relation to our fellow men, Percy demonstrated some of the disordered ways people attempt to deal with their contradictory longings for both autonomy and interrelated dependence on others.

Many people choose a more temporary form of escape from the bonds of community. What Percy labeled "misplacement" is the act of moving to and living somewhere different than one is used to, preferably an exotic place, and hoping for something to change in one's life or perspective. Like everyone else, writers hope to be inspired by a new locale, to see something new about themselves or their old home that otherwise would remain invisible or unspeakable (*SSL* 4–5). In this case, a writer might relate to the locals as a person with a real identity from somewhere else, but the more extreme the misplacement, the less likely this would be meaningful to any of the people involved. The author would be a stranger and not yet a member of any community, with all the possibilities and perils this implies.

Percy provided an example of this in *Lost in the Cosmos*: a movie crew and its actors, misplaced through their time in a small Midwestern town for the duration of filming. He related this story by way of asking why it is that these actors, finding themselves stranded far from Los Angeles or New York "found themselves playing enjoyable roles in the town . . . the roles of the superb human beings the town folk believed them to be." This move made for a particularly profound change in a famous actress, one known for being a difficult person. She "became a very model of friendliness and graciousness," but nonetheless after six weeks in the town, grew tired of the place and its people (*LC* 37–39). Percy asked his readers to consider, first, what made for the change? and second, why the actress so quickly tired of her new "role" and pined for a return to city life?

People can only be misplaced strangers for a short while. The novelty of being a famous person working in small town is a special case. He emphasized the ways that the heightened reality of being in a new place for what one knows will be a short time produces temporary changes in people that are often quite dramatic. The escape from the normal routine of one community into another sometimes mitigates alienation, but this is only a temporary fix. Time reduces the strangeness of strangers, new places become ordinary, and boredom returns in force. The person's sense of feeling out of place returns.

Of course, one can build a new community in one of these non-places that Percy described, continue a tradition of living totally placed in a town drenched in its own history, or go from being a misplaced outsider in a city to member of some neighborhood's civic life. But Americans often live in a way that makes these options very difficult. The typical middle-class American's relative prosperity liberates them from being permanently bound to any particular community, but these habits of moving in pursuit of financial opportunity or to get away from family also may undercut our ability to actually form bonds with those where we do live. Those that consider their homes temporary do not develop the habits of affiliation that make an eventual move harder. They avoid putting down roots to escape the eventual pain of leaving them behind. Think for a moment of Tocqueville's account of how Americans relentlessly move to pursue their dreams and improve their economic lot:

> It is odd to watch with what feverish ardor the Americans pursue prosperity and how they are ever tormented by the shadowy suspicion that they may not have chosen the shortest route to get it.
>
> Americans cleave to the things of this world as if assured that they will never die, and yet are in such a rush to snatch any that come within their reach, as if expecting to stop living before they have relished them. They clutch everything but hold nothing fast, and so lose grip as they hurry after some new delight.[5]

Being liberated allows for this kind of dubious freedom, but settling into a community and forming ties of friendship and family takes time and the acceptance of responsibility that Americans all too often deny themselves. Our very independence may prove the death of our community life.[6]

The difficulty community presents to modern Americans lay in the fact that both deep bonds and the complete absence of civic ties come with their own costs: the most closely tight-knit societies cannot help but look upon many of what denizens of liberal democracy see as personal matters as public business. The kinds of obligatory and deep community that are common in history often serve as a kind of nostalgic communitarian paradise because of the way the total placement of such order enforces that community's particular virtues.[7] By contrast, highly mobile or socially distant communities encourage people to live with benign neglect toward one another—a sort of libertarian ideal that in Percy's idiom we might call "non-placed non-intervention." In a 1984 essay on New Orleans, Percy compared the city to New York and

Mobile, and makes an important claim about the nature of public and private spaces in each sort of place:

> The space in question is not the ordinary living space of individuals and families but rather the interstices thereof. In New York millions of souls carve out living space on a grid like so many circles on graph paper. These lairs are more or less habitable. But the space between is a horrid thing, a howling vacuum. If you fall ill on the streets of New York, people grumble about having to step over you or around you. . . . Mobile, Alabama, unlike New York, has no interstices. It is older than New Orleans. It has wrought iron, better azaleas, an older Mardi Gras. . . . Yet it suffers from the spiritual damps, Alabama anoxia. Twenty-four hours in Mobile and you have the feeling a plastic bag is tied around your head and you're breathing your own air. Mobile's public space is continuous with the private space of its front parlors. So where New York is a vacuum, Mobile is a pressure cooker. (*SSL* 10–11)

Percy exaggerated the extremes, but each of these general options comes at a cost: New York (or any other major American city, for that matter) certainly allows its residents the possibility of choosing and forming small knots of fully chosen community. On the other hand, if a family prefers to ignore their neighbors, they expect that choice to be respected, and indeed, the community may strongly encourage this distance between neighbors. The fact these bonds remain optional leaves us isolated and shut in upon ourselves, a condition only reinforced by many of our economic and social choices actively undermine our desire to take on the responsibility of making a community at all. In the Mobile Percy described (and presumably innumerable small towns across the nation), if a person cannot leave and does not like the enforced community, they have little choice but either accepting the Mobile way of life or ostracizing themselves from the group—and their reputation for being "un-neighborly" will follow them.[8] Percy presented the community found in New Orleans as a kind of compromise between these two kinds of communities, but he also thought the tenuous balance of cities like this is always fragile and may give way to the evacuated center of Los Angeles or New York urban and suburban life.

Percy further complicated the picture of community life by noting that even beyond the difficulty of "placing" oneself in the right community and finding a home with the appropriate public interstices between homes, people still evince a restless quality. Rather than dwelling in a place and not expecting salvation or perfect happiness from it as Percy suggested wayfarers should, now we *consume* them: "Places are consumed nowadays. The more delectable the place, the quicker it is ingested, digested, and turned to feces" (*SSL* 5). Hyperbolic, perhaps, but this analogy of consumption explains many

American attitudes not just toward home and place, but also about our views on vacation. He pointed to one extreme that presents itself in Kerouac's *On the Road*. Percy observed that over the period covered in a single book, Kerouac "careens back and forth between New York and California—with one Mexican detour" and never finds more than a temporary solace via his consumption of each place and its people (*LC* 148–149).

In a world where we expect temporal satisfaction and delight almost as a right, Percy argued we demand more from our places and our people than before, and invest meaning in them in a way that guarantees their failure to satisfy. Our attitudes also leave us less likely to see the clues about the imperfection of any actual community for what they are. Percy's first published novel, *The Moviegoer*, offers more insight into this phenomenon.

CONSUMING PLACES

Percy's best fictional representation of how an alienated man might respond to "place" appears in the *Moviegoer*'s Binx Bolling. Binx is a character fully invested in the practice of "consuming" places as a way of escaping his everyday sense of dislocation and boredom. As the novel progresses, Binx becomes increasingly aware of the difficulty of finding meaning in places and activities. He finds even less comfort in his family and broader community in which he lives. That is not to say Binx is a cast-off or social dropout. He rightly claims the title of being a "model tenant, and a model citizen," and derives pleasure from fulfilling his obligations in different environments. Rather than affirming his bonds to specific places and people (Percy presented his reader a couple dozen friends and relations that Binx kept at arms' length), Binx explains his desire for belonging in an entirely abstracted way: "It is a pleasure to carry out the duties of a citizen and to receive in return a receipt or a neat styrene card with one's name on it certifying, so to speak, one's right to exist" (*MG* 6–7). This seems a paltry proof of one's existence, labeled by membership in groups, in our credit rating, and under the auspices of various authorities. Binx suggests that we want not just ourselves but our places "certified" by the myriad authorities of popular culture. After seeing a film, Binx explains:

> Nowadays when a person lives somewhere, in a neighborhood, the place is not certified for him. More than likely he will live there sadly and the emptiness which is inside him will expand until it evacuates the entire neighborhood. But if he sees a movie which shows his very neighborhood, it becomes possible for him to live, for a time at least, as a person who is Somewhere and not Anywhere. (*MG* 63)

Binx's identity—and Percy implied, that of many other people—is bound up with being recognized by others, but unlike many Americans, Binx believes this is insufficient to even start to live well. Sensing something is missing and unable to quite name it, Binx begins what he calls his "search."

Binx's search, which he describes as "what anyone would undertake if he were not sunk in the everydayness of his own life," remains focused on his sense of self and his relations to places. He hopes to be like a castaway on a strange island and "miss" nothing about his surroundings. He desires to fully experience every detail so he might relive it and fully savor it later in his mind. Binx's search poses at least two difficulties: first, his quest focuses not on any sense of wonder at the mysteries of his world, but rather revolves around fleeting moments of novelty, excitement, and consumption. Second, Binx's search also revolves around his attempts to make places and his memories of them into sources of fulfillment. He abstracts himself from his surroundings in doing this, always lost in memories and connections between the present and other times (*MG* 13–14). Such mental images cannot satisfy his longing to belong; nor can his nostalgia. His rebellion against "everydayness" draws him back to these odd experiments, and only their repeated failure alongside the intrusions of a woman who desperately needs him, his lifelong friend Kate, leads him on a different path.[9]

Yet at the outset of the novel, Binx remains unmoved by his surroundings and unattached to those around him. He understands that his life is comfortable and prosperous, if understated; he tells us his "apartment is as impersonal as a motel room" because of his care in avoiding possessions (*MG* 78). He has a sports car, plenty of money, and spends his free time reading great books or in the company of the essentially interchangeable beautiful women he employs as secretaries. He parts from the women he dates as soon as the anxiety and thrill of novelty wears off. Binx's intellectual endeavors do not help either: he only reads books that cover "fundamental" subjects, and always provide general theories that give him no help in answering the questions he asks about life. Beyond offering him prosperity, his work as a stockbroker presents him with intellectual challenges. Yet Binx is convinced that he has only escaped what he calls "everydayness" once in his life—when he lay bleeding in a Korean ditch, wounded in combat (*MG* 145). In his successful postwar life, he only seems to find meaning or joy in evanescent moments: in the fleeting experience of new love, in the consumption of things and places, or in the balancing of what he calls "repetition" and "rotation." These moments and activities remain a far cry from any sense of real satisfaction, but Binx indulges in them until his search leads him elsewhere.

The activities of repetition and rotation bear importance for understanding what Percy meant by suggesting people can consume a place, and for most of the novel, Binx's search for events that break up the everydayness of our world works itself out largely in his frustrated acts of repetition and rotation. As the label implies, repetition looks back:

> What is a repetition? A repetition is the re-enactment of past experience toward the end of isolating the time segment which has lapsed in order that it, the lapsed time, can be savored of itself and without the usual adulteration of events that clog time like peanuts in brittle. (*MG* 79–80)

The desire to abstract oneself out of particular events to, as Binx puts it, "savor" time bespeaks a hope he cannot quite name. He links it to his desire to "miss" nothing in the world. His hope seems to be that by acutely observing all the novel and exciting things in the world, he will "find" what he seeks. What he misses in this endeavor, however, is the possibility of attenuating his alienation through concrete relations to others. Indeed, trying to experience time without the "adulteration of events" is especially peculiar because those events and the people we encounter in them are the markers we use to remember.[10]

To re-experience lapsed time this way cannot help but add to one's sense of being out of place—it is an act of nostalgic self-abstraction from one's circumstances. He describes achieving that nebulous feeling as a successful experiment in repetition, but it leaves him as cold as when he started; these moments never satisfy him. Binx does not explain the difficulty of "clogged" time directly, but if the goal is to escape the everyday, one must abstract oneself from what actually happened and forget the ties one has with places or people. They serve as the metaphorical clog in the process. This may allow the person who embraces repetition to transcend themselves and the everyday confusions that comes with life, but what have they achieved besides a temporary sense of their own annihilation?

Binx hopes for another sort of transcendence from the act of rotation, which aims at satisfying the needs of the search through an encounter with the unexpected:

> A rotation I define as the experiencing of the new beyond the expectation of the experiencing of the new. For example, taking one's first trip to Taxco would not be a rotation, or no more than a very ordinary rotation; but getting lost on the way and discovering a hidden valley would be. (*MG* 144)

Mere novelty does not suffice for this. Binx's idea that life is better outside the everyday is a clue: we travel to new places as a vacation and do "vacation things" there, then once the place is consumed, we go home and do our "home things." This poses a problem for Binx because these are routine and expected events, and he indicates in his travels that this sort of experience wore thin quickly. But to really shake oneself out of the everyday, we need not just the new but the *surprising*. The difficulty he faces stems from his inability to predict this feeling, and Binx's continual dissatisfaction with how long it lasts: being surprised and off the beaten path prove only the most temporary resolutions to Binx's alienation.

Binx Bolling represents a strange case of what Percy saw as the stereotypical American problem of seeking a solution to the problem of community by turning to extremes of rotation and repetition. In his essays Percy argued our conflicting tendency to seek novelty was just as difficult to overcome. Binx discovers this, eventually, and Percy believed that his path could be ours. But this would require that we rethink our attitudes toward community and avoid futile quests like his repetitions and rotations through the world.

These exercises cannot satisfy him or anyone else because they never bring the person to the end of seeking moments of perfect satisfaction in the world. At the same time, they also fail to chasten the desire for escape that stands at the heart what drove Binx's initial search to transcend the "everyday." Percy suggested that Binx was correct—as the existentialists were—when he said he was "onto" something with his search. But for most of the novel, instead of seeing his confused longings as clues to the impossibility of escaping his alienation entirely, Binx assumed he could eventually find the right balance to his acts of theory and consumption. Only at the end, with his marriage to Kate Cutrer and acceptance of responsibility as a member of a family does he find some peace.

THE CONTRARY LONGINGS FOR COMMUNITY AND AUTONOMY

Part of what makes *The Moviegoer* compelling reading is that Percy understood the ways that so many Americans long for perfection just like Binx did. At the start of the novel, Binx genuinely believes as many of us do that we can have it all: a happy, materially fulfilled, and spiritually satisfied life, if only he could hit on the correct balance of technical means. But a merely technical means like the kind both Binx and Will Barrett attempt will not do. Percy argued that at least part of our nature longs for community—as long as we freely choose the members and place. At the same time, most people rebel against the intrusiveness such communities demand.

The situation for modern people in relation to community is difficult because these anxieties about belonging exist alongside what Percy saw as actually happening to many American communities: the tendency to standardize. The trouble starts with Percy's claim that the capacity to "place" oneself in a community bears at least some relationship to the *character* of the city.

Mobile's public spaces may be oppressive, but at least they have a distinctive identity, while for Percy, New York or Los Angeles lack this trait. This certainly seems a dubious point: convinced New Yorkers and Angelinos—many of whom make communities out of their neighborhoods—would disagree. All places develop a culture. Percy does not have to be correct in his polemical judgment of America's largest and most cosmopolitan cities to understand the phenomenon as a whole. The question is whether the culture present in a community helps its members overcome their desire to seek a permanent remedy to their alienation.

Percy's general point may hold in the sense that Americans today are united by a common popular culture and increasingly relate to one another via abstract connections. Social media in particular may draw people away from particular physical communities into a sense of being that reflects the influence of no place in particular. Percy certainly worried that abstract connections like these might only exacerbate the alienation people already feel on a daily basis. He argued that one sure but only partial antidote remained: attaching oneself to a specific place and people, and accepting the obligations, joys, and pains of a physical community.

Percy believed the South had retained a "greater sense of place" than that of other regions in the United States, but this difference stood under threat of being effaced by the march of uniformity, that it might be "losangelized" like so much of these rest of the country (*CWP* 214, *MCWP* 138). Uniformity threatens community by undermining the distinctive places and relationships people form with companies, workplaces, and what makes their community different from others. It is possible that a chain diner or a Starbucks can serve as a distinctive place of gathering for members of a community, but as businesses, they are much less likely to be owned and operated by the same people over many years or decades. We might work for the same business for an entire career, but when large companies encourage their employees to move repeatedly for advancement, this can only harm our bonds with other people. Finally, the very pattern around which planners design cities can undermine our affection for them: if any one grid-based town is more or less interchangeable with another, does that not increase our ability to move on when opportunities present themselves?

The South's distinctiveness was both a matter of place and a matter of its moral culture. The two reinforced one another. This is crucial because Percy saw the South as a possible bulwark of virtue, but only if it both retained the legacy of the honor culture and reinvigorated its commitment to a real Christian faith. While the spread of Protestant faith throughout the South is no longer in doubt, Percy feared that the distinctive differences of Southern culture that allowed a traveler to recognize when they crossed the Mason-Dixon line might fade (*MCWP* 138). And yet, despite watching the same television shows, viewing the same films, and making connections through common social media, regions still appear to retain distinctively different cultures (*SSL* 295–6). Distinctiveness may not be enough, however.

In his 1977 *Esquire* magazine self-interview, Percy noted that "ordinary life in an ordinary place on an ordinary day in the modern world is a dreary business" (*CWP* 167). This is a clue to understanding Percy's ambivalence about community. So perhaps a reading of Percy today suggests a different line of inquiry than one that emphasizes the contrasts between either cities and suburbs or distinct national regions: if we grant that our relationships to place are very complicated, and that modern Americans seem to ask either too much (some form of deeply transcendent connection) or too little (privacy and amenities like garbage removal) from their communities, the key is to understand what we really need from our lives in common. Percy savaged the conventional way of understanding a community as a place where we can develop some sort of progressively improving "maturity, creativity, autonomy, rewarding interpersonal relations, and so forth," and severely doubted that the idea of man as a wayfarer retains much of a role in our culture today (*SSL* 208). This excessive pursuit of improvement opens the door to equally extreme oscillations within the human heart.[11]

Binx Bolling's search highlights these oscillating extremes: he desires to use places to transcend "everydayness," and at the same time fears the way creeping ordinariness sets in among even the closest relationships people have to one another. Percy implied through the story that the correct attitude to community might be one that takes the clues about our nature where we find them: the fact we feel equally uneasy in cases of total placement and total nonplacement should orient us to a wayfaring sensibility that sees all communities as by themselves insufficient for a decent life. Yet even if community is insufficient by itself as a basis for happiness, a sense of some obligation to community remains a *necessary* condition for living well. Americans often rebel against this as deeply as Binx Bolling did, and this desire to escape from "everyday" communities also provides a clue to understanding our existence.

Across his writings, Percy emphasized three general types of escape from community. The first, and most common, is the attempt to leave the everyday life of a community through diversions and excitement. This rests at the heart of Binx Bolling's self-aware "rotations," but Percy returned to this notion many times in very different ways. For Percy, this longing to jar oneself out of ordinariness places us in moral danger precisely because it suggests the necessity of treating the people we encounter and the places we live merely as objects of consumption. Think of the problem at the heart of this: if a person constantly uses their friends and neighbors solely as vehicles for disrupting their boredom, they reduce these people to objects rather than co-celebrants of the world. Here, Binx's treatment of other people throughout *The Moviegoer* as elements of a sociological experiment stands out as an example: it not only undermines his capacity to live with alienation, but deepens it along with that of his friends and acquaintances as well. [12]

A second form of desire to flee from community rests in acts of transcendence. As we saw earlier, this requires either a metaphorical or a literal escape: scientists and artists can do this without leaving home because their work, in essence, leads them into an abstract world they share with their fellows. Scientists might have an easier time of this than artists, but both share a difficulty: the joys of science and the pleasure of art rarely provide a lasting basis for taking delight in ordinary human life. In fact, having transcended ordinary life in their work, the return home after a day of thought or creation might be all the more trying on actual relationships. But what of the man or woman who lacks the talent or training that allows them to partake in these acts? One example of this comes in the predicament of the lay Freudian, the person who reads just enough to feel superior to ordinary folk by understanding their "real" motives, and thus gains a shadow of real transcendence at the expense of his or her bonds with others. Such a person reads just enough to believe he holds the key to other minds, but in the process impoverishes his actual ability to see other people as more than abstractions to be studied (*LC* 117–19). This theoretical devaluation of human life bears other consequences on communities, as well.

In the *Moviegoer*, Binx Bolling's cousin Nell Lovell seeks a justification of her life and reassurance that she has done what she should. A fortyish mother of two grown children, Nell turned to philosophy. But she did this not from the perspective of a search, or even of challenging her settled ways of life, but rather to confirm her own dispositions about how to live. Encountering Binx at the library, and holding a book reputed to offer a depressing view of the world,

> "I don't feel a bit gloomy!" she cries. "Now that Mark and Lance have grown up and flown the coop, I am having the time of my life. I'm taking philosophy courses in the morning and working nights at Le Petite Theatre. Eddie and I have re-examined our values and found them pretty darned enduring. To our utter amazement we discovered that we both have the same life-goal. Do you know what it is?"
>
> "No."
>
> "To make a contribution, however small, and leave the world just a little better off." (*MG* 101)

Nell's self-study leads her to a kind of naïve optimism and accommodation with the world in which she lives. Her readings emphasize certainty rather than mystery, and so amount to a kind of oscillation between theory and consumption rather than a real change in perspective.

Giving up television and reading Khalil Gibran aloud in the evening may indeed divert her and her husband from ordinary life, but not in any way that might reconcile their sense of alienation. Binx silently assents to her claims but reacts violently. Nell's self-description as a satisfied seeker troubles Binx to the point that he sees her as engaged in a lifeless activity: "why does she talk as if she were dead?" (*MG* 102)[13] Percy leaves the reader with the sense both of them are lost: Binx might be in a slightly better position because he is aware something is wrong in his life (but looks in the wrong place), whereas Nell seems to embrace her values as a way of putting off recognition that anything is out of place at all. Percy implied her restlessness would return once the novelty of being a philosopher wore off.

A second form of escape can be seen in *Love in the Ruins*. Doris More presents the reader with a variation of this theme: she attempts her own escape from the everyday through the pursuit of Eastern philosophy and a new life.[14] Doris's story is a failed mirror of Binx Bolling's: she also sees ordinary life in suburban Louisiana as spiritually dead and sought a way out of her marriage and Feliciana Parish. Tom More recounted this exchange:

> "I'm going in search of myself."
>
> My heart sank. This was not really her way of talking. It was the one tactic against which I was defenseless, the portentous gravity of her new beliefs. When she was an ordinary ex-Episcopalian, a good-humored Virginia girl with nothing left of her religion but a fondness for old brick chapels, St. John o' the Woods, and the superb English of the King James Version, we had common ground.
>
> "Don't leave, Doris," I said, feeling my head grow heavy....
>
> "Why do you have to leave?"
>
> "We're so dead, Tom. Dead inside. I must go somewhere and recover myself." (*LR* 65)

Like Binx Bolling, Doris was engaged in her own search. She saw the same death-in-life Binx observed in his fellow men—and worse still, saw it in Tom, who at that point in his journey can only be considered a kind of deranged scientific expert. Doris's search took her down a very different path, however, in that study alone never sufficed for her. She moved beyond the scientist or artist's metaphorical escape to a physical one to the island of Cozumel, where she eventually died. Her marriage could not survive her attempt to find total escape from the pain of their lost daughter, suburbia's discontents, and her own alienation. The failures of escape through transcendence need not be so dramatic, but all of them share the desire to break the ordinary, and if we follow Percy's argument, all of them must inevitably fail almost as a law of nature: that which goes up, must come down.

A third form of escape is possible, that into a total community, a move driven by the longing to join a perfectly unified society defined by a cause or belief. In this utopian mode, people stake everything on interactions with others and with the world (*LC* 114). Here, consider Father Rinaldo Smith's confession in *The Thanatos Syndrome*. A member of the remnant Catholic Church in Feliciana Parish, Louisiana, Fr. Smith takes a position as a watchman in a fire tower to help sustain his ministry, and at one point in the story, refuses to come down. Tom More, as his old friend and parishioner, is sent to help. But instead of receiving help from Tom, he tells Tom about his past—a tale that helped Tom see the flaws of his own position.

In this story, Fr. Smith tells Tom More about his trip as a young man to Europe in the 1930s and his attitudes toward his home. Fr. Smith pitied his father and mother and "couldn't stand Louisiana, and New Orleans . . . its phony French *laissez le bon temps rouler*, let the good times roll, which masked a cold-blooded marriage of moneymaking and social climbing, rotten politics and self-indulgence" (*TS* 243). Smith's deeply anti-bourgeois attitude did not let him see the possibility of joining a "lesser" form of community there—their goods were unworthy ones. Travel provided a possible escape. In Germany, he and his father stayed with their cousins, the Jäger family. Smith recounts his loathing of the *Sturmabtelilung* (the SA, or brownshirts) and his distaste for the bourgeois intellectual community in which the Jägers lived. Fr. Smith's relationship with the Jäger family's youngest son Helmut bears special mention.

Helmut was a handsome, intelligent eighteen-year-old man at the end of his days in the Hitler Jugend with aspirations to join the *Waffen-SS*.[15] Fr. Smith deeply admired Helmut and marveled at his readiness to die for his cause. It is important to note that Fr. Smith's warning to Tom More emphasizes not the theory of National Socialism so much as the honor-loving, violent community it helped form (*TS* 247). Fr. Smith ended his story with a confession:

> This is my confession. If I had been German not American, I would have joined him. I would not have joined the distinguished Weimar professors. I would not have joined the ruffian Sturmabteilung. I would not have matriculated at the University of Tübingen or Heidelberg. I would not have matriculated at Tulane, as I did, and joined the D.K.E.'s. I would have gone to the Junkerschule, sworn the solemn oath of the Teutonic knights at Marienberg, and joined the Schutzstaffel. Listen. Do you hear me? *I would have joined him.* (*TS* 248–49)

The allure of this sort of commitment—a bond that provides its members with a purpose, and above all, with *enemies*, bears importance. Percy emphasized that in times of sentimentality and boredom such as our own, bourgeois people might find violence increasingly appealing as a form of escape. He saw communal bonds formed around a real or potential struggle as a perennial hope for some, as we see in the conversation Tom More shares with the black radical Uru in *Love in the Ruins*: Uru believes that once he and his comrades start an African-American revolution and kill their white oppressors, they can begin again with a clean slate (298–299). In the story, Percy suggested that the difficulty with this plan is that Uru and his comrades would ultimately face the same intractable alienation and fallible political life as people always have. Moreover, the pattern set by founding a community on violence is not so easily escaped. Whatever the appeal of destruction, one cannot build lasting communities out of the ashes of war and death—the habits these actions create ultimately leave a dangerous and lasting stamp on our character.[16]

However, this form of escape can also lead to relatively innocuous communities, like the commune Tom More visits early in *Love in the Ruins*. In the novel, a group of misfits from various walks of life retreated from the world, exiting into something they imagine to be like Rousseau's state of nature. Forming a new community, based on simplicity and love, these individuals often turned to More for help, and one evening, a couple from this commune came to seek treatment for their dehydrated infant:

> They speak freely of themselves. . . . They've given up city, home, family, career, religion, to live a perfect life of love and peace with a dozen others on a hummock with nothing else for shelter in the beginning other than an abandoned Confederate salt mine. (*LR* 47)

The rebels Percy invented are not misfits or failures in the conventional sense. Chuck Parker, the father of the child, is a brilliant MIT dropout; his companions were all college graduates. These young people yearned for a simpler life and hoped to escape the supposed mistakes of their parents. Chuck and his friends attempt to persuade More to stay, and one member of this community, Hester, takes a romantic interest in him. Confused as he is, Tom has little notion of why he should not stay, but seems to have the intuition that something dangerous stands at the heart of the desire to start over in an entirely new form of community with a blank slate (*LR* 49–51).

New communities, unencumbered by a sense of history or past membership pose a danger because they see only the possible, fugitive perfection just over the horizon—and often turn to murderous coercion to bring about the new order. Tom remains in civilization, and late in the novel, discovers that another so-called "love community" perpetrated a number of gruesome murders, despite their leader's professed but highly abstract belief in "love, the environment, and freedom of the individual" (*LR* 386–7). This episode from the novel serves as a comment on the relationship between utopian ideals and violence: despite their apparent achievement of utopia, Percy's reversal of the ideals of the "love communities" in his story suggests no one truly gets to clean the slate and return to nature. With this example, Percy showed that even a peaceful radical community like this can fall prey to excesses as dangerous to the soul as the one Helmut Jäger chose—and that Fr. Smith might have followed as well. The temptation to escape to a new life, one that others provide with intense purpose and deep meaning, merely evades the uniquely human problem: no community is ever quite enough to satisfy the longings of the human heart.

Those who desire to lose themselves and escape their alienation through immersion in a cause or community may find a temporary place of belonging, but must always find themselves frustrated with the results. Since there is no perfect completion in a group, the effort will always fail. This incompleteness must remain in both success and failure: the successful cause may leave its adherents empty and in need of a new crusade; and in most cases, the perpetual failure to achieve a satisfactory conclusion or closure to a cause must inevitably lead to disillusionment or despair (*CWP* 277–8). Even if these are successful, the individual escapes the loneliness and weakness of the self by *subsuming* their life into the order of the group, community, or cause, which seems a rather steep cost. A man can imagine himself to be united utterly with a tribe or community, but Percy cast doubt on how this or any other escape can last as a form of remedying alienation.

Moreover, all three forms of diversionary escape face this challenge of incompleteness. Accommodating one's life to consumption and justifying it with theory as Binx Bolling and his cousin Nell Lovell did only provides a temporary fix: we can defer boredom, but eventually, places and things get "used up." While attempts to transcend the ordinary world hold more promise than mere consumption, they present both political and personal dangers. Not all of us can be great performers or scholars, reveling in art or science, but even these chosen few often find themselves vexed by their attempts to flourish in normal life. For the rest of us without those gifts, the hope for real transcendence remains slim, and often ends in the destruction of concrete relationships and communities that might attenuate our longings. Finally, escape into total community often leads to a sense of entrapment, of being in a place without possibility of exit—insofar as such a community succeeds in binding its members together, they lose themselves completely.

PLACES OF REST?

However much he deplored the deformed versions of community so prevalent in modern America, Percy also showed that even decent community can only do so much to salve the wounds of our existence. Mostly because Percy saw our alienation from others and sense of being out of place in any community as the legacy of our status as fallen creatures, his account of what we can really gain from community remains ambivalent. What we actually need most from our places and their social life are persistent reminders about the limits of human life, and a chastening of our desire to control and dominate our environment. Ultimately, he demonstrated the value of community understood simply as a place for wayfarers to take moments of rest. A few examples will demonstrate how Percy accomplished this.

Despite the difficulties Tom More faced, he ultimately remains in his hometown of Paradise and marries his former nurse, Ellen Oglethorpe. More recounts his reasoning:

> I stayed because it's home and I like its easygoing ways, its religious confusion, racial hodgepodge, misty green woods, and sleepy bayous. People still stop and help strangers lying in ditches having been set upon by thieves or just plain drunk. Good nature usually prevails, even between enemies. As the saying goes in Louisiana: you may be a son of a bitch but you're my son of a bitch (*LR* 386).

For most of the novel, More dreams of salving all of his hometown's wounds with his ontological lapsometer, heaps scorn upon his neighbors, and generally wallows in drunken misanthropy. In the epilogue set five years after the main action of the novel, Tom and Ellen More live in poverty, but are happy. He has grown content with the work he has serving different communities in Feliciana Parish, and notices a small change in the way he and others live in the aftermath of American decline:

> Here's one difference between this age and the last. Now while you work, you also watch and listen and wait. In the last age we planned projects and cast ahead of ourselves. We set out to "reach goals." We listened to the minutes of the previous meeting. Between times we took vacations. (*LR* 381–2)

He evokes the idea of a slower life, but also one where men and women recognize the limitations of their lives and places. Tom himself gives up at least part of his scientific ambitions—he tinkers with his lapsometer, but refuses to use it until he gets it right. Life may be no simpler than before, but his bonds with family and friends keep Tom from seeking escape.

None of Percy's protagonists achieve a perfect community; his stories do not really end with a tidy resolution to the characters' difficulties living with themselves or one another. The characters always face challenges and incompleteness in their lives going forward. Usually they turn to some restored faith—though not always an orthodox, clearly Christian one. All of them begin by seeking a remedy for their alienation in the wrong place. Binx Bolling's search goes comically awry just as Tom More's adventures in scientism did. Binx's failure sets him onto a more stable path of marriage alongside a newfound realism about his life. But in every case, the characters' resolution does not come from joining some totalizing community. Their transformation does not appear in their relationships with others. This change does not even emerge through their restoration of faith. Percy depicted all of these modes as ultimately flawed but cumulatively helpful places of rest that help his seeking characters realize their place as wayfarers.

In depicting flawed communities and our desire to escape them, Percy reminded his readers of both the personal and social dangers of seeking perfection. For individuals, the longing for escape from ordinary life can deprive them of sanity; for society as a whole, the ideologies and practices that tend to spring up as a way of satisfying our longings make recognizing the prudent limits of community far harder. Percy suggested that the most serious and viable option to viewing human life as an exercise in wayfaring comes in the embrace of honorable stoicism like that he so often encountered in the South, and that he learned deeply from his guardian and teacher, William Alexander Percy. Percy suspected that disaffected modern bourgeois people might increasingly turn to an imprudent alternative in reconstructed honor patterned off of this ideal. This fear forms the subject of chapter 4.

NOTES

1. Alexis de Tocqueville, *Democracy in America*, ed. J.P. Mayer, trans. George Lawrence (New York: HarperCollins, 1969), 50–54.

2. Robert Putnam, *Bowling Alone: The Collapse and Revival of American Community* (New York: Simon and Schuster, 2000). See also Robert Nisbet, *The Quest for Community: A Study in the Ethics of Order and Freedom* (Wilmington: ISI Books, 2010) and Marc J. Dunkelheim, *The Vanishing Neighbor: The Transformation of American Community* (New York: W.W. Norton, 2014).

3. On this, see Sherry Turkle, *Alone Together: Why We Expect More from Technology and Less from Each Other* (New York: Basic Books, 2012). Also see Nancy K. Baym, *Personal Connections in the Digital Age* (New York: Polity, 2010).

4. For an articulation of a position between these extremes that fits with Percy's sensibility, see Ray Oldenburg, *The Great Good Place: Cafes, Coffee Shops, Bookstores, Bars, Hair Salons, and Other Hangouts at the Heart of a Community* (Emeryville, CA: Avalon Publishing Group, 1999).

5. Tocqueville, *Democracy in America*, 536.

6. On Percy's recognition of the modern scandal of being dependent on others, see Peter Augustine Lawler, *Stuck with Virtue: The American Individual and Our Biotechnological Future* (Wilmington: ISI Books, 2005), 146–153.

7. See, for example, Amitai Etizoni, *The Spirit of Community: The Reinvention of American Society* (New York: Touchstone, 1994).

8. On the peculiar perils of this status in small-town life, see Robert C. Ellickson, *Order without Law: How Neighbors Settle Disputes* (Cambridge: Harvard University Press, 1991), 207–229.

9. Binx's family relationships are somewhat complicated: after Binx's father died, his overwhelmed mother sent him to be raised by her wealthy her sister-in-law Emily Cutrer. Kate Cutrer is Emily's step-daughter and other characters often refer to Binx and Emily as cousins. But while Binx and Kate spent a significant portion of their youth together, they are not related.

10. Eviatar Zerubavel, *Social Mindscapes: An Invitation to Cognitive Sociology* (Cambridge: Harvard University Press, 1997), 100–110.

11. I borrow this language of oscillation from Joshua Mitchell. See his *Fragility of Freedom: Tocqueville on Religion, Democracy, and the American Future* (Chicago: University of Chicago Press, 1995), 3–11.

12. On Binx's treatment of others and their relationship to his escape from alienation, see John F. Desmond, *Walker Percy's Search for Community* (Athens: University of Georgia Press, 2004), 45–46 and 62–63.

13. John Desmond argues that the worst element of Nell's view is its denial of "the mystery and wonder of being," which she expresses in part through her clichéd philosophy (*Walker Percy's Search for Community*, 48).

14. On Doris as a disembodied Gnostic seeker, see Gary M. Ciuba, *Walker Percy: Books of Revelations* (Athens: University of Georgia Press, 1991), 149–50.

15. The "armed" SS was a branch of the infamous organization usually detached to military service and renowned for their ferocity in combat. Perhaps underselling their ideological nature, Percy uses them as an example of honor-bound militancy in both *The Thanatos Syndrome* and *The Second Coming*.

16. On the distinction between friendship and comradeship in war (and why the latter is so fleeting), see J. Glenn Gray, *The Warriors: Reflections on Men in Battle* (Lincoln: University of Nebraska Press, 1998), 89–90.

Chapter 4

Stoicism and the Honor-bound South

Throughout his works, Walker Percy vividly dramatized the ways that Americans strive to escape their sense of alienation and anxiety. Americans turn to theories of the self that purport to make them whole, and when those fail to satisfy their hearts, they seek to escape the human predicament through drugs, or travel, or new experiences. Sometimes Americans turn to deep communities, and at other times, they throw themselves into work. The common thread throughout these efforts to escape our predicament is the search for a perfect solution to life's troubles.

When these attempts fail, only two major alternatives remain: the first can be found in Jewish and Christian faith, either of which Percy believed to be difficult for most people to embrace. Indeed, he argued the traditional defense of Catholicism and other faiths through a rational apologetic, "however valid it may be, is generally unavailing for reasons both of the infirmity of language and the inattentiveness of the age" (*SSL* 308–9). Abjuring faith, Percy suspected that the religious skeptic who disdains both the incoherent theories of the self and the unfulfilling life of consumption might be drawn to some concept of honor.

This chapter deals with Percy's presentation of Southern honor as the best viable alternative to Christianity or Judaism as a basis for wayfaring worldview. He nevertheless believed that when honor defines the scope of a society's morality, this comes at a significant cost to justice. In particular, honor can undermine the ground for moral recognition and sympathy in any society that embraces as the dominant ethical code, which explains to a great degree why Southerners faced such profound difficulties in dealing with the legacy of slavery.

As a moralist, Percy viewed the South through the lens of its great sins; at the same time, he believed that the South had retained a culture that respected place and community in a manner much of the nation did not, and maintained hope that Southern culture and its ethos might be rallied in a defense of America's many virtues. These two thoughts stand in tension because the moral legacy of slavery directed Percy to question the Southern way of life as well as its default assumptions about race, hierarchy, and especially honor. But more generally, his struggle with the South's traditions led Percy to some deeper insights into the dangerous blind spots not just of Southern culture, but also of any society's attempt to live in a morally coherent manner on the basis of honor.

Throughout his adult life, Percy grappled with the place of what he called "Southern Stoicism" and its relationship to both honor and Christianity. Walker Percy inherited this stoicism from his cousin and guardian, William Alexander Percy (usually referred to as "Uncle Will"), whose memoir *Lanterns on the Levee* distills the worldview Walker found so powerful and yet so impotent in the face of grave injustice. (In this chapter, I adopt the convention of referring to the two Percys as "Walker" and "Will." In chapter 5, I return to using "Percy" to identify Walker alone.)

Walker saw this distinctively Southern cultural inheritance as the source of both promise and peril for a renewal of community that could help attenuate alienation and restore the wayfaring sensibility. The South's disrespect of equality undermined the possibility of using the Southern way of life to construct a theoretical defense of human dignity in an age of "theory and consumption," but Walker nevertheless believed that the South gave us some clues about the way community can bind people together and give them practical reasons to defend one another's dignity.

Walker thought Southern honor might have once served as an antidote to the failures of the various senses of the self I discuss in chapter 1. The promise of such a way of life rests in its capacity to cultivate high virtue and excellence against the world's decay, yet Walker insisted that without genuine acceptance of Christianity into this way of life, it could never rise beyond a kind of mournful nostalgia, one that would always remain tainted by the legacy of racism. Without such a change, Walker feared the South might remain forever torn between its love of the Lost Cause and the march of an increasingly standardized commercial existence like that found in Los Angeles or Dallas.

Walker's account of honor is important on its own terms because it explores one of most curious moral problems in American history: above and beyond the material interest some shared in maintaining slavery, why did the supposedly Christian South find it so hard to recognize the seemingly obvious conclusions of the Christian faith against slavery?[1] Walker's answer, one reinforced in interesting ways by at least one historian of the American South, rested on the notion that for a wide swath of Southern whites, Christianity as a moral doctrine—particularly understood as a source of *equality*—never played a profound role in shaping the public culture.[2]

Thus for Walker, the "Southern gentleman did live in a Christian edifice, but he lived there in the strange fashion Chesterton spoke of, that of a man who will neither go inside nor put it entirely behind him but stands forever grumbling on the porch." Instead, Walker claimed they lived and died with Stoic honor at the heart of their lives and that this central fact explains the Southern white gentleman's gradual transformation from paternalistic defender of the blacks to their greatest enemy (*SSL* 84). Walker's analysis of this "grumbling" union of external Christian forms with an internalized Stoicism remains an important contribution to our understanding of honor as a moral and political force in America, not only the past, but upon some contemporary arguments as well. In the wake of the political and moral stresses placed upon American society since September 11, 2001, perhaps we should not be surprised by renewed claims that we need to reinvigorate a national interest in honor and clarify our understanding of the virtues that flow from its codes. This renewed attention has come from very different sources. To cite just two examples, James Bowman and Kwame Anthony Appiah point Americans toward honor not simply to understand its role in the past, but also to use it to shape us in the present and future—and they do so by elevating honor to be *the* dominant moral force in legitimate political life. Appiah's approach focuses on the idea that honor is the source of serious moral action, and places honor in the service of progressive ideals; Bowman adopts a more conservative position and ties honor to the vanishing possibility of manly assertion in the present day.[3]

These authors are some of the latest in a long line of thinkers who recall Plato's understanding that honor, or spiritedness, forms an essential part of a well-developed human character: it is the seat of the trained, noble emotions. Appiah, and to a lesser extent Bowman, understand the difficulty Plato identified: our reason alone is too weak to control our conduct, and it is our spirit, or as C.S. Lewis put it perhaps more aptly, our "chest" that develops first in childhood, and reason develops alongside of it later.[4] Honor, then, is prior to any rational attempt to understand moral duty, and therefore takes on extraordinary importance as a guide and teacher for human life. The difficulty with the way Appiah, Bowman, and others render this argument rests in the way they tend to slight the necessity for honor itself to be checked by some other forces in our moral and political life. One scholar of German literature hinted at this by rewriting the Beatitudes in an honor-loving key:

> Blessed are the rich, for they possess the earth and its glory.
> Blessed are the strong, for they can conquer kingdoms.
> Blessed are they with strong kinsmen, for they shall find help.

> Blessed are the warlike, for they shall win wealth and renown.
> Blessed are they who keep their faith, for they shall be honored.
> Blessed are the open-handed, for they shall have friends and fame.
> Blessed are they who wreak vengeance, for they shall be offended no more, and they shall have honor and glory all the days of their life and eternal fame in ages to come.[5]

When framed in these terms, honor's limitations as a moral code become clearer. Because of this creed's overwhelming reliance on socially accepted norms, it all too often fails as a source of justice.[6]

Walker's analysis of Southern culture cast doubt on the efficacy of honor as a viable way of life or source of morality for a republican people, particularly one concerned with defending liberal constitutionalism and equal rights. The South's manly code of honor, driven as it is by what Walker called "broadsword virtues"—such as strength, good manners, and attention to one's reputation—come at the expense of viewing justice as universal. Walker claimed those driven by honor tend to subordinate matters of equal justice to concerns of propriety and status. That is to say: the right thing to do becomes far less about our reasoning with regard to a moral standard, and far more about how the act we might contemplate reflects upon us and how it reflects on our relative status before others (*SSL* 84–5).

This relational morality serves as a source of great strength for communities bound by honor. One way to escape the failed theories of the self that Walker criticized is to seek to understand oneself primarily in relation to the experience of a place and its people. Instead of rooting one's identity in either theory or consumption, Walker argued that American Southerners had the opportunity to experience relatively balanced community that forces human beings out of their recurring sense of alienation, without too deeply threatening their longings for autonomy. Percy argued people oscillate unhealthily between individualism and furious engagement in the world.[7] As a place with a history and strong remnants of civil society working together to counteract these negative aspects of American individualism, Walker saw the South as uniquely well suited to teach other regions of the country how they might cope more stably with both the permanent ills of human life and the extraordinary ones we so commonly inflict on ourselves.

Part of this difference in social life rests in the nature of Southern communities: they have no firm limits on what Walker calls their "zone of obligatory social encounter" (*SSL* 99). The examples he supplied evoke the idea of a small town where the category of one's private life becomes blurred with that of the town's common life and gossip; at the same time, however, Walker argued that even after World War II, large Southern cities retained this peculiarly intensive sense of the necessity of social bonding. Recall Walker's analysis of the difference between Mobile and other cities: as a sort of "pressure cooker" that limits the space for privacy, the intrusiveness of a deep community can be quite overwhelming (*SSL* 11). This suggests one difficulty that flows from honor-driven communities: while the Southern community alleviates feelings of loneliness and being out of place that Walker feared might become the new American norm, the intrusiveness of the community into one's affairs comes at a moral cost. The honor that helps bind the community contributes more to "good manners" and acting with propriety than it does to cultivating a belief in universal justice.

Walker contrasted the experience of education in other regions to that of the South in the 1920s to the 1960s: outside the South, a "public high school is a place where one goes primarily to acquire certain services, just as the A & P is a place to acquire certain goods. One may, of course, make friends in school, have dates, but this is far more of an option, far more segregated, if you will, from the business at hand" (*SSL* 99). The public and private spaces of Southern students blur because "the social body almost coincides with the student body," in the same manner that the society sees everyone's conduct as their business. Walker observed that at least for whites of his generation, the small-town Southern high school was "an extremely pleasant, humane, democratic institution." He argued this formed some of the difficulty for moving beyond racial hostility in the South: since the whites saw schools as a social club and shared living space more than as a public institution in the conventional sense, integration seemed a deadly threat to their way of life (*SSL* 99–100).

This ought to give us some sense that at least in the South, community retained a somewhat different meaning and place in people's lives, one that allows us to consider the value of being rooted in a place. Walker held out the possibility that the South in particular offered its native children an ethos distinct from that of the North or the West, one rooted in the experience of being immersed in a place's memory and culture, and knowing one's family lineage and its ties to that place.

The difficulty the South presented Walker, and anyone who thinks it might offer us something today, rests not only in the difficult moral legacy of slavery and segregation, but also in the limitations of Southern moral culture. In certain conservative and libertarian circles for instance, there is a tendency to depict the story of the Civil War as a struggle between a noble, plucky, freedom-loving South and a Northern oppressor aiming at the destruction of the Constitution.[8] Many of these authors, to be sure, deplore slavery, but the political lessons they draw from their imagined South rest on a sanitized version of how Southern honor worked as a code in the first place. Moreover, like Bowman and Appiah, these thinkers often vastly overestimate the degree to which honor might be recaptured as a motive for action in our society, and fail to see the dangers recreating it ideologically might create.

Looking at Southern history through today's lens confuses matters, for we might mistake the spread of evangelical churches for what Walker argued came before: a long-standing attempt in the South to limit the public space and authority ceded to religious morality. This might have been something like a gentlemen's agreement where the society as a whole encouraged a degree of public observance toward Christian teachings on sex, drinking, gambling, and the like, but refused to accept the idea we must love our neighbor in any challenging way (*SSL* 87).[9] Instead, the Southern creed rested heavily on a kind of Stoic honor code, moderated only with a tiny dash of Christian morality shorn from the love that gives it real meaning. A look at Will Percy's memoir *Lanterns on the Levee* will illuminate the stark limitations this position holds for its adherents, as well as what Walker thought might allow it to hold a legitimate place in our moral imagination.

UNCLE WILL'S LONG SHADOW

As a Southern planter, lawyer, poet, and freethinking critic of virtually every dominant trend in American political life, Will Percy (1885–1942) gives us an important glimpse into a kind of fading aristocratic and honor-loving character type that dominated the upper ranks of Southern cultural life in the nineteenth and early twentieth centuries.[10] *Lanterns on Levee* highlights Will's views on the value of stoicism and honor and his disdain for Christian teachings. Rather than preach reliance on the mechanisms of law and justice, Will emphasized honorable violence as a necessity for the maintenance of social order. He also explored the appeal of war as a purpose-generating and almost aesthetically enlivening experience, a notion that reappears as a powerful concern in Walker's political thought.

Orphaned at the age of fourteen, Walker and his younger brothers LeRoy and Phin came to live with their cousin, Will Percy in Greenville, Mississippi. Looking back on this as an adult, Walker wrote that Will gave up "the freedom of bachelorhood," and "taking on the burden of parenthood without the consolations of marriage," proceeded to raise the boys as his own (*SSL* 55).[11] For Walker, Will became a teacher, mentor, and "fixed point in a confusing world" (*SSL* 56), shaping his views on art, literature, and morality. Walker's early notions concerning the virtues of the South also owe a great deal to Will's teachings, but he ultimately could not accept them as adequate to the challenges of a moral life.

Will lived with a creed that blended stoicism and personal honor, one that placed a high emphasis on the vitality of a personal sense of truth, of the reality of good and evil, and the necessity of virtue for a life well lived. He utterly denied the relevance of orthodox religion for achieving virtue, and in fact implied that it often stood in the way of taking responsibility for the cultivation of virtue in one's own life. Will's account of his own life relegates religious faith to his childhood, observes that while the nuns who taught him brought "Machiavellian heroism and saintly mendacity" to their effort at saving his soul, he could only say "Bless them, I wish they had succeeded" (*LL* 80–1). Will implied in this passage that if they had succeeded, it might have given him a less anxious existence. As a teenager enrolled at the University of the South, Will shed the remnants of his faith and developed an understanding of life rooted in Greek and Roman philosophy.[12]

Over the course of his memoir, Will sketched this turn to Greco-Roman concepts of honor and virtue as the work of his adult life. But as he recounts his story to the reader, the arrival of his young cousins and his new role as their guardian elevated Will's moral anxieties to a new level of urgency. In pondering what to pass on to his young charges, Will considered his life's work and sense of his own philosophy, and found himself suddenly "unprepared, with the responsibility of directing young lives in a world that was changing and that seemed to me on the threshold of chaos" (*LL* 310). Will knew his duty: "to direct them toward the good life" as he understood the notion (*LL* 312). Will's first instincts pointed him to passing on an honorable "pattern of living" in an age where all such authoritative patterns had fallen into disrepute. In such circumstances, how might this actually happen? His reservations and fears abounded:

> But what good life that I had ever glimpsed was suitable and effective for this world where the children must earn a living and fashion their own happiness? The old Southern way of life in which I had been reared existed no more and its values were ignored or derided. . . . I had no desire to send these youngsters of mine into life as defenseless as if they wore knights' armor and had memorized the code of chivalry. (*LL* 312)

Unsure of his own capacity as a teacher, Will initially sent his young charges to church, with unpromising results. Will notes that "[i]t seemed to matter little what sect they sought for guidance: they and their young friends returned confused, resentful, and distressed," and instead of looking to local ministers or priests, the boys turned to Will for wisdom and instruction (*LL* 313–4). Will had attempted to live within a distinctive neo-classical ideal rooted in virtue and governed by honor—and despite his misgivings, it was this creed that he worked to convey to Walker, LeRoy, and Phin.

Will filled his memoir with pointed examples of honor's power as a sustaining creed regardless of the world's failures. In Will's world, men settle issues between themselves with noble violence. At Harvard Law School, he found himself astonished by the prevalence of an openly dishonorable culture where "a Harvard man's prominence was gauged by the number of men he could afford to cut"—that is, snub—publicly. With an obvious tone of approval, he described how a roommate from New Orleans delivered a response to a particularly egregious offender: "He delivered the *Mayflower* princeling a sock on the jaw and a bit of advice which I recall but can't repeat" (*LL* 117). While not the culture of the duel so common to the antebellum South, in Will's worldview social insults demand repayment in some measured violence, and threats demand an answer.[13]

Will recounted one particularly illustrative event from his youth in this regard. During his family's 1920s struggle against the Ku Klux Klan in Greenville, Will's father and mother came under threat, and his father LeRoy very nearly fell prey to an attempted kidnapping and murder. In response, Will took action:

> I went to the office of the local Cyclops. He was an inoffensive little man, a great Mason, and partial to anti-Catholic tirades. I said, "I want to let you know one thing: if anything happens to my father or to any of our friends you will be killed. We won't hunt for the guilty party. So far as we're concerned the guilty party will be you." (*LL* 236)

Looking back, Walker saw this as the epitome of the broad-sword honor tradition within which Will lived. Five feet, two inches tall and 110 pounds, barely able to meet the minimum standards for military service in World War I (and presumably no more imposing thereafter), Will Percy nonetheless threatened a senior member of a dangerous organization to protect his family. Of course, after facing Germans in combat, the Klan may have seemed somewhat underwhelming. A serious threat demanded a serious response; honor demanded no less (*CWP* 154).

These attitudes toward violence formed only one part of the honor code in which Will believed. In his world, no Machiavellian division of public and private morality would do: he found it "sophistry to speak of two sets of virtues," when "there is but one: virtue is an end in itself; the survival virtues are means, not ends." However, Will drew a distinction between those virtues of mere survival, higher virtues necessary for security, and the noblest virtues of "honor and honesty, compassion and truth" for these "are good even if they kill you, for they alone give life its dignity and worth" (*LL* 313). This is worth dwelling on for a moment because this hierarchy was unusually well suited to the stoical creed to which Will adhered: virtue itself remains tied to its contexts. His worldview allowed no moral universals, only contextual virtues and vices, allowing his view to be quite tolerant of everything but bad manners. Will remained an aesthete and a cultural relativist his entire life, albeit one who adhered to a very firm set of standards concerning his duties as a man and citizen.[14] Taste, character, and judgment would then reign supreme in his understanding.

Because of his adherence to these values, Will disdained the usual marks of achievement in the American South. After graduating law school, he tells us that he hunted about for a goal, a "good ambition." Conventional bourgeois goals did not quite satisfy him; he felt none of the usual allure people see in comfort, prestige, or social influence. Not money, because even though his future was far from completely assured, the pursuit of wealth "wasn't interesting and it wasn't worthy"—and worthiness here must be understood in terms of its intrinsic virtue to a man of good character. Fame in his chosen profession mattered little because he cared nothing for the opinions of other lawyers. Beyond a vague notion of helping one's fellows, he was at a loss for how to proceed (*LL* 127–8).

Will denied the authority of mere public opinion, and rightly saw social honor creeds as potentially falling prey to mass sentiment—think here of the vulgarity of the Ku Klux Klan. Unlike most followers of an honor code, Will's sense of honor remained an inner creed, one found not in theology or philosophical doctrines, but the self:

> There is left to us, no matter how far defeat pierces, the unassailable wintry kingdom of Marcus Aurelius, which some more gently call the Kingdom of Heaven. However it be called, it is not outside, but within, and when all is lost, it stands fast. To this remaining fastness I knew I should help the children find their way. (*LL* 313)

From Will's perspective, religious hopes and motives made little difference in how we ought to live from day to day. We should pursue virtue regardless of the benefits or costs it carries. For him, the absence of certainty about any higher purpose or reward to our lives ought not to result in despair, but a battle for justice to the last days of our lives:

> We survive or we are annihilated, and all our anguish cannot undo our fate one way or another. . . . Our dread and torment in this life we lead are its apartness, its eternal isolation. We try to rid us of ourselves by love, by prayers, by vice, by the Lethe of activity, and we never wholly succeed. . . . Our concern is here, and with the day so overcast and short, there's quite enough to do. (*LL* 321)

Walker shared Will's concern with alienation and the remedies that people hopelessly undertake to move beyond themselves. But where Walker would turn to existential philosophy and eventually Christianity as a source of certainty and an anchor for hope, Will by contrast focused his ideal entirely on the cultivation of virtue in the present. The duty to fulfill one's duties as best as possible becomes the central moral measure of one's life. Will cultivated an apathy to his fate that Christians could not embrace alongside an almost obsessive attention to the duties of his station.

This is the outlook Will attempted to pass on to the Percy boys (and perhaps even to their friend, Shelby Foote, with more success),[15] yet Will always retained a hope "for the seer or saint who sees" the things that Will believes, and believed "he will come, even if he must walk through ruins" (*LL* 321). Such a position resonates deeply and dangerously with Nietzsche's aspirations for a new kind of life embodied by a philosopher of and for the future, one who might escape the world's old understandings and move forward toward newer, more honest values.[16] Will hoped for the sort of teacher might provide an answer—or at least a disposition—toward the ultimate questions Walker, LeRoy and Phin asked. For want of a better alternative, he took up this role for the children.

Will found some refuge in his sense of duty to his fellows, as "while good morals are all-important between the Lord and His creatures, what counts between one creature and another is good manners" (*LL* 286).[17] Undistinguished at law and planting, Will nonetheless found himself in one position after another of unelected but undeniably real authority in Greenville.[18] The picture Will paints of himself in these pages is one of rectitude and giving people their due as he sees it. In some cases, the letter of law might suffer—indeed he implies that the black letter of law matters little in comparison to this reckoning of personalized justice. To take one example of this, Will reported a late-evening visit in his diary: "One of police force drops in to discuss best method of handling dangerous breach of mores which is not breach of law. We agree on a course illegal but wise as it will keep the peace" (*LL* 330). Consider the contrast here between wisdom and legality: products of a popularly elected legislature, laws cannot encompass the wisdom of a virtuous man. Will explains nothing of the details in this passage, but this is an excellent example of his reasoning about public matters: the maintenance of decent manners and mores trumps adherence to universal rules or laws. Honor demands not equally applicable rules, but rather, the application of good judgment about what treatment individuals deserve. Nowhere does this distinction appear more clearly in Will's thinking than in relation to the South's lingering difficulties with the legacy of slavery.

For Will, the peculiar relationship between whites and blacks in the twentieth century was a matter of *manners* and not *morality*. Will argued that the resolution of race relations depended upon personal interactions, and therefore should have remained entirely a local concern, one to be settled through the cultivation of good manners. Understood as tied to reason and universality, morality allows—if not demands—that whoever has the capacity to do so should judge and involve themselves in the righting of wrongs. By contrast, good manners have everything to do with one's place in life—both in the sense of their geographic location and in their relative rank or station in life. The latter recognizes and perhaps demands inequality, bearing particular importance for matters of race in the South.

In Will's mind, to live in the South came with the clear recognition that blacks were the "inferior race," and race relations required something special that no outsider could ever provide. In a 1919 letter to editors of *The New Republic*, Will wrote in response to their coverage of racial strife in Knoxville, Tennessee that questions of race have no simple answers:

> To solve these questions in wisdom, justice, and kindness is difficult under any circumstances, but there are thousands of unadvertised leaders of thought in the South capable of working out such a solution if left to themselves—not quickly or easily, but through the years. And they are the only people who can: it is their problem, their burden, their heavy heritage. (*LL* 228)

In the letter, he argued that it is men like him, "who by training and opportunity" see themselves as the friend of the African American who can work out this "solution." For Will, the lingering difficulties of life in the South will only find a resolution through the spread of good manners and the cultivation of decent character. For him, the attempt to remedy race relations in the South on the basis of universal moral grounds runs aground on the realities of life in mixed-race communities. Will claimed a resolution to the lingering difficulties of slavery could only proceed on the basis of recognizing the "fact" of inequality and provide no "short cut": "It is in the first place education for the whites and in the second education, simple and practical, for the Negro. For the rest common kindness must be the guide in this as in all human affairs" (*LL* 229). It is precisely this insistence on a principle of racial inequality that Walker would later reject. Yet at the same time, he retained the idea that only personal and relational efforts toward racial reconciliation and justice would bear any fruit.

Will believed that the fight against the Ku Klux Klan in Greenville required citizens with the right sensibility in manners, as well as decent characters. The correct attitude here was one of white paternalism, where African Americans could never hope for equality, but would be treated with the relative kindness due to inferiors. In terms of character, opposing the Klan required honesty and bravery, both of which were severely tested. Will described Greenville prior to the rise of the Klan as a place where toleration of varied beliefs and conduct reigned:

> We didn't regard drunkenness and lechery, Sabbath-breaking and gambling as more than poor judgment or poor taste. What we were slow to forgive was

> hardness of heart and all unkindness. Perhaps we were overstocked with sinners and pariahs and publicans, but they kept the churches in their places and kept the tradition of sprightliness. (*LL* 231)

By contrast, Will depicted the Klansmen as driven by ignorance, anger, and ideology rather than the sense of manners and honor appropriate to good citizens. No small amount of religious fanaticism also played a part in the Klan's desire to publicly stamp out Greenville's laxity as well as put African Americans in their "proper" place.

As Will recounts the events of this struggle, Greenville, Mississippi found itself suddenly beset by the Klan in 1922, when the leadership of the local Masonic order began actively undermining the relative harmony of the city by targeting Catholics with harassment, destroying their capacity to make a living (Klan members began firing their Catholic employees and boycotting Catholic-owned businesses), and other, mostly nonviolent, acts (*LL* 233–4). Because Klan members chose to focus their efforts not on violence, but rather on subverting Greenville's existing social and political order, they were initially quite successful. Will described their effects:

> For the next two years our town was disintegrated by a bloodless, cruel warfare, more bitter and unforgiving than anything I encountered at the front. In the trenches soldiers felt sorry for one another, whether friend or enemy. . . . But in the Klan fight the very spirit of hatred materialized before our eyes. It was the ugliest thing I have ever beheld. You didn't linger on the post-office steps or drink cokes with random companions: too many faces were hard and set, too many eyes were baleful and venomous. You couldn't go a block without learning by a glance that someone hated you. (*LL* 233)

The Klan accomplished this change in the culture of the town by adopting methods of secrecy and subversion that Will likened to what Nazi fifth columnists would later enact in Europe. Will's depiction of Greenville as filled with honorable people willing to fight for what was theirs fits with this method: only through subversion could the Klan avoid direct challenges that would humiliate their cause. But secrecy and deceit undermine honorable culture and weaken its ability to resist challenges.

Will observed that the "most poisonous thing the Klan did to our town was to rob the citizens of their faith and trust in one another." The secretive nature of the Klan and their practice of placing double-agents in local anti-Klan organizations made it difficult for anyone to know with any degree of certainty who was or was not a Klansman. Will feared that if any of these secret members "were elected judges and law-enforcement officers, we would be cornered into servility or assassination" (*LL* 237). This may not have been exactly true: when the Klan escalated their campaign to include their attempt at abducting Will's father, Will's threat of violent retribution stopped them cold. But given the way Will describes Greensville, his fear seems to have centered more on the consequences a Klan political victory would have brought about in the moral culture of the town. The culture of honor Will described depended on delicate balances between each social group and institution, each of which knew its rightful place in the order of the town and did not seek to reorder this state of affairs. People were firmly placed in their communities and kept order and decency largely through social pressure. Violence was present, but strictly limited. Being forced to deal with the Klan as a political force undermined this status quo, and turned the town's genteel modes of handling challenges on its head. Fortunately, the need was averted by the anti-Klan forces' victory in a hotly contested sheriff's election.

This episode reveals two moral weaknesses of the honor-bound community that Will defended so strenuously. Communities like Greenville that rely on a sense of shared manners and relational virtues rather than a clear belief system to bind them are very easily disturbed by small numbers of immigrants. In this case, Will notes that almost unnoticed by the residents, the town had grown to include whites from the elsewhere uninitiated into the town's mores. That their community defeated the Klan is a testament to Will and his friends' commitment and their influence as leaders and examples. But the events of 1922–24 in Greenville also are noteworthy for what Will does not emphasize. The major flaw in this system, however, is that for Will, blacks could never be truly equal partners. In this entire effort, Will never seems to have considered that blacks might provide some assistance or have an opinion of their own as to how to proceed. They were bystanders to Will's struggle, nothing more.

Will's paternalism ran deep. He saw great virtue in a sharecropping system where white managers looked out for their black partner-tenants, cared for them through the lean months, and maintained their position of *noblesse oblige*. Walker observed that

> [a]s a planter, my uncle felt that the attacks [by Northern civil rights advocates] were unjust. He believed that the sharecropper system was an outgrowth of a natural partnership between the Confederate veterans, who had nothing left but the land, and the Negroes, who had nothing but their labor. (*SSL* 333)

Walker added that Will's example and teachings always emphasized that to "behave with dishonor was . . . a detestable thing, but to mistreat a Negro was unthinkable, precisely because the Negro was helpless" (*SSL* 333). Honor demanded no less than decency to inferiors, respect to equals, and vengeance upon those who gave offense—such as the Klansmen who attempted to break this putatively noble order. Despite the harrowing nature of this struggle, though, Will almost seemed to long for something similar in his later days. It is this desire for struggle and testing against enemies that led Walker to conclude honor is a potentially dangerous creed.

Will lived his life enmeshed in a community guided by the responsibilities of active citizenship. He did his duty in Greenville against the Klan, but wondered if anything in his later life would ever compare to his service in the Great War. Will considered himself "desperately unfitted" for war—he was a small, sickly little man, but brought a will to succeed that carried him through training. He believed that the war "somehow, had meaning, and daily life hasn't: it was part of a common endeavor, and daily life is isolated and lonely" (*LL* 223). He returned home deeply conflicted about the experience and harboring a conviction that in the absence of an enemy, something would always be missing:

> It's over, the only great thing you were ever part of. It's over, the only heroic thing we all did together. What can you do now? Nothing, nothing. You can't go back to the old petty things without a purpose, direction, or unity—defending the railroad for killing a cow, drawing deeds of trust, suing someone for money. . . . You can't go on with that sort of thing till you die. (*LL* 223)

Will seems to have thrown himself into his tasks in the community in an effort to substitute for this desire for community and purpose which he could not fulfill in his career as a lawyer.

Given this attitude toward war—what Walker suggested was the ultimate "bad environment" (*MB* 3–4)—we can begin to understand the tone of mournfulness and despair that suffuses *Lanterns on the Levee*. Will stoically bore what he perceived as the utter failure of his age to sustain its moral life, but he could not let modernity's disasters pass without comment. Observations about the moral disorder and chaos of American society appear early in Will's memoir's remarks about coming of age in the South and continue throughout. Politically, the most important of these observations rest on Will's idea that a certain kind of stoic aristocrat once governed the South (his father among them), and that as these men died or lost their positions of authority, disaster followed. His memory of these leaders' meetings at the Percy home as a child points to both his political attitudes and his mournfulness at the old South's passing:

> It is not what they discussed so much as how they discussed it that makes those meetings so memorable to me—indeed, so epic. They were leaders of the people, not elected or self-elected, but destined, under the compulsion of leadership because of their superior intellect, training, character, and opportunity. . . .

> They knew leadership was a burden, they know there was no such thing in the long run as public gratitude for public service, they also knew that unless the intelligent disinterested few fought for good government, government would be bad. (*LL* 69)

Character formed the basis of such political judgment rather than a principled formula or scientific system: "Being convinced no system of government was good without good men to operate it, they considered it their bounden duty, their prime obligation as members of society, to find such men and elect them to office," and when none could be found, run themselves, as Will's father did (*LL* 73). No explicit political philosophy drove their actions, only an implicit stoicism that insisted one must pursue the good to the end, regardless of the odds of success (*LL* 75).

The North had destroyed his forebears' way of life, and Germany came along in due course to destroy his old genteel world (*LL* 156). Will's father and his peers died, and no one rose to replace their greatness. The vulgar, both rich and poor, took their place. When Will's father lost his bid for reelection to the U.S. Senate, Will judged this his "first sight of the rise of the masses" (*LL* 153).[19] This upending of the world's natural order portended other changes to come. Abroad, Will highlighted the example of mass movements taking center stage in Germany and Russia. At home, he observed the insolence of both "organized labor" and "capital," both of whom he saw as examples of the "herd on the march," a mob that will have blood and destroy beauty (*LL* 153). In this new world, when good men go to political defeat, "[t]he intelligent are cynically amused, the hoi-polloi are so accustomed to victory, they no longer swagger. The voters choose their representatives in public life, not for their wisdom or courage, but for the promises they make" (*LL* 153). Democracy cares little for honor—indeed, the premise of equality that stands at its center makes a mockery of the genteel honor Will held so dear.

Unsurprisingly, Will had no taste for a world without manners. Worse still, he abhorred the trends of the 1930s, which he saw as possessed by totalitarian projects and driven by "tyrants who laughed at the security virtues and practiced the most vile of the survival virtues with gangster cynicism." Perhaps more relevant to the South he loved, Will despised the growth of democracy, which he feared had grown "so busy providing itself with leisure and luxury it had forgotten that hardihood and discipline are not ornaments but weapons" (*LL* 312). In a world descending into madness, Will found his only hope in the small pockets of order a virtuous person might protect, and ultimately, in that "unassailable wintry kingdom" stoicism provides (*LL* 313). Will retained his memories, and little else, for they "lose nothing of their luster in this time of doom. A tarnish has fallen over the bright world; dishonor and corruption triumph" (343). Will left an impressive—if highly illiberal—legacy of thought and deeds, but Walker eventually argued that it never really sufficed as a guide to life in the postwar South, or for anywhere else. This resulted in devastating consequences for the moral life of the South in the 1950s and onward.

WALKER PERCY AND THE FAILURE OF A MORAL TRADITION

Will's stoic honor shaped Walker's morality such that even when Walker embarked upon criticism of honor as a way of life, he always emphasized the manner in which it provides those who embrace it with a substitute for the mishmash theories of the age, one that might actually sustain them. Honor allows for a coherent theory of the self, mysterious in origins, but defined relationally by being true to the "wintry kingdom of the self," one's family, and one's place (*SSL* 85). It also provides a stern moral code, within which people know how to behave in the ambiguous situations that contemporary society finds so difficult to navigate.

Will's ideas inform part of Walker's understanding of Southern morality, but Walker also observed that the South, is "perhaps the only section of the United States where the public and secular consciousness is still to a degree informed by the theological habits of thought, the old notions of sin, of heaven and hell, of God's providence, however abused and shopworn these notions may be" (*SSL* 328). Walker may have been uncharitable to large sections of the country on this point, but his perception that some of these elements of public culture are fading seems apt. Walker saw a great deal of tension in Southern culture between stoicism, honor, and Christianity. He argued that this amalgamation of beliefs present in Southern Stoicism resulted in a kind of moral blindness, and in particular an unwillingness to embrace either any conception of universal natural law, or a Christian notion of the moral equality of human beings.

However, Walker argued that Will's beliefs—those of the Stoic aristocratic class that led the South through the Civil War and for some time after—actually served as "the major ideological source of racial moderation in the South," and that its fatal weaknesses in moral sympathy led to its collapse (*SSL* 331). When those leaders of thought passed away, they left their children nothing of equivalent moral substance to replace this vision. Walker believed that this ought to have forced Christians in the South to reexamine their beliefs about the proper place of their religion in moral life, but he observed that for the most part, this self-criticism did not take place. As a result, race relations deteriorated as whites found themselves assailed by civil rights activists, pastors, and the rising tide of national public opinion. The children of Will's generation found little in their parents' moral teaching to help them navigate these currents.

The post-World War II "Stoic-Christian" churchgoer experienced a profound change in the North's attitude toward their peculiar treatment of blacks.[20] This renewed effort to advance civil rights seems to have simply puzzled the old Southern Stoics at first, but became utterly offensive when white religious leaders within the South became involved in the struggle. Thus, on Walker's account of events, when the Archbishop of New Orleans criticized typical Southern attitudes about segregation or labor relations, the typical Stoic-Christian could not "help feeling that religion is overstepping its allotted area of morality" (*SSL* 87). As Walker puts it, even though the Southerner is apt to "inherit, almost despite himself, a theological turn of mind," the Southerner's sense of religious morality mainly remained limited to "sex and alcohol, to the exclusion of ordinary human cruelty" (*SSL* 328). Elsewhere Walker added gambling to this list of "allowed concerns." This rather limits Christ's commandments to love one's neighbor; it also authorizes the maintenance of a public ethos of honor instead of one driven by Christian love and oriented toward justice.

The peculiar moral synthesis of an essentially private Christian ethos with a public creed based in Stoic honor may have allowed for a "comfortable modus vivendi" between white Southerners, but allowed no space for improving the social condition of African Americans. Honor appeals to distinctly un-Christian motives such as pride and manly self-assertion. While most adherents to this code may have abandoned its most violent expressions (such as the duel), at best honor nonetheless only appeals to each individual's personal virtue, and at worst, it leads men to be motivated solely by pride and reputation. Honor cannot provide a standard of universal justice, much less to a chastened conscience. Recall Will's description of Greenville, where everyone kept religion "in its place": at most, such a faith can help the cultivation of good manners; it provides no a significant challenge to moral evils like racism (*LL* 231). Moreover, the Southerner who subscribed to this mixed ideal could only be "confused and obscurely outraged when Christian teaching is applied to social questions." As a result, as Walker put it, such men reacted as if "a gentleman's agreement had been broken" when this came to pass (*SSL* 87). The old order had put questions of manners and private virtues far above any sense of higher law or justice. Their adherence to honor-bound inequality made the moral challenge of civil rights into a scandal of the highest order.

The peculiar weakness of Stoic honor and morality rests in "its exclusively personal character and its consequent indifference to the social and political commonweal" (*SSL* 332). Personal, in this instance, does not mean individual: the point is not that this "wintry kingdom" fosters a kind of individualism—indeed, if it did, Walker's admiration for Will would be perplexing.

Instead, the moral difficulty of Southern honor rests in the social nature of its morality and the way that it is rooted in pride. In a 1965 article, Walker argued that the

> very man who will get up at all hours to get Ol' Jim out of jail, and even risk his life to protect Ol' Jim from the lynch mob, is also outraged when Jim's sons demand better schools and better police—not come hat in hand, but demand them as ordinary rights of a citizen. And, of course, the fact is that many of the old-style "good" people, both Christian and Stoic, have now turned against the Negro because of what they deem his "insolence." "If the Negro had not become aggressive," a good Christian man told me the other day, "I'd still be on his side. It is these demonstrations, his *demanding* rights of me, which changed my attitude." Of *me*? Here is the heart of the matter certainly: it is where the rights are deemed to come from which causes the offense. (*SSL* 334–5)

To Walker, if we base our morality in a principle, we can understand right and wrong through universal rules of social intercourse that we then adapt to particular circumstances. But in the absence of such a standard, people with a sense of honor develop and enforce manners as replacements for a more definitive creed. To the Stoic honor-lover, the idea that someone has a claim to universal moral standing apart from visible evidence that they deserve respect is simply offensive. Obvious excellences of character deserve respect, as do specific or familial achievements, but extending moral recognition to those who display neither of these traits appears to the honor-lover as an absurd inversion of the proper moral order. As Will put it, this meant placing the bottom rail of society on top and undoing the entire basis of honor (*LL* 153).

In the South, Walker remarked, everyone knew "someone like Atticus Finch in *To Kill a Mockingbird*, with his quite Attic sense of decency (and his correspondingly low regard for Christianity) and his courage before the lynch mob" (*SSL* 334). Such people act out of magnanimity, not charity; their decency flows from their sense of self-righteousness, and not from any loftier moral principle. For such a man, there *is* no higher duty beyond that owed to one's clan, and ultimately, oneself (*SSL* 46). In a world fallen into hopeless decay, the mood such individuals bring to both their public and private lives is one of "poetic pessimism," one that finds "a grim satisfaction in the dissolution of its values—because social decay confirmed one in his original choice of the wintry kingdom of the self" (*SSL* 85). This satisfaction reinforces the honorable sense of superiority, and redoubles their sense of detachment from the struggles of lesser beings. Worst still, it may even generate some glee in seeing them fall as a result of their own choices.

Observing doom and decay comes with pleasures, as prophets who observe our impending destruction sometimes betray their joy "by a telltale gleam in the eye and moistness of the lip" (*SSL* 263). Though society may fall into decay, in the meantime the wise stoic can revel in their steadfastness against the end and superiority over those that caused the disaster. Thus, Gary Ciuba observes that such characters "become as self-obsessed as the age, isolated in the sanctuary of their own inner integrity."[21] Walker depicted this descent into moral isolation pointedly with the character of Emily Cutrer in *The Moviegoer*. Emily's example rounds out Walker's case against the characteristic moral failures of the South, and can also help direct attention to a deeper danger in the Stoic or honor-loving tendency to nostalgia and the hope for a revival of the old ways.

Binx Bolling's aunt and adopted mother Emily Cutrer embodies the Stoical, honor-driven South to which Walker addresses his criticisms.[22] Emily never understands Binx's confusions about how to live. She knows her place and how men and women ought to conduct themselves; she regularly reminds those in her orbit of their duties as she sees them. The formality with which Emily undertakes this duty makes for some humor. Emily sends memos to those in her circle, like the following:

> Every moment think steadily as a Roman and as a man, to do what thou hast in hand with perfect and simple dignity, and a feeling of affection and freedom and justice. These words of the Emperor Marcus Aurelius Antonius strike me as pretty good advice, even for the ornieriest young scamp. (*MG* 78)

Her ethos echoes Will's and she amplifies some of his sentiments and criticism of the America's increasing disorder. She hails from Aurelius's wintry kingdom, and from this position launches into periodic tirades against the decadent world.

Over the course of the novel, Emily always attempted to view Binx's actions in a Stoical framework—she imagined him to be just like her. In a soliloquy set at the end of *The Moviegoer*, Emily does more than merely express her confusion at Binx's attitudes. Emily sets herself apart from a world she believes to have gone mad. She reveals her mournful understanding that she cannot even rely on the idea she shares the same meanings of words with Binx and his kind, for in her worldview, "among certain people, gentlefolk I don't mind calling them, there exists a set of meanings held in common, that a certain manner and a certain grace come as naturally as breathing" (*MG* 222). Yet while her stepdaughter Kate and young ward Binx grew older and further from the dictates of honor, drifting in their own confused way, she remained focused on her inner kingdom, and these common meanings had fallen away. Through Emily, Walker conveyed the assumption that Will and others also embraced: that manners trump morals, and that these unspoken notions remain the source of all public order. For Emily, this set of manners remains idealistically embodied in a small group of people, "our kind of folks," all of whom shared "a native instinct for behavior, a natural piety or grace" (*MG* 222). These natural aristocrats define what it means to possess class—for Emily, this way of being placed them in a state of natural superiority over the rest of American culture (*MG* 223).

Yet, Emily's sense of superiority did not only rest on the abstract notion of her people's intrinsic virtues. She linked this sense of worth to noble attitudes and actions in the world, especially in terms of the honorable people's relations to others:

> The charge is that people belonging to my class think they're better than other people. You're damn right we're better. We're better because we do not shirk our obligations either to ourselves or to others. We do not whine. We do not organize a minority group and blackmail the government. We do not prize mediocrity for mediocrity's sake. . . . Ours is the only civilization in history which has enshrined mediocrity as its national ideal. (*MG* 223)

Emily's assault thus not only enshrines her class as the moral standard of the wider society, but she also lays out a significant criticism of the politics and culture of the democratic age. Without excellence as our guide, mediocrity—the "ordinary man"—becomes our political lodestar, with devastating consequences. Emily describes a coarsening of moral character which runs alongside an expressive emotionalism in politics; in her speech, these together undermine the self-discipline and strength of will of any people who hobbles themselves with these attitudes. In the Southern Stoic's mind, the importance attached to equality in such circumstances must naturally grow out of all proportion—destroying the natural hierarchy people like Emily and Will saw as necessary for a decent social order.

While Walker came to support racial equality, he nonetheless harbored the suspicion that the most dangerous and least justifiable part of the North's response against the Southern way of life had to do with the contempt for all traditions some progressive-minded thinkers and social critics brought to the problem (*SSL* 90–1). Walker argued the old ways came with certain benefits that flowed from an agrarian society, "a tradition which at its best enshrined the humane aspects of living for rich and poor, black and white" and that put emphasis on the maintenance of "stable family life," a kind of "sensitivity and good manners between men," and a "chivalry toward women" (*SSL* 91). All of these virtues follow nicely from Will's worldview, but the honorable basis for this way of life rested on foundations that largely disappeared with coming of World War I, and that were completely destroyed in the aftermath of World War II.

As his depiction of Emily Cutrer suggested, Walker believed that the remnants of 1950s Southern decency all too easily became bound up with nostalgia rather than any capacity for moralizing. This appeared especially true when literary men or philosophers attempted to explain the merits of this old system, or criticize some aspects of the new civic order. When people attempt to revive the old ways, Walker noted:

> It was often with the sense of a nostalgic revival of a way of life, or else undertaken with the skill of a great novelist in portraying a belief which he did not necessarily subscribe to. I am thinking in particular of the Southern Agrarians and of Faulkner's Dilsey. . . . We are all familiar with an entire literature about the ennui of life in suburbia and the split-level nightmare. Yet this literature is generally even more boring than the life it portrays. Aside from the worth or lack of it in such novels, I cannot escape the suspicion of a degree of bad faith in both the novelist and his characters, that, in short, for all their complaints, neither of them would dream of changing places with the nineteenth-century housewife or the low-paid nineteenth century novelist. (*SSL* 209–210)

Thus, what remains of the Southern Stoic or honor-loving way of life is most emphatically not something the contemporary author really wishes to bring back. Walker implied that since this old way of life flowed from the stability of prewar Southern communities, it might not be possible to recover this sense of honor in industrial times without tremendous acts of will and violence. These efforts might simply reflect a desperate desire for something solid in a world that has lost its old bearings.

As a possible source of respect and support for stable family life, a sense of attachment to place, and a commitment to certain virtues, what Walker calls Southern Stoicism has some value (*MCWP* 105–6). He also consistently argued that this tradition carries within it many dangers that grow especially worrisome without the moderation of a Christian ethos. If the Southern Stoic simply conceded greater ground to his ostensibly Christian beliefs, many of the worst aspects of life in the south would diminish in their effects. The desire for honor could take its rightful place, subordinate to the greater truths about our existence that Will Percy and Emily Cutrer intimated, but never fully accepted. At the same time, Walker feared those honor-lovers who might attempt to abandon their uneasy attachment to religion, making the idea of honorable violence in the name of restoring the old ways more compelling, even desirable. He saw this as one possible path through which the scourge of fascism might return to the postwar world. His novel *Lancelot* develops the links between catastrophe, violence, and renewal, and for these reasons it deserves extended examination.

DISENCHANTMENT, VIOLENCE, AND LANCE LAMAR'S THIRD REVOLUTION

As Walker put it in a brief essay on *Love in the Ruins*, the "prospect of catastrophe has its attractions" (*SSL* 249). Think for a moment of the prevalence in various media today of stories focused on the last days of earth, or post-apocalyptic settings where humanity must begin anew or the popularity of documentary programs such as *Life after People* (History Channel, 2008–2010). These might simply be imagined resources for thinking about the world in a new way. But against these, Walker argued that one type of doomsayer deserves special mention: the anxious and trembling culture critics who function as "professional gravediggers of the West" (*SSL* 263). Yet this excitement concerning destruction and renewal might go beyond these disingenuous critics, and benign fans of post-apocalyptic television. Instead, we may see a resurgence of acts by those whose goal is cultural renewal through destruction and a substitution of their putatively "new" values for those of the old, decayed world.

Through the story of Lance Lamar, a patient in a mental hospital coming to the end of his stay, Walker's novel *Lancelot* presents this possibility in a vivid form as a monologue where Lance, with a silent audience in a childhood friend turned Catholic priest named Percival, recounts what brought him to the asylum. Lance was a moderate in all things: reading, liberalism, drink, music, and even the pursuit of happiness (*L* 24). Prior to his institutionalization for mental illness, this was a man that held nothing to be certain. He lived by no truths. Over the course of the book, Lance slowly remembers and reveals, albeit somewhat unreliably, his discovery that it was impossible for his daughter Siobhan to actually be his biological child, and his revenge, a tale which ends in the destruction of his home and Lance's murder of his wife and several others. Walker's tale has all the elements of a mystery, but the weight of the story rests on a set of pointed challenges to those who have lost powerful reasons to believe in their regime and way of life: If we accept the impending demise of our society, its moral decay and weakness, why defend it? Why not embrace something else besides moderate liberalism and the comfortable life of bourgeois prosperity (*CWP* 154–5)?

Lance embarks upon a search for meaning amid the obvious failure of his marriage and what he depicts in his narrative as the corrosion of virtue in the world. But his quest does not really resemble Binx Bolling's—a search for enlivening meaning that breaks one out of the ordinariness of life. Lance quests after something darker and more compelling. After relating the realization of his wife's infidelity, Lance asks the silent priest whether one "might undertake a search not for God but for evil?" (*L* 51) Not recognizing the nihilism implicit in this question, Lance goes further:

> You people may have been on the wrong track all these years with all that talk about God and signs of his existence, the order and beauty of the universe—that's all washed up and you know it. The more we know about the beauty and order of the universe, the less God has to do with it. . . . But what if you could show me a *sin?* A purely evil deed, an intolerable deed for which there is no explanation? Now there's a mystery. People would sit up and take notice. I would be impressed. You could almost make a believer out of me. (*L* 51–2)

This search leads Lance—as he recounts his actions in the hospital—into the realization that if he cannot follow the path of the church, of man's moral equality, and the need for forgiveness, he must develop his own harrowing path to revival. But why look to evil for answers?

Lance's realization hinges on an observation: we live in an age of "interest," not one oriented toward truth. In proclaiming himself the "Knight of the Unholy Grail," Lance hoped to overcome the present era's incapacity to see that the passive, fleeting attachments we display for one theory or consumer item after another lead nowhere. He poses Percival another question: suppose for a minute that a Harvard professor found and authenticated the Holy Grail. Would this make any converts? Lance thought that this would have no effect. People get "into" spirituality, history, archaeology, and a thousand other fleeting passions; they "show interest." But apart from those in scientific disciplines, people pursue no truths as such, allow no claims on themselves that might transform their very souls (*L* 137–9). In an age where everyone pursues happiness and seeks material fulfillment, "everything and everyone's either wonderful or sick and nothing is evil" (*L* 138). Under such conditions, good and evil lose all meaning. Lance suggests that at the time, he had no idea how this quest would change him and expresses scorn for his own mentality: "[t]here I was forty-five years old and I didn't know there was 'evil' in the world" (*L* 139). Modern people might speak of healthy and sick, good and bad, but never of evil. If they cannot identify any willfully wrong acts as such and call them evil, the only category left open is insanity.

In the process of searching for the immoral truth of his life and his wife's betrayal, Lance rediscovers another older path. His way forward points not toward nihilism—indeed, he agrees with Nietzsche that would be an apt label for his enemies—but rather back toward an ethic of honor stripped of limitation and bound up in the will of the higher, new man. As Walker put it, "the miscarriage of his search issues, quite logically . . . in his own peculiar brand of fascism" (*SSL* 383). Though Nietzsche scholars and devotees would disagree with this interpretation, Walker suggested that this might be one practical way a Nietzschean ethic might grow to life in the world.

In an interview with Jan Nordby Gretlund, Walker described his experience of spending the summer of 1934 in Nazi Germany. He noted that there "was tremendous excitement at the 'rejuvenation' of Germany, and the creation of new values in the Nietzschean sense: the death of God, the death of old values, and the creation of new values. . . . Lancelot is a conscious combination of something quite positive and quite evil" (*CWP* 208). Walker's reading of Nietzsche conflicts with much recent interpretation that emphasizes the more aesthetic and less violent implications of his thought. The trouble that Walker identified is that once we accept Nietzsche's claims, one man's beauty can be another's nightmare and there are no legitimate grounds for judging between them. As he reveals his acts of vengeance to Percival, Lance lays out his creed of violent renewal alongside a bitter critique of modern society that extends Emily Cutrer's beliefs beyond a resigned, Stoic acceptance of the nature of our times to a more transformative ethic of revolution.

Lance's transformation from the quintessential liberal bourgeois citizen into an unholy crusader rested on the recognition that he had never really noticed his profound dissatisfaction and boredom with the comforts of our world. The reality was now much simpler: "I couldn't stand it. I still can't stand it. I can't stand the way things are. I cannot tolerate this age. What is more, I won't. That was my discovery: that I didn't have to" (*L* 154). This passage shares some profound resonances with various quotes attributed to Will Percy, but lack the sense of duty and restraint Will brought to all his relationships. Walker implied that this shift is not an accident because Will may have had no logical moral reason to accept the limitations his sense of duty imposed. Lance Lamar may have been an image of what Will Percy or Emily Cutrer could be like if their faith in virtue faltered. Rather than accepting the passing of honor with stoic resignation as they did, Lance yearned for the days of what he saw as an easier clarity, where one responded to insults with violence rather than lawsuits. At least in that situation, one "knows where one stands and what one can do," for even "defeat is better than not knowing" how to live from day to day (*L* 155).

Liberated from the sorts of limitations and duties that constrained the old sort of honor-lover—the Will Percys or Emily Cutrers of the world—Lance is free to contemplate his new order without reference to history. In Nietzschean fashion, Lance tells Percival that "[t]here is going to be a new order of things," and admonishes him to neither confuse it with anything that has come in the past, nor diminish the boldness of the project he has in mind. At least in his mind, Lance's new world will resist comparison to any other kind of social order:

> Certainly not with your Holy Name Society or Concerned Christians Against Smut. This has nothing to do with Christ or boycotts. Don't confuse it with the Nazis. They were stupid. If in fact there was a need to clean up the Weimar Republic and if in fact they did in part, they screwed everything up by getting off on the Jews. What stupidity! The Jews were not to blame. The Nazis were clods, thugs. What they should have done was invite the Jews. Half the Jews would have joined them—just as half the Catholics did. Don't confuse it with the Klan, those poor ignorant bastards. Blacks, Jews, Catholics—they are all irrelevant; blaming them only confuses the issue. We'll invite them and you. (*L* 156)

From Lance's perspective, this would not be a revolution launched in the name of any particular "ism" or on behalf of a master race. It would transcend ideology by restoring manners and proceed on the basis of Lance's conviction that he has the freedom to act on his repugnance for our time, and that out of their common disgust with our society, many would follow him into a purifying struggle for a new code of honor and a twisted kind of meritocracy based upon virtue.

Such a man brings a revolution with his deeds rather than with his words, and hopes to craft a new world out of sincerity and sobriety. Lance states that "[s]ome act, assassinate, bomb, burn, etc., but they are the crazies" (*L* 156). Given his past acts of murder and destruction, this seems more than a little peculiar. Lance argues that his violence and rejection of the old world would serve to restore the rule of honorable manners:

> But what if one sober, reasonable, and honorable man should act, and act with perfect sobriety, reason, and honor? Then you would have the beginning of a new age. . . . We? Who are we? We will not even be a secret society as you know such things. Its members will know each other without signs or passwords. No speeches, rallies, political parties. There will be no need of such things. One man will act. Another man will act. (*L* 156–7)

Lance remains vague about what sorts of actions might generate his new world. His assertion that change might occur without assassinations or bombings stands in tension with the undertone of purification and violence present in his words. The incoherence and lack of self-awareness here might be called insanity, but consider again its resonance with Carl Schmitt, whose insistence that all the ordinary things Lance suggests we associate with politics—the "speeches, rallies, political parties"—pale before the friend-enemy distinction. Schmitt and his followers are often ambivalent about the logical consequences of this thinking. Action trumps words in this thinking.

The fact that Walker conveys this idea through an unreliable character Lance tells us something about how liberal, tolerant people today tend to categorize such thinking as insanity. This is an example for Walker of our society not taking words and deeds seriously, and he conveyed a double warning to the reader in this passage about our tendency to medicalize or psychoanalyze evil, and of the threat of novel forms of honor. Lance tells Percival that he and others will recognize one another clearly through their common convictions to which they adhere and upon which they act:

> a stern code, a gentleness toward women and an intolerance of swinishness, a counsel kept, and above all a readiness to act, and act alone if necessary. . . . The new order will not be based on Catholicism or Communism or fascism or liberalism or capitalism or any ism at all, but simply on that stern rectitude valued by the new breed and marked by the violence which will attend its breach. (*L* 157–8)

Lance wraps his goals in what he sees as virtue, but Walker believed they cannot breed anything but monstrousness. Even Lance's attempts at magnanimity fail to recognize the danger of living with honor that lacks moderation. The way he subordinates women to his vision stands as just the most obvious example.[23] Gentleness and charity cannot grow out of Lance's inflexible brand of honor. Indeed, it is difficult to conceive of what basis one might use to moderate this imagined revolution's pursuit of purity and rectitude.

Lance's invitation to all noble souls carries a threat. He must see all those too weak to stand with the great men, or too wedded to the comforts of our present day to see the "rot" as enemies (*L* 160). He only dimly realizes the depth of what he proposes, denying the degree of violence it might take to bring about a new world order, and then likening himself to Christ as one who speaks "with authority" (*L* 159). Yet in place of the "good news" at the center of the Christian message—the forgiveness of sin and the possibility of eternal life—Lance can only announce the condemnation of vice and destruction of the old order.

At the root of honor-codes stand men, men who decide the rules and clarify every person's place in the world, and in each case, they will not only declare right from wrong but impose it on the world: "You will do right, not because of Jew-Christian commandments but because we say it is right" (*L* 178). Having laid down the law by which all people should live Lance and his honor-lovers would reorder all relations. Women would choose between becoming ladies or whores, and men would face a no less important choice:

> And we will value them [women] exactly as much as they value themselves. They won't like it much, you say? The hell with them. They won't have anything to say about it. Not only are they not strong enough. They don't care enough. . . . The men? The best of them will be strong and brave and pure of heart, not for Christ's sake, but like an Apache youth or a Lacedemonian who denies himself to be strong. The others can whoremonger and screw whom they choose. But we will prevail. (*L* 179)

This crusade to establish the reign of the brave New Man and chaste New Woman over lesser beings cannot end in toleration of difference or the acceptance of vice. The idea we might love our neighbors despite their flaws holds no power over his honor, at least until he accomplishes the necessary cleansing: "Don't talk to me of love until we shovel out the shit" (*L* 179). Lance's victory means death for those who offend the noble honor-lovers.

One might wonder whether we ought to take Walker's nightmare vision of honor gone mad so seriously. After all, this is a story recounted by a man in an asylum about a revolution unlikely to happen. Lance proposes a world that renders compromise unnecessary and politics obsolete—a sentiment repeated many times in the classroom by disenchanted students, to say nothing of the rhetoric of domestic terrorists such as Timothy McVeigh, or the shooters at Columbine High School in 1999. This ideal also appears in the writings of Weimar-era veterans disenchanted by democracy.[24] Is this not a compelling ambition for someone who despairs of liberalism? Even if we accept that it is unlikely an individual would actually attempt Lance's "Third Revolution," Walker's tale still demonstrates the ultimately dangerous logic of honor and all the ways this perspective remains tied to classes and individuals that deem themselves the adequate judges of virtue.

The Emily Curtrers of the world may moderate the demands their honor places on the world around them, but Walker focused on the idea that people like Emily have no *logical* reason to stop short of crusading for a new world (*CWP* 209–10). Even if most individuals fail to follow Lance on his quest for evil, the story implies that settling matters decisively through violence retains an appeal to some: first in the apparent decisiveness of action rather than conversation or compromise; second, in the sheer excitement and fullness in the moment of action; and finally, in the sense of sovereignty and escape from constraint such acts grant the honor-lover. The very survival of an "antiquated" concept such as honor might be clue to some of the darker aspects of human nature and its hopes and dreams. This observation it might also lead us to ask about the persistent place of destruction in the human heart.

HONOR AND THE ESCAPE FROM BOREDOM

Walker's method of analyzing our present discontents gives us some insight into the nature of the "authentic thrill of the Bomb and the Coming of the Last Days" (*MB* 84). But we need not embrace Lance's quest for a world made pure and noble or live in hope of a decisive moment where the destruction of the world as we know it opens up new vistas to appreciate both the danger and appeal of honor. Walker argued that in an age filled with people who live with sentimentality and boredom moments, that shake us out of our ordinary lives—especially through violence—will retain an appeal seemingly inexplicable through the standard theories of our time (*SSL* 310).

Having looked at Walker Percy's understanding the popular theories of the self in chapter 3, and one promising, but tremendously dangerous attempt to live a life with integrity in the present, we can see how he returns time and again to the notion that a people grown sentimental and bored will fall prey to the desire to transcend their condition—sometimes in an extravagant and terrifying fashion. A creature of the present age "can become so frustrated, bored, and enraged that he resorts to violence, violence upon himself (drugs, suicide) or upon others (murder, war)" just to *escape* (*SSL* 312). In the context of such a world, the standard answers all sorts of people give to questions about their nature and destiny fall short. The South in particular may have something to offer the world, but only if they renounce their uneasy, honor-bound compromise with—or, more pointedly, repudiation of—Christian faith.

Walker opened his essay collection *The Message in the Bottle* with a curious set of questions focused on the myriad causes of sadness in the twentieth century. Seemingly good environments produce boredom and yearning for something more meaningful, while putatively bad environments appear to enliven us and heighten our enjoyment of the little things in life. Walker extended this logic to war, and noted that Will responded rather curiously to the advent of World War II:

> Why is it the only time I ever saw my uncle happy during his entire life was the afternoon of December 7, 1941, when the Japanese bombed Pearl Harbor?
>
> Why did he shortly thereafter become miserable when he learned that he was too old to go to Europe to shoot at Germans and stand a good chance of being shot by Germans?

> Why is it that the only time he was happy before was in the Argonne Forest in 1918 when he was shooting at Germans and stood a good chance of being shot by Germans? (*MB* 4)

Judging from *Lanterns on the Levee*, Walker did not exaggerate his account of Will's sadness. But the questions Walker raised about the link between honor and violence lead him to peculiar lines of inquiry in his nonfiction and striking representations in his fiction, perhaps the most important of these being: Does war have greater appeal in a comfortable age precisely because it conveys meaning to lives lost in materialism and easy living?

NOTES

1. On this point, the best history of this problem can be found in Mark Noll's *The Civil War as a Theological Problem* (Chapel Hill: University of North Carolina Press, 1996).
2. See Bertram Wyatt-Brown, *Southern Honor: Ethics & Behavior in the Old South* (Oxford and New York: Oxford University Press, 2007). For Wyatt-Brown's more specific arguments relating the Percy family to the Southern experience, see his *The House of Percy: Honor, Melancholy, and Imagination in a Southern Family* (Oxford and New York: Oxford University Press, 1994).
3. Kwame Anthony Appiah, *The Honor Code: How Moral Revolutions Happen* (New York: W.W. Norton, 2010) and James Bowman, *Honor: A History* (New York: Encounter Books, 2006). For other accounts attempting to define or grapple with the legacy of honor in historical or anthropological terms, see Frank Henderson Stewart, *Honor* (Chicago: University of Chicago Press, 1994), Wyatt-Brown, *Southern Honor*, and Joanne Freeman, *Affairs of Honor: National Politics in the New Republic* (New Haven: Yale University Press, 2001). Another work related to Bowman's inquiry is Harvey C. Mansfield, *Manliness* (New Haven: Yale University Press, 2006).
4. C.S. Lewis, *The Abolition of Man* (New York: HarperCollins, 2001), 24–25.
5. George Fenwick Jones, *Honor in German Literature* (Chapel Hill: University of North Carolina Press, 1959), 40.
6. For two other examples, see Richard Ned Lebow, *A Cultural Theory of International Relations* (Cambridge: Cambridge University Press, 2008) and Sharon Krause, *Liberalism with Honor* (Cambridge: Harvard University Press, 2002). Both perceptively look to honor to help understand the limits of conventional understandings of politics, and as a source of potential restraint in political life.
7. There are significant similarities between Percy's concerns and those of Tocqueville. While Walker does not use explicitly Tocquevillian terms, his general mode of discussing the idea of people shut in on themselves, turned to solipsism and comfortable consumption echoes Tocqueville, who points toward a kind of individualism which is "a calm and considered feeling which disposes each citizen to isolate himself

from the mass of his fellows and withdraw into the circle of family and friends; with this little society formed to his taste, he gladly leaves the greater society to look after itself." See *Democracy in America*, ed. J.P. Mayer, trans. George Lawrence (New York: HarperCollins, 1969), 506.

8. Here I would mention the work of M.E. Bradford in particular. See, for, instance, *The Reactionary Imperative: Essays Literary and Political* (New York: Open Court, 1999). Many other writers, both popular and scholarly, have emulated his approach. For other representative examples, Thomas J. DiLorenzo, *The Real Lincoln: A New Look at Abraham Lincoln, His Agenda, and an Unnecessary War* (New York: Crown Forum, 2003) and Claes G. Ryn, *America the Virtuous: The Crisis of Democracy and the Quest for Empire* (New Brunswick: Transaction Publishing, 2003).

9. At least in 1957, even though Walker Percy believed in racial equality and always held out hope for respect and comity between races and cultures, he opposed the method by which integration proceeded after *Brown v. Board*. Walker's point here was that if high school in the South served as a place of obligatory and deep social encounter, it was thus the place where racists would see the greatest threat to their way of life because it opened up the possibility for interracial coupling. He argued that this failure to understand the South's culture could only be seen as the result of ignorance on the federal government's part. He suggested that kindergarten might have been the appropriate place to start the process of integration and the slow changing of hearts on the issue of racial equality (*SSL* 98–99). On this, see Brendan P. Purdy and Janice Daurio, "The Second Coming of Walker Percy: From Segregationist to Integrationist," in *A Political Companion to Walker Percy*, ed. Peter Augustine Lawler and Brian A. Smith (Lexington: University Press of Kentucky, 2013), 207–236.

10. Today, Will attracts more scholarly attention for his sexual attitudes and quiet life as a homosexual in a place and time extremely hostile to that lifestyle. The only major biography of Will focuses quite heavily on his sexual orientation and his opinions on matters related to this: see Benjamin E. Wise, *William Alexander Percy: The Curious Life of a Mississippi Planter and Sexual Freethinker* (Chapel Hill: University of North Carolina Press, 2012).

11. On this time in Walker Percy's life, see Patrick Samway, S.J., *Walker Percy: A Life* (Chicago: Loyola Press, 1999), 28-66; and Jay Tolson, *Pilgrim in the Ruins: A Life of Walker Percy* (Chapel Hill: University of North Carolina Press, 1992), 64–108.

12. For a brief account of Percy's childhood and college years, see Wise, *William Alexander Percy*, 30–58.

13. On the duel's place as resolver of dispute, see Wyatt-Brown, *Southern Honor*, ch. 2, 25-61. On the broader culture of honor and dueling in the early American republic, see also Freeman, *Affairs of Honor*, Ch. 4, 159–198. Appiah also devotes a section of his book to the problem of the duel, see his *Honor Code*, Ch. 1, 3–51.

14. On Will's aesthetic vision and its ties to his morality and rejection of Christianity, see Wise, *William Alexander Percy*, 66–67.

15. Foote lived more closely to Will's ideal than Walker or his brothers, noting in an interview that it "sounds terrible to say so, but art is what I worship, in all its various forms." On Foote and Will's relationship, see *Walker Percy Remembered*,

ed. David Horace Harwell (Chapel Hill: University of North Carolina Press, 2006), 124–126, quote above at 137.

16. Consider Lawrence Lampert's readings of Nietzsche on this point. As a convinced Nietzschean, Lampert echoes some of Will's desires. See his *Nietzsche's Teaching: An Interpretation of Thus Spoke Zarathustra* (New Haven: Yale University Press, 1986) and *Nietzsche's Task: An Interpretation of Beyond Good and Evil* (New Haven: Yale University Press, 2001).

17. Will makes it very clear he does not believe in any conventional religious faith. Elsewhere, he references the "High God" (*LL* 348). If anything, *Lanterns* suggests that Will was a deist of some sort—but did not seem to think that this deity had any moral role in human life.

18. On this point, see chapter twenty-five in Will's memoir, "A Bit of Diary," which depicts an exhausting array of little visits, consultations, and small exercises of authority on Will's part (*LL* 322–331).

19. LeRoy Percy was the last indirectly elected senator from Mississippi, and his opponent, James K. Vardaman, the former governor, a populist and supporter of Klan activities would be the first senator of the state elected by popular vote.

20. This is not to suggest that segregation and racism was a peculiarly Southern difficulty, for Walker recognized that it certainly was not, expressing his "opinion that local Yankee racists are even worse than Southern racists; they don't even like Uncle Toms or Aunt Jemimas. One can only wonder how Abraham Lincoln ever talked these people into fighting a war to free slaves" (*SSL* 8). My point here is to emphasize the ways that Walker argues the South faced particular challenges, and draw some lessons from his account.

21. Gary M. Ciuba, *Walker Percy: Books of Revelations* (Athens: University of Georgia Press, 1991), 15.

22. Walker's lifelong friend Shelby Foote suggested to at least one interviewer that Emily *is* Will Percy, disguised and slightly re-imagined (*CWP*, 64–65).

23. John Desmond, *Walker Percy's Search for Community* (Athens: University of Georgia Press, 2004), 162–163.

24. For a compelling account of this, see Jeffrey Herf, *Reactionary Modernism: Technology, Culture, and Politics in Weimar and the Third Reich* (Cambridge: Cambridge University Press, 1984).

Chapter 5

Dreaming of the End Times

Anxiety concerning the decline and fall of civilization appears throughout Percy's body of work. It may be that he shared this trait with all serious moralists.[1] What sets Percy's account of this issue apart from others rests in not only his preoccupation with depicting actual disaster for what it might tell us about human nature or our politics, but also his focus on mining our obsession with the end of our society as a clue that might help explain our predicament in modern times.

> The contingency "what if the Bomb should fall?" is not only not a cause of anxiety in the alienated man but is one of his few remaining refuges from it. When everything else fails, we may always turn to our good friend just back from Washington or Moscow, who obliges us with his sober second thoughts—"I can tell you this much, I am profoundly disturbed"—and each of us has what he came for, the old authentic thrill of the Bomb and the Coming of the Last Days. Like Ortega's romantic, the heart's desire of the alienated man is to see vines sprouting through the masonry. The real anxiety question, the question no one asks because no one wants to, is the reverse: What if the Bomb should *not* fall? What then? (*MB* 84–85)

As a novelist and essayist, Percy saw his role as reading the signs of our spiritual and social disorders, and rendering them intelligible to an audience that increasingly possessed a language inadequate to understanding the situation.

Percy's method here matches his understanding of the limitations of current language. He suggested that if you tell a contemporary American he or she suffers from alienation, he or she probably will not understand your point. Indeed, without recourse to therapeutic or medical terminology, it is unclear that he or she could comprehend the diagnosis. By contrast, Percy suspected that a writer who depicts alienation in a story that engages the reader's emotions, naming the situation in relatable terms, might have some ability to reveal the notion to his readers. Percy explained how he viewed his ambition as a writer in the following terms:

> A serious novel about the destruction of the United States and the end of the world should perform the function of prophecy in reverse. The novelist writes about the coming end in order to warn about present ills and so avert the end. . . . If he did not think he saw something other people didn't see or at least didn't pay much attention to, he would be wasting his time writing and they reading. This does not mean he is wiser than they. . . . The novelist is less like a prophet than he is like the canary that coal miners used to take down into the shaft to test the air. When the canary gets unhappy, utters plaintive cries, and collapses, it may be time for the miners to surface and think things over. (*MB* 101)

When authors attempt this warning function, however, Percy insisted that a direct approach cannot easily avail itself of success. Scholars may warn about the dangers of environmental collapse, financial instability, political corruption, and the like using clear terms and unambiguous argument. But how can a person with a deeply impoverished language, and hence, a limited notion of how to think about her existence, see her spiritual predicament?

Percy argued that depicting characters bent and misunderstood by their times serves as the best starting point for demonstrating our situation. Seeing the "fault lines in the terrain, small clues that something strange is going on, a telltale sign here and there" becomes an increasingly important role in times like our own, in part because the sketching the appearance of apocalyptic moments and images of decaying social order provide important contexts within which we might examine ourselves and our political life (*SSL* 155). Indeed, the very technique of presenting such notions as real stories or thought problems,

> not only makes for ordinary good adventure but for interesting theological experiments. What is good and bad about wiping out the whole crazy edifice of Western civilization? What realities, good and bad, does a survivor confront who finds himself alone in a rest stop off I-80 in Utah? (*MCWP* 131)

When we dismiss patterns of thought like this as evidence of insanity, we miss the chance to understand the motives behind the longing and the social and political disturbances they might portend. Percy believed that to address these ideas head on, in a directly moral or theological key, is to end the possibility of conversation with most modern people. The best way to address the real crises of the present comes from *not* talking about them at all—discuss the situation around them in a distorted way, and perhaps one might provoke a thought about the dilemmas we face about how to live (*SSL* 158).

BOREDOM, ALIENATION, AND THE IDEA OF DEATH-IN-LIFE

People often feel strangely out of place in the world they have tamed for their use. One source of our alienation rests in the ways that the very material objects and goals modern people pursue rarely satisfy us for long (*LC* 80–2). Indeed, once we secure them, boredom sets in, and creates one of the conditions under which the desire for disaster might creep into our consciousness. In *Lost in the Cosmos*, Percy offered several possible explanations of this condition. He noted that the very word boredom did not exist prior to the eighteenth century and asked why this might be, suggesting this answer as a possibility:

> Is it because there is a special sense in which for the past two or three hundred years the self has perceived itself as a leftover which cannot be accounted for by its own objective view of the world and that in spite of an ever-heightened self-consciousness, increased leisure, ever more access to cultural and recreational facilities, ever more instruction on self-help, self-growth, self-enrichment, the self feels ever more imprisoned in itself—no, worse than imprisoned because a prisoner at least knows he is imprisoned and sets store by the freedom awaiting him and the world seems to be open when in fact the self is not and it is not—a state of affairs which has to be called something besides imprisonment—e.g., boredom. Boredom is the self being stuffed with itself. (*LC* 70–1)

Two crucial elements emerge in this description. First, Percy sketched out some of the spillover effects of scientism and materialism. An objective, empirical-oriented, and materialistic theory of the person as want- and need-satisfier faces significant challenges if the various wants and needs the human person fulfills have the unintended effect of increasing their alienation from others. Second, Percy implicitly suggested here that the "softening" elements of modern progress—the elimination of inequality, struggle, violence, and so on—might actually contribute to our distress. Comfort may not deliver the happiness we initially trust it might provide. With this in mind, consider how Percy argued alienation relates to boredom.

In part because of the indifference they face both from ordinary citizens and those in real positions of authority, Percy contended that American writers usually suffer deep alienation. Paradoxically, they feel a kind of envy for actually persecuted writers. Speaking of the 1960s and 1970s American protest novelists in particular, Percy wrote: "My theory is that he secretly envies Aleksandr Solzhenitsyn, despite the terrible ordeal Solzhenitsyn suffered, despite his rightest [*sic*] sympathies. He envies the fact that a novelist can so irritate the state that the state will go to a great deal of trouble to get rid of him" (*SSL* 171). We might further distinguish Percy's point from that of strict materialists: an obsession with material causes misses a critical dimension of this problem in that no one is totally reducible to their set of material circumstances. If they were, alienation would be subject to surer and more permanent remedy.

This all bears importance because as we have seen, Percy defined alienation in relation to the objective-empirical mode of self-understanding that characterizes scientism and materialism. He termed our recognition and naming of our alienation as a "reversal" of that anxious and out-of-place feeling (*MB* 84). By naming the phenomenon, the human person momentarily restores their sovereignty and sense of agency—they are no longer totally subject to the nameless circumstances of the moment. Reversal is an appropriate description of Percy's concept of alienation in two senses: first, that it literally inverts the materialist assumption that a good environment breeds happy people; second, it focuses on the opposite concerns, beginning from the heart and soul of the person and only secondarily considers the environment in which the person lives. If we accept this point that individuals can satisfy all their physical needs and fulfill most or all of their material wants, we ought then to consider some of the motives and feelings that the objective-empirical approach cannot easily comprehend, like the misplaced ghostliness of alienation and its near cousins, envy and despair.

Percy shed considerable light on the strange features that come with living in boredom and alienation. In his novels, he presented two brief, fairly dramatic renderings of alienation as an unnamable, but harrowing condition. In *The Second Coming*, one of the protagonists, Will Barrett, recounts a discussion with his father about alienation and the state of being within which modern Americans must live:

> One night after the war and during the Eisenhower years the father was taking a turn under the oaks. The son watched him from the porch.
>
> "The trouble is," the man said, "there is no word for this."
>
> "For what?"
>
> "This." He held out both arms to the town, to the wide world. "It's not war and it's not peace. It's not death and it's not life. What is it? What do you call it?"
>
> "I don't know."
>
> "There is life and there is death. Life is better than death but there are worse things than death."
>
> "What?"
>
> "There is no word for it. Maybe it never happened before and so there is no word for it. What is the word for a state which is not life and not death, a death in life?" (*SC* 126)

The idea that we might be biologically alive and nevertheless emotionally dead to significant aspects of reality recurs throughout Percy's novels, but here Will's father articulates above all the pain of not being able to name his dilemma. What distinguishes this account is the insistence we can be like ghosts still haunting the earth, ill at ease with our condition but incapable of escaping it, either. Alert to something, Will's father ultimately refuses to countenance this state of affairs and commits suicide.

Twenty years earlier in *The Moviegoer*, Percy presented a similar account through Binx Bolling's observations about how he and others deal with ordinary conversations. Binx does not know how to deal with small talk, and Percy's presentation of his disposition bears some examination:

> For some time now the impression has been growing upon me that everyone is dead.
>
> It happens when I speak to people. In the middle of a sentence it will come over me: yes, beyond a doubt this is death. There is little to do but groan and make an excuse and slip away as quickly as one can. At such times it seems that the conversation is spoken by automatons who have little choice in what they say. (MG 99–100)

This is not just an introvert's protest against small talk. The death Binx describes is that of which follows from philosophical materialism: an alienated people who do not see themselves as capable of choice and reflection are left with little more than idle observations about the weather or the market—forces beyond their control. People pronounce their bland opinions, seek to avoid offense, and this for Binx is another sign of their inner death.

However, this does not reach the depth of Binx's confusion and irritation at this state of affairs. He has an easier time dealing with "negative" emotions such as anger and hate than the sort of bland kindness one often encounters in our world. He explains this curiosity:

> Whenever I feel bad, I go to a library and read controversial periodicals. Though I do not know whether I am a liberal or a conservative, I am nevertheless enlivened by the hatred which one bears the other. In fact, this hatred strikes me as one of the few signs of life remaining in the world. This is another thing about the world which is upsidedown: all the friendly and likeable people seem dead to me; only the haters seem alive. (*MG* 100)

Opposition is at least lively; hate reflects a certain presence of will that all too many alienated wanderers lack. If individuals might escape alienation and boredom through a lively but potentially destructive emotion like hate, the objective-empirical approach of the social sciences as much as the kindness of a New Age toleration may not measure up as antidotes to our era's spiritual malaise. If the standard remedies to our unhappiness—seeking comfort, pleasure, and wealth—only make alienation worse, where might a person turn for an alternative?

Percy argued that many of the possible paths of escape from alienation and boredom defy our ordinary, bourgeois understanding of happiness. Despairing of one's condition may be the beginning of wisdom and a search for a better way to live, but without an adequate language or theory of the self to cope with this condition, the despair may naturally lead to suicide. The moral and political danger Percy identified here rests in the fact that the easiest forms of escape from alienation result from some of the darkest motivations in the human heart. Envy is the most prominent of these.

ENVY AS RESPONSE TO ALIENATION

The persistence of alienation does not prevent people from attempting to live by weak theories of the self or by immersing themselves in acts of consumption that never quite satisfy their longings. Thankfully, most people do not throw themselves wholeheartedly into radically illiberal or anti-bourgeois ideas or political movements. But at the same time, people do not simply embrace the fact of alienation and attempt to cope. Instead, Percy argued that the most common and easiest response to this feeling takes the form of envy, which results in moral and political harm to any community possessed by it. Envy erodes the basis upon which human relations flourish, but it confers curious pleasures on those that embrace it as a way of relating to others.

Percy addressed the subject of envy most pointedly in his 1983 satire *Lost in the Cosmos*. His analysis of the subject began with a broad definition, as he reminds the reader of "the root sense of envy: *invidere*, to look at with malice" (*LC* 57). Thus, as a phenomenon envy incorporates not just the comparisons people make between themselves and others, but also situations where we judge past and present circumstances against one another. Think here of the way Percy used all kinds of invidious comparison between circumstances in *The Moviegoer*—Binx Bolling continually contrasted being mired in the everyday against the exceptional and novelty against what had become stale. He consumed these experiences until nothing remained but the fading memory. By sketching this mode of envious experience, Percy suggested that a searcher like Binx might constantly undermine the dignity and worth of his present relationships and places by contrasting them against a fugitive standard of perfection. The trouble Percy identified is that envy is pleasurable, though, so we all too often fall prey to its allure.

Percy began his discussion of envy in *Lost in the Cosmos* with an example of how we might rethink the concept:

> Everyone remembers what he was and what he was doing when he heard the news of the Kennedy assassination—or, if he is old enough, Pearl Harbor.

> Why?
>
> The self deceives itself by saying that it is natural that such terrible events be etched in the memory.
>
> It is not so simple.
>
> The fact is that the scene and circumstances of hearing such news become invested with a certain significance and density which they do not ordinarily possess and with which ordinary events and ordinary occasions contrast unfavorably. (*LC* 57)

Perhaps it is in the nature of such comparison that the present usually comes up short when we measure it against the exciting moments of our past. The density to which Percy referred here seems to center on pain: people compare their awful past to the boring present, and strangely, the past seems better. This provokes myriad dissatisfactions: we remember exciting and exceptional moments with a kind of vividness denied to our recollections and experience of everyday life, so those humdrum occurrences naturally lose value. Binx Bolling's desire to "savor" the passage of time springs to mind here. If we constantly engage in rumination and comparison between the vivid experiences of our past, the ordinary present almost always suffers.

Percy argued that as a result of this way our memory tends to distort the past and color our view of the present, a kind of nostalgia for the horrible past creeps into our lives, such that he asked the following question:

> Why did French and German veterans of Verdun, a catastrophic battle in which one million men were killed, keep returning to Verdun for years after the war, sit quietly at the café at Lemmes on the Sacred Way, speaking softly of those terrible times, and even camp out for a week in the shell hole or trench where they spent the worst days of their lives? (*MB* 6)

Given Percy's descriptions of this phenomenon, it is easy to imagine individuals looking back and thinking, "at least then I knew my place and purpose." Will Percy's sensibility concerning war fits this notion as well—it was misery but vital, mysterious, and offered charms that civilian life could not. Immersion in such purposeful circumstances offers a way out of our boredom. The memory of that past can cast a shadow on the present, devaluing it in a way that makes it difficult to partake in communities or friendships that might guard us against the worst elements of our alienation.

Our envy toward others follows a similar pattern as this nostalgic longing: we look to others and imagine we see something better or less everyday than our own circumstances and feel anger or disgust at our life—or we see misfortune befall others and feel delight. Neither variation makes it easy to treat one's neighbor as a full partner in conversation and community. To take one of Percy's examples, imagine that our neighbor Charlie has received multiple pieces of good news today, and relates them to us with joy. At best we can express sympathetic happiness for Charlie. Percy asked his readers to ponder: "how much good news about Charlie can you tolerate without compensatory catastrophes, heroic rescues, and such" (*LC* 65)? Is it possible for us to really feel good all the time for our friends when they win in life? Percy's account of misfortune and envy focused on the comparisons we make in part because he suspected that the average alienated, depressed, anxiety-ridden person of our age can always interpret other people's misfortune in at least two ways (*LC* 60).

First, we can see such bad news as "unrelievedly bad," and express some real sympathy toward those suffering in the event. He offered the example of a UFO destroying Omaha, Nebraska. A person given to view the situation in this category would have to "see nothing good about the loss of several hundred thousand people" (*LC* 60). This is at least the moral response to such a circumstance. Percy believed that this is sometimes a difficult attitude to maintain, and that our temptations toward envy of interesting circumstances run deep. Percy's second way to view an unfortunate event, that of the "putatively bad," poses a challenge to us in part because there is a species of news which "by all criteria should be bad but in which you nevertheless take a certain comfort." The value here springs from the excitement new and dangerous circumstances generate. This relates back to nostalgia for war: death and disaster restore our appreciation for life, but only because of our general malice and indifference. So, when the aliens attack, Omaha might be nothing more than a crater, but an individual might say to himself that "I don't know anybody in Omaha," and become excited that the world just became a more interesting place because aliens are real (*LC* 60).

In the case of bad news, Percy believed that people face serious temptations to feel excitement at others' misfortune. In the opposite case of someone else's good fortune, they face the equal and opposite temptation to want the other person to suffer some disaster. The malice in both of these circumstances allows for a kind of imaginative escape from the everydayness of our own circumstances. In the case of bad news, Percy thought that the value this creates for the envious person comes from the resulting experience of seeing the world in a new light. So, for example, if aliens are real and may come to destroy our city next, that may cause us terror, but also brings about great excitement. More importantly, it restores unalienated focus to our lives. This notion is important because it helps clarify what so many scholars strain to explain: Why so many Europeans volunteered for World War I with such excitement and remained wedded to a view of the war as liberating or transformative for so many years.[2]

In the case of others' happiness, the fact we often cannot easily enter into their experience presents one barrier to fellow feeling—after all, it is *their* moment of happiness, not ours. The act of sympathy requires we consider how we might feel under the same circumstances, and then for us to abstract outward, feeling happiness for someone else. Clearly people sometimes fall short of this capacity: not only does this leave the sympathetic friend in their alienated state, but also they have to watch their friend temporarily escape into exultation. Percy thought envy often followed.

In both cases, we face the temptation to view destruction and chaos as a positive good simply because it offers us an escape from our alienation and boredom with ourselves and our environment. If we have to live with our condition and face no possibility of conventional escape from the everyday, the exceptional might have charms. People might embrace at least the idea of that escape perhaps even if that event will bring unimagined horror. Percy suggested that the mildest and most likely outcome is that we retreat into exceptions from the everyday in more mundane ways: through our imaginations, in our conversations about news, and in our attitudes—overt and covert—toward disaster.

DAYDREAMS OF CATASTROPHE AND THE DESIRE FOR ESCAPE

Perhaps because the specter of nuclear holocaust remained all too real for most of Percy's career, one feature of recent popular culture he did not discuss at great length was the American fascination with apocalyptic film and television. A cursory glance at the advertisements for upcoming movies rarely fails to involve at least one disaster scenario—with zombies playing a particularly prominent role as the bringers of disaster in recent years. But given his analysis of our psychology, Percy probably would not have been terribly surprised at this phenomenon. In comparison with our bored, alienated lives, contemplating our society's destruction, the end of the world, and even suicide bears certain charms.

Imagining these events in a healthy manner might have some salutary effects. Thinking seriously about the decline and fall of our society may not just prompt the hypothetical, "what if we could do this …?" that liberates our thinking from convention; it may also have the important effect of helping shape ideas that forestall catastrophes and reinvigorate politics and society. When Percy wrote about the nature of creating apocalypse in fiction and likened his role to that of a canary in a coal mine, he also claimed that his goal was to avert the end before it arrived (*MB* 101). This is also the sort of hypothetical one might bring to bear on one's own life—and that might allow us to genuinely appreciate the gifts that life can offer and restore the concept of wayfaring to dignity.

Seriously contemplating suicide can have a peculiarly enlivening effect on the mind. In his discussion of suicide, Percy asked the reader to invert the usual hypothesis about depression, and instead, consider the possibility that any human being who is *not* depressed in our era deserves to be called deranged (*LC* 76). Percy considered undertaking a mental experiment with deadly seriousness:

> Now consider, not the usual therapeutic approach, but a more ancient and honorable alternative, the Roman option. I do not care for life in this deranged world, it is not an honorable way to live; therefore, like Cato, I take my leave.
> Now notice that as soon as suicide is taken as a serious alternative, a curious thing happens. *To be or not to be* becomes a true choice, where before you were stuck with *to be*. Your only choice was how *to be* least painfully, either by counseling, narcotizing, boozing, groupizing, womanizing, man-hopping, or changing your sexual preference. (*LC* 77)

The reality of the choice—one that Percy implied people seldom contemplate with any frankness—is fairly monstrous. Percy did not think suicide a noble act by any means. Yet, he argued that contemplating and ultimately rejecting suicide "dispenses" the contemplative soul: "Why not live, instead of dying? You are free to do so. You are like a prisoner released from the cell of his life. . . . Where you might have been dead, you are alive" (*LC* 77–78). The act of contemplating this enlivens the mind and lets us reconsider our situation, perhaps awakening the possibility of a search for a place of actual rest rather than the usual American journey toward fugitive perfection.

Percy claimed an "ex-suicide" knows that he does not *have to* live, and can appreciate the small moments in their life and grapple with their alienation on better terms than others might. The person who drifts through life in acts of theory and consumption actively flees from recognizing this. Indeed, if a man chooses to live with the theorist-consumer belief that he is merely the product of an environment, if he grows depressed, on what basis could he resist the lure of suicide if the tools of psychiatry and therapy do not help him? Such a man might seek fulfillment by being either an immanent body seeking pleasure, or a transcending mind searching for complete answers. Both paths ignore our embodied nature and the real needs of the soul. While the ex-suicide can potentially see this, most of Percy's characters initially do not—and fall into more destructive patterns.

Percy explored this need for ever-increasing danger at the beginning of *The Second Coming*, where Will Barrett, deeply depressed, alienated, and suffering from inexplicable fainting episodes, plays a dangerous game with his father's old Luger pistol. In earlier times, he tells the reader that simply firing the pistol into a gorge had previously shocked him out of his "spells," but by the outset of the novel, the effect had diminished. So Will acted more dangerously still, and contemplated something more drastic:

> He shot again, holding the Luger closer and firing past his face. The sound was louder and flatter; a wave of hot air slapped his cheek. The gun bucked, hurting his bent wrist. He held the muzzle against his temple. Yes, that is possible, he thought smiling, that is one way to cure the great suck of self, but then I wouldn't find out, would I? Find out what? Find out why things have come to such a pass and a man so such down into himself that it takes a gunshot to knock him out of the suck. (*SC* 14)

Only the real contemplation of self-destruction gives Barrett a few moments of respite and clarity, but he does not find any renewed appreciation of his circumstances in them. He accepts the possibility of exit but has no way of comprehending what this might tell him about his life. This "remedy" promises no communion with others, only a slight escape from alienation and the tedium of an ordinary Tuesday afternoon. At best it provides a possibility; a moment for a person to reconsider their choices in life. An external threat, however, sometimes proves more fruitful.

Percy thought that people usually fear pain and often fear death, but violence itself serves as a catalyst for escaping our alienation and boredom in the world. Fear and violence provide a concrete escape from the everyday alienation we feel; not everyone fears violence. One illustrative example from *The Moviegoer* demonstrates this well. In it, Binx Bolling recounts how boredom and alienation beset his life, and only a serious combat injury in the Korean War freed him:

> Everydayness is the enemy. No search is possible. Perhaps there was a time when everydayness was not too strong and one could break its grip by brute strength. Now nothing breaks it—but disaster. Only once in my life was the grip of everydayness broken: when I lay bleeding in a ditch. (*MG* 145)

Binx's quest to escape the everyday fails repeatedly; he finds respite only through accident and the memory of becoming a war casualty.[3] Binx does not give voice to why this is the case. Being injured and surviving focuses one's attention on all the details of one's surroundings, because only there does a man "miss nothing." In Binx's case it enlivened his mind. But if this becomes the standard for what being "cured" of everydayness entails, ordinary life must always suffer. Accidents can serve a similar function. Percy explored this through an incident in Will Barrett's life in *The Second Coming*.

Returning home after experimenting with the Luger, Barrett comes under rifle fire in his garage, suffering a cut from the ricochet. He notices two things about his life in the moments around the shot. Before the shot, he had observed a cat and realized that the problem with human beings is that unlike the cat, "for whom one place was the same as any other place so long as it was sunny," human beings are constantly out of place. Moreover, unlike man's perception of his own personhood,

> the cat was exactly a hundred percent cat, no more no less. As for Will Barrett, as for people nowadays—they were never a hundred percent themselves. They occupied a place uneasily and more or less successfully. More likely they were forty-seven percent themselves or rarely, as in the case of Einstein on the streetcar, three hundred percent. All too often these days they were two percent themselves, specters who hardly occupied a place at all. (*SC* 16)

Percy presented a fascinating analogy for alienation here, one that provides an explanation for how people float between immanent, embodied pleasure and transcendent mental states. The idea that our selves need to be rejoined with our bodies in order for us to truly feel at home in the world echoes his account of why people use drugs and alcohol to achieve a cat-like effect. They anesthetize the feeling of being out of place and can simply abide as bodies free from the peril of consciousness. By contrast, one can transcend one's momentary existence by becoming immersed in a world of fantasy or ideas. But neither lasts, and neither allows us to actually live with the reality of human everydayness, with what Barrett calls living as "forty-seven percent themselves."

Returning to the shooting, Will notes that when the shot rings out, he noticed a paradoxical difference in response between him and the animal:

> Quicker than any drug, in the instant in fact of hearing and recognizing the gunshot, he was, as he expressed it, miraculously restored to himself. The cat of course had jumped four feet straight up and fled in terror, as any sensible animal would, reduced instantly to zero percentile of its well-being. But Barrett? The missing ninety-eight percent is magically restored! How? By the rifle shot! (*SC* 17)

Animals respond with alarm and fear at bad environments, but the same circumstances can heighten human reality in some ways. Fear and violence can move us out of alienation and into a sense of liveliness that was lacking before, especially if the events are not random but purposive. Indeed, Barrett betrays his disappointment that the stray shot came from a poacher, and not from an enemy wishing him harm (*SC* 18–19).

Percy thought that people often find the retelling of more distant disaster diverting as well. Percy's most Nietzschean character, Lance Lamar, called the anticipation he felt on watching the nightly news "the sweet horrid dread we had been waiting for" (*L* 72). Using Lance, Percy intimated that alienated, bored, and sentimental people may not easily admit this longing, but that they enjoy hearing of disaster. But this distant and vicarious experience does not suffice for some people: if news alone sufficed, people would not stare at accidents or rush to disasters to look upon them in person (*MB* 6–7). Even this, however, stands at a remove from experiencing a disaster, violence, or accident oneself. Actually feeling the thrill of danger may be even better. In a 1990 interview, Percy observed:

> In Louisiana we have hurricanes. My theory is that people enjoy hurricanes, whether they say so or not. In a hurricane terrible things are happening, but there is a certain exhilaration. It comes from a peculiar sense of self, the vividness. As Einstein said, "Life is dreary as hell." Somebody asked him why he went into quantum mechanics. Well, to get away from the dreariness of life. Louisianans enjoy hurricanes, if they're not too bad. (*MCWP* 240)

Percy posited a curious relationship here: the closer the danger and nearer the experience, the greater the escape from the ordinary. Natural disasters will come and go. The political danger here rests with the desire to not just embrace the exceptional circumstances when they crash in upon ordinary life, but rather to pursue them in a way that makes danger or violence the norm. In this vein, consider again the works of Carl Schmitt and Ernst Jünger, both of whom defended a form of social and political life ordered around a war-like mentality.[4] Americans might not want to admit publicly to seeing value in this sensibility, but Percy's point in drawing our attention to these feelings is that our seemingly innocent longings of the heart all too often spill over into politics.

One reason Percy argued people actively enjoy disaster more than they let on is that in moments of excitement and disaster, like the ex-suicide, they become dispensed from their old activities. In that moment, their relations to other people change; seemingly authentic community becomes a possibility. Percy used the example of a commuter on a train to explore this. Consider an ordinary commuter's situation, riding on the eight-fifteen morning train through Metuchen, New Jersey. He is in the city, but not really there. As Percy put it, the fact of commuting erects a "partition" between those passing through and those that actually live there. The commuter takes this train every day with the same people, but no one speaks to the strangers beside them:

> As is especially noticeable on the subway, the partition exists as well between oneself and one's fellow commuters, a partition which is impenetrable by anything short of disaster. It is only in the event of a disaster, the wreck of the

> eight-fifteen, that one is *enabled* to discover his fellow commuter as a comrade; thus, the favorite scene of novels of good will in the city: the folks who discover each other and help each other when disaster strikes. (*MB* 87)

The fact that this describes a cliché of film, television, and novel plots does nothing to diminish the reality of the change that occurs when something turns out wrong and strangers find themselves forced to work together to escape, survive, or in less-drastic situations, to simply pass the time until help arrives. Being thrown into comradeship by circumstance is not usually the basis for genuine friendship, however. It may collapse the usual boundaries that stand between people in ordinary life, but almost always falters when the moment of need passes.

There is a paradox of choice here that requires some discussion. Percy emphasized that often people feel at a loss in relation to the very freedom and wide-ranging choice available in their surroundings. Middle-class life in the United States. allows for the consumption—in many cases on-demand with no waiting—of a tremendous array of relatively inexpensive media; the ability to instantaneously communicate with friends, acquaintances, and even strangers; access to a wide range of educational and cultural opportunities; and the opportunity to pursue a decently paying and physically undemanding if not always particularly engrossing form of work. None of these possibilities for consumption or interaction alleviate our alienation. But the fact remains that day after day, our society forces us to choose which path to take. The necessity of making a living compels us to work, but no authoritative pattern in our society tells us what to do, or how to cope with this range of choice. No one would want to lose *all* choice, but Percy suggested in his work that freedom and leisure give us additional mental space within which we can recognize our alienation.

In a world of near-endless possibilities, often the temporary *loss* of such endless options comes as a peculiar kind of relief from our everyday alienation. After all, Percy observed that the young, who so often seek "a new life of joy and freedom" in actions and ways of living that differ from their elders, still remain a pretty sad lot (*MB* 7). Little or nothing really changes about their condition, as they have made choices that only slightly differ from their parents' decisions. If Percy is correct on this point, an era of abundance is paradoxically an era of the greatest anxiety concerning what to do and how to live. The allure of danger comes from the fact that it brings necessity back into life, and with it, our place and purpose suddenly become clear.

The problem remains deeper, though. Communities born out of emergency or necessity all too often fade when either the crisis recedes or even when terrible circumstances become the new normal and our alienation creeps back in. Nowhere does he explore this more pointedly than in his many observations on the nature of war as a possible source of escape from boredom and alienation. We cannot exempt ourselves from this analysis: whether we consider nuclear terrorism or contemplate the eventuality of great power war, the specter of destruction remains, making it extremely important as a window into the political importance of catastrophe.

WAR AS AN ANTIDOTE TO ALIENATION

War is in some respects the ultimate "bad environment." For that reason, Percy argued that even in our comfort-obsessed bourgeois world, war retains certain appeals for some people. Consider the usual assumptions bourgeois people of whatever political persuasion make about war today: most scholars who study war have little appreciation for Percy's idea of alienation, and seem to ignore the idea that people often feel good in materially bad environments. Normally, modern people conceive of war in various rational ways: as tragic, but useful; the destructive product of miscalculation, but largely unavoidable; or perhaps as the foolish or inhumane acts of a few against the unenlightened majority's real interests. Such people would find it very difficult to see war as a positively valuable event the way many thinkers from the ancient world to the present day maintained.[5] It seems no exaggeration to say that people who follow this line of reasoning would conclude at the outset that only the mentally ill would value war as a possible path out of whatever bothers them about their own society—and yet, a deep study of the intellectual culture surrounding World War I reveals a broad spectrum of European intellectuals of all nations embracing exactly that ideal.[6]

Understanding war's appeal in terms of alienation and boredom, the first and perhaps most obvious source of its allure must rest in the excitement it generates, an energy that defies the objective-material understanding of the human being. Consider first Binx Bolling's claim that the only time he ever felt lifted out of his everydayness was at the moment of his injury in the Korean War, or Percy's recollection that his Uncle Will was happy on December 7, 1941 and sad again when he realized he was too old to fight (*MG* 145, *MB* 4). This theme recurs constantly in Percy's writings, perhaps most directly in a brief exchange between Tom More and an elderly veteran in *The Thanatos Syndrome*. After recounting some of the local history of the Civil War and waiting until his niece Lucy leaves the room,

> the uncle leans close and won't let me go.
> "You know what they're always saying about war being hell?" he asks.
> "Yes."
> He leans closer. "That's a lot of horseshit."

> "Is that right?"
> "Let me tell you something. I never had a better time in my life than in World War Two." (*TS* 142)

In the context of the story, Percy implied something was disordered about this situation, but *not* with the characters that state their love of war; he seemed intent on forcing his readers to confront the love of war and man's reasons for embracing it as an escape from ordinary life. The fact those with no exposure to war disbelieve in the possibility people might enjoy it, and that many veterans keep silent only contributes to this sense of disquiet.[7]

Percy's representations of the war bear a great deal of similarity to his brother Billups Phinizy ("Phin") Percy's recollections: Phin served as a patrol boat commander in the same unit as John F. Kennedy and then transferred to the submarine service, two of the most dangerous branches of the navy during the war. He "liked combat," was awarded the Silver Star and Bronze Star for heroism, and at the end of hostilities, left the navy despite being offered the chance to stay, as once "the game was over" he saw little point.[8]

Percy observed that the risk of death and excitement that comes with war's destruction also sharpens the participants' focus on savoring experience. He argued that while many social scientists ignore this, novelists have some advantages in that in order to write, they have to notice the peculiar, unstated assumptions people carry with them:

> Everyone admits the atrocities of the [twentieth] century, which we like to think of as horrifying, inexplicable, and occurring at a great remove from us. True, every century has its horrors, but what the novelist notices, peculiar fellow that he is, is that in these strange times people, himself included, seem to experience life more vividly, most immediately, remember places best, on the occasion of war, assassination, hurricanes, and other catastrophes. The real question is seldom asked. It is not: How do we prevent the final war? but: What do we do if we succeed? Can man get along without war? (*SSL* 162–3)

This reference to the vividness of life experience recalls Will Barrett's explanation of what sorts of experiences make man more or less "himself" at different times. Unlike the other modes of orbit or escape I discuss earlier, for Percy war might be the only social endeavor that creates a community of brotherhood while immersing its direct participants in an experience that summons their full personhood. If man can "get along" without war, this implies that he has found a better way of coping with his sense of alienation. Until that happens, war and dangerous events that generate comradeship will always retain an appeal. In relying on objective-material methods of studying human life or other reductive assumptions about human beings, today's scholars often fail to grasp this.

To provide a concrete example of how war changes our observations of places and people, in one of Percy's thought experiments in *Lost in the Cosmos*, he contrasted viewing the Parthenon under two very different circumstances. In the first, Percy noted that tourists visiting the monument are most likely to be bored and compare it unfavorably to the pictures they have seen. By contrast, Percy imagined the following difference:

> Now imagine under what set of circumstances a viewing of the Parthenon would not be a bore. For example, you are a NATO colonel defending Greece against a Soviet assault. You are in a bunker in downtown Athens, binoculars propped on sandbags. It is dawn. A medium-range missile attack is underway. Half a million Greeks are dead. Two missiles bracket the Parthenon. The next will surely be a hit. Between columns of smoke, a ray of golden light catches the portico. Are you bored? Can you see the Parthenon? (*LC* 71–2)

Percy illustrated here the difficulty of seeing and appreciating extraordinary parts of our world under our normal conditions.[9] By cutting out our boredom and alienation and shocking us out of our everyday conditions, we can see things anew. War heightens reality, and this contributes to its appeal.[10]

Percy also subtly emphasized the ways that war fills in the emptiness of ordinary life by granting the aimless a purpose and the alienated a concrete, relational role in which to live. In a world of wide-ranging choice and freedom, Percy argued that both of these matter more than we might suspect. Moving from a world of strangers to one of comradeship helps alleviate loneliness. Percy used the backdrop of the American Civil War to note these themes. That war in particular, fought for the soul and direction of a nation, inspired unprecedented sacrifices (*SSL* 72–3). One of the attractions war holds is the meaning and self-understanding it brings to the participants lives. In describing the enduring fascination related to the American Civil War, he wrote:

> Yet, with all the horror, or perhaps because of it, there was always the feeling then, and even now as we read about it, that the things a man lived through were somehow twice as real, twice as memorable as the peace that followed. . . . In the ordeal the man himself seemed to become more truly himself, revealing his character or the lack of it, than at any time before or after. If a man was secretly cowardly or secretly brave, stupid or shrewd, that was what he was shown to be. The War infallibly discovered his hidden weakness and his hidden strength. (*SSL* 74–5)

Thus, in Percy's view, war can serve as a kind of testing ground for human virtue and vice, or a place of self-discovery or self-disclosure. In times of comfort and peace, the implication follows that we do not easily learn things about ourselves that struggle reveals. Small wonder, then, that alienation and boredom find such frequent expression in literature and drama centered in affluent suburbs.

As I noted in the previous chapter, in *The Thanatos Syndrome*, Father Rinaldo Smith explained his attitudes as a young man from New Orleans visiting Germany. Smith bitterly criticized the phoniness of his home, the home of "let the good times roll, which masked a cold-blooded marriage of moneymaking and social climbing, rotten politics and self-indulgence" (*TS* 243). Smith's account of his parents and home excoriates the weakness and ill-defined purposes of living in the inter-war years as an American in good suburb. Smith marveled at his experience in Germany in part because through his friendship with the officer cadet Helmut Jäger, he found something entirely new, what a life with warlike purpose might entail:

> I was aware of a serious and absolute dedication in him which I had never encountered before. He showed me his SS officer's cap with its German eagle and death's-head. It dawned on me that he meant it. He was ready to die. I had never met anyone ready to die for a belief. . . . He was planning for war even then. Who could I compare him to? An American Eagle Scout? No, because even a serious Eagle Scout is doing scouting on the side, planning a career in law, insurance, whatever. Certainly death is the farthest thing from his mind. (*TS* 247–8)

The heart of Fr. Smith's confession to Tom More rests in the claim that if he were German (and implicitly, even if he knew the way World War II would unfold), he would still have joined Helmut and the SS to pursue that life filled with martial purpose (*TS* 248–9). Percy asked his readers to contemplate the uncomfortable possibility that some of us would make a similar choice, not so much out of racism or the desire for political glory, but rather as a means of escape from our everyday alienation.

We need not contemplate such extremes to see Percy's point: if alienation rests primarily in our sense of misplacement and purposeless in relation to other people and the places which we inhabit. War carries with it certain properties that no other situation can offer as an escape. Catastrophe lowers the barriers between individuals and strips away our abstracted awareness of ourselves as separate from our environment: at least for as long as it lasts, disaster dispenses us from carrying much of the emotional baggage with which the alienated self commonly lives (*MB* 83–84). As a kind of extended disaster, war shatters many of the barriers between individuals that exist in civilian life. Moreover, those people that find peacetime life unsatisfying because of their own needs for struggle and violence—the man like Will Barrett's father, who was "born with a love of death and death-dealing," but had "no enemies"—find release in war (*SC* 146). These ideas represent more than fictional speculation on Percy's part. In the inter-war years in Germany, for instance, some of the soldiers' movements that fostered National Socialism made a domestic political creed out of the experience of frontline combat in World War I. Ernst Jünger developed a kind of civic militarism that exemplified this line of thinking by claiming the community and shared purpose of war transformed its participants for the better.[11]

Percy's thinking on this point poses troubling questions for individuals who hope to eliminate war, but also those who think of violence as an aberration explainable only through the disordering of the human psyche. It is certainly possible for such theorists to attempt reductive explanations of why we wish for catastrophe and war, but all of those would point to the disorder of the individual caused by bad environmental or social inputs. Instead, by inverting the usual scientific hypothesis, the desires for violence will always be with us. Will Barrett's question about what individuals in a mild bourgeois society do when they have a love of death provides some insight as a starting point. Unless moderated by some other force, presumably this sort of person commits suicide (as Will Barrett's father did), or turns to a life of violence against others (*SC* 146–9). Percy would probably suggest such thinking may help explain the prevalence of affluent children of the Western world joining radical or revolutionary causes, and perhaps give some insight into the prevalence of nihilistic terrorism of various kinds since the dawn of the Industrial Revolution.[12]

Percy raised no objection to the idea that wars happen for legitimate reasons of state. He was more concerned with the latent psychological and moral dispositions prevalent in society that might encourage the love of war than he was with any high-level political explanation of why nations make war. Indeed, when discussing the causes of war, Percy regularly dealt with it through *reductio ad absurdum*. Consider the following question from *Lost in the Cosmos*:

> (a) Will World War III happen absurdly, by an accident in a purely technological, sexually liberated age, e.g., by computer malfunction, misinformation, misbehavior by a small-time Qaddafi madman?
>
> or (b) Will World War III erupt because of the suppressed fury of the autonomous self, disappointed now even in the erotic, that demoniac spirit which is overtly committed to peace and love but secretly desires war and apocalypse and nourishes hatred of all other selves and perhaps of its own self most of all?
>
> (CHECK ONE) (*LC* 192)

Taking the satire with a grain of salt as we might, this line of reasoning might nevertheless lead us to question whether the objective-material hypotheses that drive most scholarship on war do not miss something about the underlying desires and motives that make war thinkable in the first place. War may be irrational or wasteful in some objective-material sense, but decrying it on those terms may miss the point. We ought–like the depressed person–invert the normal hypotheses about what makes war so common in our world: it may or may not be that wars happen so often because nations fall into irreconcilable clashes over interest, but there may be some value in pondering whether the desire for escape from normal social order through the violence of war does not make the recourse to conflict more *likely*.

Yet, the central difficulty remains the fact that people are reticent to confront our tendencies directly. These arguments suggest at least part of the reason we choose not to confront the fact that our age "is the most scientifically advanced, savage, democratic, inhuman, sentimental, murderous century in human history" (*SSL* 309). Or rather, we choose not to confront this in a clear-eyed manner: indeed, perhaps because of how difficult it is to portray this easily in the present, Percy resorted to a science fiction fable in *Lost in the Cosmos* to explore this point most clearly. In it, he argued our sentimental, alienated, potentially murderous nature would be the first and most alarming thing an alien species might notice about us (*LC* 206–217). We need not agree with the extremity of this claim, but failing to acknowledge the persistent appeals of war does real damage to our ability to understand political life.

POLITICS AND THE ESCAPE FROM THE NORMAL

Percy's observations about the attraction of catastrophe may sometimes seem hyperbolic, but they make an important point. The fact we cannot forego the allure of enviously dreaming about and even hoping for disaster bears political importance. To some degree, the permanence of these desires provides justification for our own tendencies to detach and flee the real, fragile, and all-too-flawed communities within which we actually must live. Percy's characters often exhibit a detachment from their family, neighbors, friends, and colleagues that seems to flow naturally from their unease with the world as it is and anticipation that things might fall apart.

Consider the examples I presented in previous chapters of how individuals attempt to satisfy their longings with theory or affiliation to different ideals or new communities and how the love of apocalypse plays a part in them. For the apostle of scientism, like Aristarchus Jones in *Lost in the Cosmos*, who proposed that the survivors of Earth's final war form a colony on Jupiter's moon Europa, the possibility of renewing the existing society holds no appeal. Instead, Jones emphasizes the possibility of departure from the old way of things:

> With a bit of luck, we can colonize Europa in much the same way as Europe colonized the New World, *except that*—and here is the exciting part!—there is no reason why we cannot develop a society . . . based on reason and science, and do so without repeating the mistakes of the past, for example, the Dark Ages, two thousand years of Plato and Judaism and Christianity—a sexually free and peace-loving society where the sciences and arts can flourish freed from the superstitions and repressions of religion. (*LC* 246)

Perhaps the appeal of disaster at its extreme rests in this hope for a new order, purged of the previous beliefs we have come to know.

Percy emphasized that the aspiration to change the world through or after apocalypse always glosses over the human cost of these endeavors. In the story above, Aristarchus Jones planned to abandon all those damaged by the radiation to their fate on Earth. The abstract hope to redeem the world trumps such "petty" considerations. The pretention to being able to control people and events sufficiently well to transcend the old order dies hard: readers might be repulsed and amused by Percy's depiction of Lance Lamar's deranged, fascistic hope for revolution, but Percy implied that despite Lamar's insanity, it is almost certain that someone dreams in a similar manner. Any inquiry into politics must take these thoughts seriously because sooner or later, people will act on these desires.[13] In Part III, I attempt to sketch his remedies to this and other threats.

NOTES

1. For a survey of the prevalence of this theme in Western history and thought, see Arthur Herman, *The Idea of Decline in Western History* (New York: The Free Press, 1997).

2. On this, see George Mosse, *Fallen Soldiers* (Oxford: Oxford University Press, 1990). Mosse strives to explain the way soldiers saw value in the war as a consciously constructed myth, but Percy might lead us to rethink this point.

3. Another example where Binx is dispensed from alienation through violent accident comes during Binx's drive with Sharon Kincaid, when they have an accident and Sharon cares for him (*MG* 124–128).

4. For the clearest statement on Schmitt's position, see *The Concept of the Political*, trans. George Schwab (Chicago: University of Chicago Press, 2007). Jünger's war memoir *Storm of Steel* remains noteworthy for its expressions of love for the war itself, but in the inter-war years both advanced a politics modeled to a great degree on the front experience of World War I. For an account of both thinkers, see Jeffrey Herf, *Reactionary Modernism: Technology, Culture, and Politics in Weimar and the Third Reich* (Cambridge: Cambridge University Press, 1984), 70–108 and 115–121.

5. One path largely left by the wayside in our age is the sort of civic militarism the Greeks and Romans embraced, where moral educators view military service in

general and war in particular as the vital element allowing the virtues of citizenship to form. On this phenomenon, see Doyne Dawson, *The Origins of Western Warfare: Militarism and Morality in the Ancient World* (Boulder: Westview Press, 1996). Not all liberal moderns would reject this notion, however: both Adam Smith and Alexis de Tocqueville, for instance, retained the idea that military service, if not the actual conduct of war can promote noble virtues.

6. On this point, Roland Stromberg's *Redemption by War: The Intellectuals and 1914* (Lawrence: The University Press of Kansas, 1982) is particularly important, arguing that this was a common goal among European intellectuals, particularly those in uniform, throughout World War I.

7. On this, see Jonathan Shay, *Achilles in Vietnam: Combat Trauma and the Undoing of Character* (New York: Touchstone Books, 1994).

8. See David Horace Harwell's interview with Phin Percy in *Walker Percy Remembered: A Portrait in the Words of Those Who Knew Him* (Chapel Hill: University of North Carolina Press, 2006), 155–158. It bears noting that Percy's female characters usually disdain this logic. Consider Lucy's response to her uncle in *Thanatos Syndrome* (143–44). In interviews, Percy also claimed that women have better sense than men in this respect and rightfully hate war (for example, see *MCWP* 80).

9. Related to this point, elsewhere Percy discusses his theory that the last place we might really understand and be charmed by Shakespeare is an English literature classroom, just as a biology lab is the last place we can discover nature (*MB* 56–59).

10. On this point, see J. Glenn Gray, *The Warriors: Reflections on Men in Battle* (Lincoln: University of Nebraska Press, 1998), 30–34.

11. On this, see Herf, *Reactionary Modernism*, esp. 72–80.

12. Consider that the emergence of such movements runs parallel to a profound expansion of wealth and comfort alongside an acceptance of the bourgeois ethos in the West. There is no way to prove their interrelation; had he lived long enough, it is easy to imagine Percy having written a novel about terrorism.

13. This is not an idle speculation. At the fringes of our politics today, the "alternative right" culture embodies virtually all of what Percy attributed to Lance Lamar. For one influential member of this subculture, see Jack Donovan, *The Way of Men* (Cascadia: Dissonant Hum, 2013) and *Becoming a Barbarian* (Cascadia: Dissonant Hum, 2016).

Part III

COPING WITH ALIENATION

Percy adopted a two-pronged approach to addressing the obstacles to building a moderate political life based on the wayfaring sensibility. As we have seen the dangers Percy outlined were both intellectual and rooted in the spirit and relationships of men. A remedy hoping for success in the one sphere still faces considerable challenges from the other. In my final chapters, I divide my account of Percy's prescriptions for change accordingly.

Objective-material attempts to understand the place of catastrophe, disaster, and disorder solely as malformed responses to our condition cannot come to grips with many of the behaviors Percy depicted in his stories. To take the most extreme example he uses, perhaps only a small percentage of men truly love war. But what if those men come to power? This has clearly happened in the past, but a purely materialist social science can only see Hitler's Germany in reductive terms, or view the power of a militarist ideology with roots in war and death as an outlier. Percy identified the gaps in many other areas of materialist analysis, and thus, one problem that Percy set out to address was what questions and methods a new social science might use to address the lingering disorders of our world, and chasten our hopes for radically transforming our condition. In chapter 6, I develop an argument about how Percy's critical analysis of social science and suggestions for reform might help us conceive of a better kind of social science that does not suffer from the blind spots of pure materialism. In exploring this, Percy's theory of language emerges as a key to moving social science away from the tools and logic of the natural sciences and instead recognizing the distinctiveness of human culture.

Given Percy's insistence on moderation, it should be no surprise that one of the hallmarks of a reformed social science would be an appreciation for its limits as a vehicle for social improvement and change. My account of Percy's culturally sensitive social science naturally leads back to a renewed understanding of what family, community, and faith can provide us as wayfarers.

In chapter 7, I turn to these themes again, aiming to show the proper role our relationships and beliefs might play in a wayfaring sensibility, as well as the potential excesses flawed human beings are especially prone. This chapter brings together themes from across the book to show the ways that the remedies available to us as wayfarers never quite satisfy our longings. Embracing the life of the wayfarer opens up a future of realistic limitation concerning what politics might achieve, and it also holds out the promise of rest against the overly exuberant tendencies of modern American life.

Chapter 6

Toward a New Social Science

In Percy's wide-ranging essay "The Delta Factor," he turned to language as the central empirically obvious phenomenon that sets human beings apart from all other creatures:

> In the beginning was alpha, the end is omega, but somewhere in between came Delta, man himself. Man became man by breaking into the daylight of language—whether by good fortune or bad fortune, whether by pure chance, the spark jumping the gap because the gap was narrow enough, or by the touch of God, it is not for me to say here.But it happened, and to this day man knows less about what happened than he knows about the back side of the moon. (*MB* 45)

Percy argued that we know so little about this event because the prevailing approaches to studying human life scientifically all tend to engage in reductive analysis. In particular, social science tends to betray its flaws most pointedly when attempting to grasp the products of human consciousness, developing weak explanations of deep belief or faith, the nature of honor, the sources of anxiety and alienation in our society, and some of the reasons communities matter so much for human life. It is not so much that social scientists *cannot* explain these things but that so many of their explanations devalue the human person's capacity for choice and agency. They undermine our sense of sovereignty against expertise. And perhaps worst of all, they often encourage a kind of fatalistic determinism and belief in the overwhelming powers of social structure for defining our life.

All of these observations flow from the previous chapters' arguments, but Percy hoped a reformed social science might overcome these difficulties. He drew upon the distinction between dyadic and triadic interaction to develop his account of where scientists often go astray. Percy argued that dyadic theory cannot take the products of human language and thought seriously, and as a consequence, undermines much social science as a path to understanding and improving the human estate. This provides support for Percy's insistence that only a social science developed in light of the reality of language and consciousness can help us understand the peculiar difficulties humanity faces, especially in the present age.

THE LIMITATIONS OF DYADIC SOCIAL ANALYSIS

Any dyadic social science must begin with the assumption that some important aspects of human activity proceed in a manner functionally similar to other interactions in nature. In Percy's sketch of the history of man's self-awareness in *Lost in the Cosmos*, he summarized one element of the typical dyadic approach to such all natural phenomena:

> Thus, all the elements and events in the Cosmos, including other organisms, could be thought of as the *environment* of the organism. The organism "responded" to those segments of its environment to which, through evolution, it had become genetically coded—hard-wired—to respond. (*LC* 90)

A significant amount of social science work conducted in the last century follows this method, not least out of the desire to apply the clean models of physical and biological science to understanding society. If we see the work of social science as tracing out how various kinds of measurable environmental stimuli condition empirically observable responses in human beings and their societies, some major consequences follow.

To begin with, this approach must necessarily take the most distinctive and empirically verifiable element of human life—language—and place it and all its related products of thought on a continuum with other organisms. To do this, an analyst has to interpret the complex nature of language itself as a series of stimulus-response interactions. Percy argued that this does violence to our understanding of human beings at the outset because while other creatures do use limited forms of communication based in gesture and sound, these always bear a direct relationship to environmental stimuli and demonstrate nothing like the complexity of human language. Percy offered the example of how in its natural state a gorilla, "can utter one of a dozen or so vocal signals which are responded to by other gorillas . . . in an appropriate fashion—e.g., the bark *wraagh* is a signal of a sudden alarming situation, such as unexpected contact with a buffalo, which signals flight in other gorillas" (*LC* 91–2). Communication of this kind in animals follows this pattern of stimulus and response and develops on the basis each animal's direct encounter with its environment. Whether learned or innate, all of these modes of communication bear the stamp of their environmental origins.

By contrast, humans develop the capacity not only to replicate sounds and phrases directly experienced, but they move beyond this very quickly, for "unlike other animals, which learn a very limited repertoire of responses, a four-year-old child can utter and understand an unlimited number of new sentences in his language"—sentences for which no simple stimulus-response model can account (*MB* 15). Human beings not only create word-representations of concrete instances of each object they encounter—tree, ball, car, etc.—but also use the word as a symbol representing not just that object but all that they encounter in that category (*SSL* 121–122). Thus, for Percy, we transcend merely responding to stimuli and early in our lives enter into a genuine "world" of choice and consciousness.

Here Percy's distinction between an environment and a world bears some discussion, as these two categories help delineate the gap between human beings (as symbol- and sign-using creatures possessing the capacity to use and understand grammar) and other animals (who communicate with signals alone). An environment consists of "those elements of the Cosmos which affect the organism significantly . . . and to which the organism either is genetically coded to respond or has learned to respond" (*LC* 99). Percy described environments as discontinuous in the sense that they differ widely from creature to creature, and are limited to those things relevant to the life of the organism. Honey bees, for instance, observe their own dancing flight patterns, but the gaps in their environment include the behavior of animals outside their normal sphere of activity. Thus, "a honey bee takes account of the bee dance of another bee indicating the direction and distance of a nectar source," but ignores the flight patterns of birds that do not prey on them (*LC* 99). As an environmental response, communication for animals serves utilitarian purposes alone, and this serves as a stark contrast to the place of language in human life.

As users of signs and symbols, human beings occupy a "world segmented and named by language," in which all "perceived objects and actions and qualities are named" (*LC* 99). Names, however, do not merely function as descriptive responses to our environment. Many words serve a simple labeling function, but others are works of art and humor where the name we assign to an object serves as far more than a description and instead becomes a form of commentary on its place in our lives. Moreover, the full use of language requires consciousness, which Percy argued can only be understood as "that act of attention to something under the auspices of its sign, an act which is social in its origin" (*LC* 105). We interpret our world through the medium of language—an act of imagination using what is itself a creative medium. These are facts about language Percy argued that scholars of language often ignore, and they serve as clues to the ways a revitalized study of man might take shape.

Without a community accepting the reality of language, consciousness in this full sense becomes impossible. In a community possessing an impoverished language, too, serious thought may be difficult. For children in particular, the act of naming, labeling, and symbol-using starts in wonder and curiosity. Language use always bears the stamp of creativity and play (*MB* 43–44, *SSL* 130–132). The relationship between individual words, their users, and the symbolic reality of language cannot be reduced to any constituent dyadic interaction, and for this reason, Percy insisted that an adequate analysis of human life requires something more complex than an attempt to reduce the elements of language to some discernable set of prior causes.

Percy's understanding of language carries profound political consequences. A state that sets out to treat its citizens as products of their environment necessarily deprives them of a kind of sovereignty over themselves. This is part of the danger of relying on others' expertise. Placing Percy's argument alongside George Orwell's view of how politics can deprive human beings of dignity through the use of language itself, the picture grows more disturbing still: a regime that not only operates on objective-materialist principles but also consciously alters language to remove the play element might end politics as we know it.[1] As a consequence, Percy suggested we ought to be attentive to the fact that much of modern social science's ways of treating human beings treads dangerously close to this mode of reasoning.

Even if the social scientist concedes the argument that no adequate theory of language exists, they would probably still argue that other aspects of human life remain relatively explicable through a kind of simple and direct, or even multi-level dyadic analysis, one rooted in a kind of objective-material approach. The commitment to that method runs into at least two kinds of difficulties, both of which scholars frequently observe, albeit not quite in the terms Percy uses.[2]

In the case of social science based on surveys, qualitative reports, tests, or other reports of opinion, the difficulty stems from the way that a great deal of social scientific analysis relies on the person being analyzed providing an accurate account of themselves. In discussing the discipline of psychology, Percy argued that no matter what particular system of analysis the psychologist uses, "they all deal, by and large, with subjective, mental, or emotional entities, events and states which cannot be seen or measured but can only be reported by the patient" (*SSL* 116). The social scientist relying on these methods must turn a person's self-reported mental states into measurable phenomena for the dyadic analysis to "work" properly. Such scholarship often tends to consider the individual and his or her social groups solely in terms of their imputed environments, placing the human person in structures beyond their control or understanding. Even though the scholar must accept the potentially unreliable nature of their study's subjects self-reporting, only the devotion to dyadic analysis requires that they view human beings as conditioned by those environments. But Percy argued that any person's actual experience of life should give them cause to pursue a different view.

Other social scientists focus on the measurable products of human action. It is understandable that scholars frustrated by the "fuzziness" of self-reported data would turn to apparently more concrete data and formal models or theories that help explain and predict human behavior. Such scholarship often falls into similar difficulties. Take the example of Kenneth Waltz, one of the most important figures in modern international relations theory, whose model of international politics denies any primary causal role for war and peace to individuals or even states. Instead, he argues that the structure of the international system pressures nations and their leadership to conform to various security-seeking, interest-based modes of action. In Waltz's argument, the distinctiveness of various political cultures or peculiarities of any individual leader take second place to the balance of power and the dilemmas the search for security and power create.[3] This sort of analysis evades the human questions about war and peace Percy emphasized. While this is not the place to debate the explanatory value of such methods, it is worth noting that the general theorizing Waltz engages in and the sort of data-driven analysis many other social scientists engage in fall prey the moral dangers of expertise I described in chapter 2.

It is certainly possible to explain—to take two examples—the development of modern bourgeois society and all its attendant comforts on the basis of self-interest rationally pursued, and in so doing, understand the individual actors in such an economy as merely following the incentives of their social environment,[4] or, alternatively, to comprehend religious experience in terms of people's demand for socialization and belonging.[5] These efforts merely dispose of the problem. This analysis comes at significant cost to our ability to see the human person in a way that reinforces good character, strong citizenship, or perhaps most importantly for Percy, a concept of the self that is capable of coping with our permanent sense of alienation in the world.

Percy pointed to what he calls "the antinomy of the scientific method" as the heart of the mismatch between the methods social scientists so often use and the natures of what they study. He asked his readers to consider the elements of culture that are liable to fall prey to the worst kinds of category error if studied through conventional social science:

> Culture, in its most characteristic moments, is not a catalogue of artifacts or responses to an environment but is rather the ensemble of all the modes of assertory activity. . . . A linguist may indeed spend his entire life compiling a

> dictionary of Kwakiutl without ever dealing with an assertion as such. . . . But the fact remains that language, when it is spoken, is a tissue of assertions. Religion is not a museum of cult objects but a living tissue of beliefs, professions, avowals. (*MB* 222–3)

A living "tissue of assertions" demands an analytical approach that takes the subjects of study seriously on their own terms rather than as events explicable through other secondary causes. But a dyadic scientist must ignore the qualitative difference between matters of thought and speech and other material interactions. The antinomy here rests in the fact that while social science may provide *some* explanation of these matters (and the practitioner of such analyses often resists other triadic explanations), this does not exhaust other, equally valid lines of interpretation.

Collapsing the distinction between the spheres of language and the objective-material leads scholars to evaluate artifacts of culture in very different modes than those which make sense of lived experience. The terms of such an analysis force the scientist to dismiss or devalue the actual content of human speech—after all, if all products of language and thought can be resolved into the environment from which they arise, they cannot reflect the truth of things or a reality *apart* from that of the initial experience out of which they arise. Such an analysis cannot consider statements and actions reflecting the truth or falsehood of a belief or the rightness or wrongness of a way of life in any moral or theological sense, which may be the primary way a practitioner of a faith or philosophy considers their actions. Instead, such scholarship resorts to utility and function as the basis of analysis: "Thus a 'genuine' culture (and a genuine myth) is a culture which is viable, satisfying the spiritual and emotional needs of the culture member; a 'spurious' culture fails to do so" (*MB* 225). A belief "works" in this sense apart from its correspondence with reality—the social scientist must conceive of them as fulfilling certain practical or psychological needs but cannot evaluate them in terms that reflect their own internal logic.

The desire to use the dyadic methods of science in a social setting makes for little-observed difficulties. Dyadic analysis appears to easily comprehend events that take place in a specific and observable moment in space and time. Social scientists often fall prey to the seductive observation that many of the things human beings do every day seem to plausibly fit dyadic explanation. We eat, sleep, make love, eliminate waste, and a thousand other things that one can more or less fold into the rubric of objective-material analysis. Language does not quite fit this model, as Percy noted an "assertion is a real event but it is not a space-time event" in quite the same way as an individual eating a meal or buying this book (*MB* 237). Words can be counted, but their qualities and meanings resist quantification. Moreover, social scientists face a deeper problem in that soon after leaving the womb, human beings develop in ways that defy a complete explanation derived from the mere conditioning of their environment. As they act, choose, and use words to explain and communicate, Percy claimed that individuals create mental worlds.

For Percy, language served as a starting point for understanding the many ways that the whole panoply of human action remains irreducible to dyadic analysis. As a result of the basic assumptions they make, social scientists have difficulty ascribing causal power to matters of language and belief. Logically, this follows: if we begin with the idea that language itself emerges out of causal dyads constituted by an objective-material environment, the "root cause" of any human activity must be "deeper," so to speak, than the arguments and principles we use to describe that activity (*MB* 235–7). To do this, however, requires we deprive our language and beliefs of any intrinsic value and meaning, and refuse to see the most basic products of our lived experience as real (*SSL* 214–5).[6] This sort of deprivation causes a kind of incoherence within any worldview originating in dyadic science. Percy offered the hope of triadic analysis as an alternative that might help individuals recover their sense of self, and which in turn might open the pathway to a deeper kind of social science.

THE IRREDUCIBLE TRIAD AND THE RETURN TO REALISM

In his essay "The Delta Factor," Percy proposed that if scholars attempted to look at human beings anew, and were to examine with an open mind only the empirically observable phenomenon of language, the full complexity of the problem might emerge. A more serious account would admit "that the current theory of language is incoherent, that the formal-descriptive disciplines of linguistics deal with the products, the corpora, of the language phenomenon, that the factual science of psychology deals with the stimuli and responses of organisms, and that between them lies the terra incognita of the phenomenon itself" (*MB* 17). What makes language terra incognita rests in the way it remains impervious to reductive dyadic study.

To explain this, Percy frequently used the example of Helen Keller's moment where she suddenly comprehended language, and in her own understanding, became fully conscious for the first time: when Helen's teacher Miss Sullivan placed one of her hands under the flowing water of a well while spelling the word "water" in Helen's other hand. Helen's leap from animal behavior into language consists in the link she made between the object of perception (the flowing water) and the sign (the word "water"), allowing her for the first time to become truly conscious of the *idea* water (*SSL* 289). Taking this relation seriously requires us to move beyond an explanation that reduces language to any of its constituent parts, and accepts that language is a qualitatively different kind of interaction than that of an organism merely responding to its environment.

People constantly name and label objects, creatures, and other human beings, but Percy argued that one reason scholars in particular (to say nothing of human beings in general) so rarely think about the nature of this event is because "symbolization is the very condition of our knowing anything, trying to get hold of it is like trying to get hold of the means by which we get hold of everything else" (*SSL* 132). This poses a difficulty, but once we understand that the social world rests on the overlapping triadic interactions of the individuals that comprise it, some clarity becomes possible. Language becomes understandable not simply as the product of each person's solipsistic mental state, touching only at the margins (as some postmodern thinkers seem to argue), but rather as an intersubjective reality as Percy argued that it ought to be understood.[7]

Percy's return to linguistic realism borrowed from C.S. Peirce,[8] but his analysis pointed toward a new form of philosophical realism, albeit with some complications. Understanding the essence of language requires us to take not just the individual triads representing language, but rather a tetrad consisting of the word, the object to which it refers, the speaker, and his or her audience (*LC* 97). The reality of this interaction allows us not only to discover and conceptualize nature (think here of dyadic analysis, applied to the right objects of study), but also a method of comprehending the social world. However, this creates a difficulty for all human beings: if our words are not merely the result of our accumulated responses to our environments, but rather the product of the choices and ideas of those participating in a social world, they can be used well or poorly, truly or falsely. The words we use to describe or analyze our world can enrich our dignity or deprive us of it.

In this vein, Percy's ideas offer modern proponents of natural law a basis for both explaining their view of the human person and for understanding more deeply why so few of our contemporaries find it easy to accept the doctrine. Percy developed his minimum working anthropology precisely to show the complex reality of language, and in so doing, the possibility of a rational morality which might help govern human life. But for social science, too, Percy held out the prospect of a return to a form of inquiry about the mental state and motivations of human beings without succumbing to the temptation of reducing people to some set of environmental stimuli.

Percy aimed at restoring a condition where human beings can take their own ideas and arguments seriously. Grappling with language requires that we move away from the study of environments alone and open up the possibility of ontology as a serious basis for analyzing human life (*SSL* 134). Language allows human beings the unique capacity to affirm and conceptualize their world, and it does so in a way with significant consequences for ourselves:

> An organism is oriented to the world according to its organismic needs, but a person is oriented to the world in the mode of truth-untruth. It is a mistake to speak of truth-untruth in connection with an organism and a sign. A duck may make an error about a sign and mistake a hunter's call for a duck's call. Yet, even if he is killed, until the moment of his death, he never ceased to be what he always was, an organism responding to a sign according to a conditioned brain pattern. But for a person the selfsame symbol which discloses being may be the means by which the being is concealed and lost. (*SSL* 135)

This is not to deny that human beings develop habits and conditioned responses to certain aspects of our world. But unlike animals, we can choose when to embark upon that kind of training as a matter of prior judgment, or work to undo earlier acts of self-conditioning. As a user of symbols, the human being can speak not only truth and falsehood, but also use language in a way that either is authentic or inauthentic to their world and life. We can define ourselves in ways that deny our own most immediate mental realities, and become an "it" under the auspices of a theory. The shift from dyads to triads requires a shift from functional analysis to a level of analysis that captures the shape and tempo of human consciousness. To do this, Percy turned to the language of existentialism to better define this way of viewing our lives.

The central measure of language rests in its adequacy for representing events in the world and in our thoughts and feelings, whether literal or metaphorical. Percy argued that our intentions matter here, as does our competency. Doing this in a way that disrespects the subjects of language or in bad faith bears certain consequences, which Percy explored in his essay "Metaphor as Mistake":

> If, as so many modern poets appear to do, one simply shuffles words together, words plucked from as diversified contexts as possible, one will get some splendid effects. Words are potent agents and the sparks are bound to fly. But it is a losing game. For there is missing that essential element of the meaning situation, the authority and intention of the Namer. Where the Namer means nothing or does not know what he means or the Hearer does not think he knows what he means, the Hearer can hardly participate in a cointention. Intersubjectivity fails. Once the good faith of the Namer is so much as called into question, the jig is up. . . . One is only trafficking in the stored-up energies of words, hard won by meaningful usage. (*MB* 76–77)

This passage focuses on poetry, but a similar moral relation inheres in all language use. People can co-celebrate the existence of a concept or feeling or event by naming it truthfully or authentically, but can just as easily break this relationship before it starts by using words that others cannot associate with the event. By using abstract, depersonalized language of the sort that treats human persons as objects acted upon in an environment rather than as choosing, thinking subjects that can disclose their world in language, social scientists often undermine the possibility for conversation and persuasion.[9]

When a gap grows between the concepts commonly used to describe everyday experience and reality as people live it, so too does their alienation. Part of overcoming that alienation comes in the words working well: the man on the train that reads a book describing his feeling of alienation at least temporarily responds with joy at the experience of seeing his condition *named*, perhaps for the first time (*MB* 83). Some major difficulties emerge in relation to this phenomenon of naming, however. Percy argued that the link between a word, a concept, and the object it names can be slippery—a person, animal or object can, as he puts it, have the tendency to become "invisible in ordinary life because it disappears into its symbol," and we have the tendency not to see it in its full color and character (*SSL* 135). An explanation of this sort sheds a great deal of light on Percy's fictional emphasis on "everydayness" and the way words grow worn out and deprived of meaning (*MG* 13–14). That sense of concepts growing worn out that people often feel in encountering others and objects in their environment means people need to take special measures to avoid lapsing into this state.

Although naming represents one of human beings' highest capacities, the act nonetheless poses certain dangers. This brings us back to Percy's use of Martin Buber: how human beings can use and abuse language in their relationships with one another, which echoing Buber, he refers to as a spectrum ranging from authentic and respectful "I-Thou" relationships to "I-It" relations, which are appropriate only for describing how people relate to objects.[10] The difficulty with social science is that all too often, its rhetoric lapses into the "I-It." How this comes about bears some explanation.

Social scientists often do human beings an injustice in the manner they name our status and explain our life. To use one of Percy's examples, a child can excitedly label a ball, a chair, household pets, and every other object in her home. She places herself in relation to objects and animals (I-It), and justly so, for neither the objects nor the animals share in consciousness. After delighting in naming all the objects in her world, a child might eventually grow bored talking about her ball and toys, no longer feeling any joy in the act of using its symbol. But when she transitions from objects to persons, some moral complications emerge. In the I-Thou relationship, human beings desire to be treated like the conscious beings we are, as "co-celebrants of the world," relating to one another personally rather than as objects (*SSL* 137). People will probably find it impossible to maintain an I-Thou relationship with everyone they encounter. If we desire to live in a way that minimizes our alienation, Percy strongly implied we must try to treat others with respect in our conduct. Even more importantly for the present argument in the language we use to describe others acquires central importance. Being placed in a world rather than treated as a creature produced by an environment "is the very condition of being and knowing and feeling in a human way" (*SSL* 127). When social scientists fail to do this, they open the door to a host of political dangers, as yesterday's social science has the habit of becoming tomorrow's social policy.[11]

Think here of how political movements and regimes so often wish to deprive human beings of the possibility of familial bonds and deeper community while also subjecting them beneath labels and abstractions that deny their dignity—Percy's intuitions here may help explain why these acts ought to offend our sensibilities. The person denied I-Thou relationships or who is taught to distrust language itself can neither name their condition honestly nor find a way to easily attenuate their alienation. Practitioners of dyadic social science do something similar: the search for a clear and rigorous methodology often lends itself to analyses that place human beings in some form of environment (cultural, economic, psychological, and so on) and reduce them to those inputs. Rhetorically, the abstract and impersonal tone of social science research encourages thinking that places human beings in a position of passivity regarding their situation—and this form of thinking appears most obviously in the ubiquity of passive voice throughout social science writing. The very labels and rhetoric social science deploys to describe people fail to match with their actual experience.[12]

But even if people consistently use language honestly and decently, human beings elude complete description through the symbols they use. Whether people use the words to describe themselves or others, something always fails to cohere in the description. No name or idea the person uses to label or describe herself fully captures that indefinable substance she calls herself: "The being of the namer slips through the fingers of naming" (*SSL* 136). In *Lost in the Cosmos*, Percy observed:

> The fateful flaw of human semiotics is this: that of all the objects in the entire Cosmos which the sign-user can apprehend through the conjoining of signifier and signified (word uttered and thing beheld), there is one which forever escapes his comprehension—and that is the sign-user himself. . . . The self of the sign-user can never be grasped, because, once the self locates itself at the dead center of its world, there is no signified to which a signifier can be joined to make a sign. The self has no sign of itself. No signifier applies. All signifiers apply equally. (*LC* 106–7)

Self-description always remains more or less elusive, which means we must rely on our encounters with others to help us understand ourselves. This difficulty in language implies that at a minimum both political figures and social scientists must pay close attention to the ways they describe human beings and make policies that respect their dignity.

The act of treating another human being as "a something in the world," rather than as *someone*, a fellow language-user with consciousness and choice, is an act of disposal (*SSL* 137). It reduces the person to an object moved by alien powers. In Percy's terms, a dyadic treatment of the human person does not just fail to provide an adequate *scientific* analysis of that person; moreover, it renders them into objects and explains them entirely in terms of their environment. Throughout Percy's novels, the act of subjecting human beings to the I-It in theory deprives them of a sense of self with which they might overcome their alienation. It robs them of the capacity to imagine the world could be different. It also creates certain other difficulties: Percy often turned to the example of the scientist who accepts a dyadic theory retains no basis for a rational defense against those who would deny human beings rights and dignity. Worse still, in this condition, the human animal, understood solely as a product of its environment, can be disposed of in reality just as surely as they were in the scientist's theory. These are both perils that Percy believed a consistent attention to the realities of human consciousness could overcome.

All of this would nonetheless strike most conventional social scientists as a kind of backward metaphysics that the humanist sneaks in to co-opt or destroy rigorous analysis. They might argue that Percy offers social scientists little more than a decent into nonsensical metaphysics, and that we should accept what the scientific facts suggest: that human beings do exist in an environment and that while our language use is not fully understood, we still respond to stimuli in predictable ways. Percy knew this argument well and regularly reminded his readers that it carries a metaphysical wager too. It is impossible to debate indemonstrable first principles. The person dogmatically committed to any kind of scientific determinism cannot be moved simply by an appeal to a different first principle. This may explain why natural law theory—particularly that of the "new" natural law—finds relatively few converts despite the rigor of its logic. Despite this, Percy pointed skeptics to clues that might suggest a better first principle.

Is it not peculiar that in an era of social scientific and medical progress, we seem no closer to eradicating alienation? Even as these disciplines gain ever-greater dominion is it strange that depression, anxiety, and a host of other difficulties seem constantly on the rise? Or think too of the political versions: despite decades of well-intentioned social welfare programs that all too often presuppose that recipients are helpless, American poverty rates remain roughly the same.[13] The social scientist might say in both of these cases that we have not yet hit upon quite the right treatment or policy. But Percy's body of work suggests that we should at least seriously consider the opposite: that the difficulty rests with applying the dyadic mentality to the social life of human beings at all.

Percy strenuously denied that his position opposed science, properly understood.[14] However, he did insist that the scientist's "ontophobia" has no rational basis. A genuine engagement with the evidence concerning the uniqueness of language would at least suggest some of the methodological dangers dyadic analysis poses when applied to human beings. As a matter of reconciling social scientists to the problem in stages, Percy would probably argue that such a social scientist would not necessarily need to accept his own conclusions about the link between language and alienation. At a minimum, he showed that social science faces some dire difficulties that require a new attitude, one where scientists would admit that language hopelessly complicates their hope for a simple and clear causal models (*MB* 239–240). On this point, Deirdre McCloskey's observation that science ought to be understood "in the wide sense of 'serious and systematic inquiry,' which is what it means in every language except the English of the past 150 years" seems apt.[15] Nonetheless, if the social scientist happened to accept such a critique, they might wonder what sort of social science even remains if we discard the dyadic methods they so commonly use. Percy's argument implies that this merely leads social science back down paths discarded—to older ideas and traditions of social inquiry.

THE RETURN TO TRADITIONAL SOCIAL SCIENCE

In the first instance, many social scientists would insist that a social science focused on words or ideas simply cannot be science.[16] But Percy argued that several lines of inquiry remain open, so long as the scholar begins with a theory of the human person and its reality—an ontology, as some constructivists prefer—that acknowledges the reality of language as a triadic phenomenon. This would not be a fully coherent philosophy or theology, but something else. In one of his earliest attempts to formulate this concept, Percy articulated the need for

> a minimal coherent working model which can accommodate both a view of man—man as organism in an environment—which he is—and also those unique, triumphant, and perverse options—options for misery and joy—to which man seems particularly prone. (*SSL* 128)

Thus, we would begin with the anthropology of man doing the uniquely human thing—talking (*MB* 11). In not reducing the talking to some other material cause, those "unique, triumphant, and perverse options" Percy mentioned might be explained in more authentic terms. But how would such inquiries proceed? What new sorts of questions might scholars ask?

Such scholarship might take its bearings from the great texts of politics and history, or at least the ones that join Percy in pointing to human beings doing the unique things they do without beginning from a fully worked-out worldview. Think here of Adam Smith or Alexis de Tocqueville, both of whom practiced what James W. Ceaser labels "traditional political science." By taking ideas and language seriously, each was able to develop a powerful account of major developments in social life without "disposing" of human beings via their theories.[17] Both of them embark on a social science that begins from observable traits of human life, but reject a narrow vision of dyadic causality; neither of them proposed what might be considered a full philosophy as the starting point of their endeavors. They did not insist on the objective-material method that has enchanted social scientists since the latter years of the nineteenth century, and both explicitly assume human beings are social creatures who must be understood in that element.[18] A brief digression into their thought will provide some basis for understanding both the lineage of traditional social science and how it compares to Percy's argument in favor of beginning with the triadic nature of language.

Consider Smith and Tocqueville's similar starting points when discussing wealth and poverty. In describing the origin of the innovations sparked by the division of labor, Smith began with human action and the products of our nature as talking, trading beings. He argued that the spread of wealth results not from some grand plan or intention, but rather the unintended consequences of elements of human nature:

> This division of labour, from which many advantages are derived, is not originally the effect of any human wisdom, which foresees and intends that general opulence to which it gives occasion. It is the necessary, though very slow and gradual consequence of a certain propensity in human nature which has in view no such extensive utility; the propensity to truck, barter, and exchange one thing for another.[19]

Human beings, then, are trading creatures, and language plays a central role in this. Beginning with this and other observable elements of human life, Smith extended the point further in one of his 1762–3 *Lectures on Jurisprudence*, noting that the heart of this trading behavior rests in our unique need to communicate:

> If we should enquire into the principle in the human mind on which this disposition of trucking is founded, it is clearly the naturall [*sic*] inclination everyone has to persuade. The offering of a shilling, which appears to us to have so plain and simple a meaning, is in reality offering an argument to persuade one to do so and so as it is for his interest. Men always endeavor to persuade others to be of their opinion even when the matter is of no consequence. . . . And in this manner everyone is practising oratory on others thro the whole of his life.[20]

So for Smith as much as Percy, our conversational nature determines many other things about our lives in a manner that merely environmental analysis would miss. A dyadic economic analysis focused on the same phenomena would begin with our needs and interests, take them as given, and proceed toward an objective-material account of the division of labor. Smith's account is far richer simply for the reason he began with language and took its products seriously.[21]

Tocqueville also provided a window into how a triadic social science worked in the past. In his discussion of how near-permanent groups of poor people dependent on government assistance emerged and grew in Europe (and especially Great Britain), Tocqueville focused not on the way man's environment shapes him in a more-or-less predictable way, but rather upon the ways our conscious nature interacts with that environment to change our felt world through habit and custom (what Percy might call culture):

> Man is born with needs, and he creates needs for himself. The first class belongs to his physical constitution, the second to habit and education. I have shown that at the outset men have had scarcely anything but natural needs, seeking only to live; but in proportion as life's pleasures have become more numerous, they have become habits. These in turn have finally become almost as necessary as life itself. . . . Among very civilized peoples, the lack of a multitude of things causes poverty; in the savage state, poverty consists in not finding something to eat.[22]

As with Smith, Tocqueville began with observable or easily inferable claims about human life. He then proceeded in a relatively commonsensical way from these claims to an argument about how we conceive of poverty. Rather than rely on an objective-material argument about the nature of poverty as an entirely physical condition of want, he explained it as a mental state and product of culture.

By beginning with arguments based upon reasoned debate and empirical observation, both Smith and Tocqueville placed themselves on ground Percy could have endorsed. Their analyses rest on language and culture in unsurprising ways: as Percy so repeatedly observed, with what else might we begin our study of human beings in their social worlds? Percy's desire to renew a social science that accepts arguments outside the objective-material as both legitimate and genuinely scientific places him in a tradition of inquiry mostly abandoned by modern social scientists. But how might a contemporary reader of this "traditional" social science apply Percy's triadic model explicitly to gain greater understanding of how to proceed?

Percy's new social science would begin with the recognition of the human being's status: in the development of a minimum working model of the human person that recognizes the distinctive function of language, and perhaps identifies certain other elements important for the development of an explanatory theory about some aspect of social life (*SSL* 129). This places him in continuity with past thinkers like Smith and Tocqueville, but would likely also challenge previous thought by insisting scholars formulate a clear explanation of their assumptions rather than merely operate on an implicit working model as Smith and Tocqueville do.[23]

Moreover, Percy also argued that a theory that cannot accommodate or explain how the theorist acquires his or her lofty analytic position over other normal people poses significant difficulties. After all, "one condition of the practice of the objective method of the sciences is the exclusion of oneself from the world of objects one studies" (*MB* 129). The scientist's pretentions run headlong into their difficulty "placing" themselves within an objective-materialist theory, much less explaining how they, a speaking, reasoning being, are best understood merely as a product of their environment. This struck Percy as "a poor show," one that no reasonable person would or should settle for in explaining their own life (*SSL* 417). More directly, a triadic social science would not allow for explanations that reduced such a thinking human being to considering him or herself merely as a product of an environment. Such a method would respect personal dignity, then, by taking seriously the products of human language, thought, and choice. This suggests that social scientists would have to become far more modest in their aims of understanding the regular patterns of life as *lawlike*, and that they might have to abandon the quest for scientifically predictive analysis (MB 221–2).[24]

One possible answer to Percy's challenge lies in social constructivism, which at least in political science stands out as a mode of analysis that at partially accepts the challenge of formulating a social science placing language at the center of the inquiry. As Richard Ned Lebow observes, however, the focus here is on the "decisive role of society in constituting actors and their identities," and not on any clear-eyed theory of the human person. Indeed, most social constructivists at least partially inhabit the dyadic paradigm by construing individuals as entirely formed by environments, and then formulating arguments that predict their conduct.[25] As critics of dyadic social science, both Lebow and McCloskey provide good examples of what a triadic approach might look like today. Lebow and McCloskey modify the narrowly social constructivist approach by building a working anthropology that emphasizes the interplay between human beings' motives for a good reputation, the fulfillment of their appetites, and the pursuit of their rational goals. In so doing, both allow for a deep move beyond an objective-material form of analysis.[26] Percy might have embraced this modified constructivism rooted in a serious theory of the human person because it allows for the possibility of taking human motivation as well as the ideas and rhetoric people use seriously.

But if social scientists accept arguments about motive and rhetoric—that is, claims about the ways human beings use words not just to name but also to reason about their thoughts and feelings, and then persuade one another to act—some other attitudes and points of emphasis might have to change as well. The conventional mode of social science analysis where scholars trace the ways an environment (dyadically understood) *determines* action could not stand. Percy suggested that the human being that says she is entirely a product of an environment defies her own subjection to theory in the insistence that we can then change things. The desire to help themselves and others obscures that for this to be true, some people must exercise power over others to shape a new reality.[27]

In place of an iron cage, new scholarship might look at instances and circumstances where individuals stretch the constraints under which they appear to operate.[28] Ironically, this might make more social science research more useful to those in authority to make policy. Consider for a moment the difficulty of applying dyadic social science's predictions to actual social and political life. Dyadic social science must deal in probabilities and general predictions; any effort at precise prediction would require too much context-specific data, which in turn would invalidate the general theory a social scientist aims at creating.[29]

Triadic analysis would force scholars to discard generally predictive models, but it does allow for a depth of description and understanding of the motives and principles that drive human choice. Under the rubric of "stretching constraint," it might lead scholars to consider possibilities for change that a person obsessed with structure and environment might not allow themselves to consider. If scholars place language and belief on the table as causes open to use in scientific analysis, then they might have to revisit all manner of explanations proposed and debated concerning every widely studied major development catalogued by social scientists in the last 150 years. This reevaluation might not only transform various debates hitherto curiously unmoved by the power of language and ideas, but also unmake some of the considerable existential hopelessness at the heart of dyadic social analysis.

Percy certainly would not have argued that the advent of a genuinely triadic social science would bring joy where only despair reigns now. Triadic social science might help mitigate social scientists' wild oscillation between optimism in the possibility of new technologies or methods of social control (and the concomitant belief that society might finally free itself from poverty, crime, and other social ills) and the gloomy pessimism occasioned by the determinism dyadic analysis so often rests within (which brings about musings that only tremendous, revolutionary action and systematic efforts can effect change). A chastened middle ground might emerge out of the more widespread acceptance that persuasive words, beliefs, and even character matters, one where scholars begin by remembering that social changes always start with individuals who accept the possibility they might persuade others to join in their cause, for good or evil. Percy hoped for such a change in the study of the human person as a starting point. The changes it might have led to in education and public culture might have then reverberated into society as a whole. A vague hope for change does little good, however. We must ask: What sorts of questions might such a revitalized social science attempt to answer?

QUESTIONS AND DIRECTIONS FOR A NEW SOCIAL SCIENCE

In a series of exchanges in "The Delta Factor," Percy asked his readers to consider what a Martian who encountered dyadic social science might say in response to its practitioners. Percy's Martian wonders why government funding and scientific interest never seems to fall on topics like:

> "Suicide in San Francisco, or the End of the Frontier: Correlations between Point of Origin, Level of Education, Time of Arrival, and Number of Rotations between New York and San Francisco of 150 Suicides Who Jumped off the Golden Gate Bridge,"
>
> or "Sadness in Suburbia: Psychiatric Profiles of Twenty-Five Housewives before and after Reading Betty Friedan,"
>
> or "Scientific Transcendence and Sexual Immanence, or the Relationship of Lust to the Spirit of Abstraction: The sexual Behavior of Twelve Scientists at Los Alamos in 1942-45, the Zenith of Transcendence of Twentieth-Century Physics Interrupted by Periodic Re-entry into the Organismic and Cultural Imminence of Santa Fe, Los Angeles, and New York; Sexual Intercourse as Prototype of Re-entry." (*MB* 28–29)

Comedic value aside, all of these questions share a preoccupation with the interrelationship between human beings understood as organisms and their capacities for language use. A science insisting on materialistic objectivity or on a functional definition of culture must rule them out, but the turn to triadic analysis opens up these and a broad array of other topics for consideration.

Such a mode of inquiry might renew attention upon the multitude of ways belief, principle, and the choices that create habits and character serve as more fundamental causes of social trends and events in our world. Without the methodological requirement that language and ideas be understood by some other, putatively deeper environmental or root cause, social science might grow more directly debatable and directly insightful to a wider audience. Minimally, scholars could begin to inquire open-mindedly about the ways these cultural causes relate to more physical and biological ones without presupposing either consistently dominates. The Martian's questions given above suggest at least some of the ways Percy speculated and wondered if this could be done. Recent historical work like that I quote above indicates a starting point for bridging the current—in their minds unscientific—gap between the humanities and the social sciences.

A new social science could inquire much more deeply than current dyadic work into what it means to live and die as a human being, not as an environmentally conditioned creature. It could take human moral purposes seriously rather than simply looking at effects and imputing bad-faith motives to the objects of study more easily. Percy's repeated emphasis on the various ways modern man lives with a kind of spiritual impoverishment suggests that a triadic account of issues like anxiety, sadness, our relations to place, and with larger social groups all could bear fruit. As a storyteller, Percy hoped to draw his readers into contemplating these perennial difficulties of human life, but he also argued that a triadic social science could help do this.

In terms of specifically triadic political science, the move away from objective-material assumptions about causation might allow such inquiry to more directly inform and affect political life. The fact political science bears so little import to policy today may reflect Percy's claim that the difficulty for most people with science rests in its ambition to provide knowledge "which can be arrived at anywhere by anyone and at any time" (*MB* 125). By aiming at objectivity and universality, scientific theory may be true within its range of competence, or false, but in any case, in social life these theories remain abstract and nearly impossible to apply to offer insight into any specific case. Percy proposes an alternative to this kind of knowledge in "The Message in the Bottle," which he labels "news," and describes as a piece of information that bears directly on the hearer's condition (*MB* 127–8).

Framed in dyadic terms, a reader who would act politically would find it hard to construe much of social science as "news" in this respect, but a triadic account of political life, framed with the intent of providing explanation and insight rather than directly predictive power might strike the same reader as news of the highest importance. To offer one example drawn from the ongoing dialogue between military historians, related social scientists, and the military profession: senior military officers regularly insist that their studies in the subject, not for narrowly predictive purposes, but rather for the cultivation of insight and the formation of their minds on the subject of war, made a tremendous difference in their professional lives,[30] and practitioners of diplomacy have often remarked on the degree to which learning about other cultures can only happen through an acquaintance with their great literature.[31] News in the political sense might mean an argument or insight that forms the politician's mind for action; one can imagine an interpretive account of some aspect of political life that awakens interest in a citizen's mind.

Given Percy's obsession with the derangement of modern times, perhaps social science that formulates an explanation of what people feel when they become subsumed in materialism or live under the auspices of bad theory would do the best immediate service to correct the dangers Percy described in his writings (*SSL* 254–5). Yet despite opening up some new possibilities for research and questions for his readers to ponder, one element in Percy's ideas about the human person's triadic nature ought to give the linguistically savvy would-be social scientist pause.

Percy explained that while individuals label and categorize their fellow human beings every day, the "self of the sign-user can never be grasped" in such a way. If abstract labels cannot fully suffice as an explanation of another human being, at some point actual encounters become necessary. He elaborates upon the difficulty in *Lost in the Cosmos*:

> You are *Ralph* to me and I am *Walker* to you, but you are not *Ralph* to you and I am not *Walker* to me. . . . For me, certain signifiers fit you, and not others. For me, all signifiers fit me, one as well as another. I am rascal, hero, craven, brave, treacherous, loyal, at once the secret hero and asshole of the Cosmos.
>
> You are not a sign in your world. Unlike all the other signifiers in your world with form more or less stable units with the perceived world-things they signify, the signifier of yourself is mobile, freed up. (LC 107)

In the context of a triadic science, this passage suggests that *all* theories of the human person share a fundamental limitation in their application to any person's life. Explaining and predicting human behavior may be a noble and important goal, but if we understand Percy's claims rightly here, this means that social science should always be oriented toward helping human beings understand the consequences of their behavior and the challenges of our life together. A theory may provide news in the sense of guidance or the sharpening of the mind that possesses it, but it cannot replace the experience of being recognized and affirmed in community with friends and family. Triadic social science might help us recognize our alienation or sadness, and if done well, direct us toward a better explanation for this than its dyadic predecessors do, but as symbol-using and thus social creatures, Percy argued that the only partial resolutions to the difficulties science might identify come through our lives together. This forms the subject of my final chapter.

NOTES

1. Here I am thinking of both Orwell's essay *Politics and the English Language* (New York: Penguin, 2013) and *1984* (New York: Penguin, 2013). But also, consider Thomas Hobbes's understanding of human nature and the links he proposes between the "strict signification" of language and the stability of the regime. See esp. ch. 46 of *Leviathan*.

2. See for example, Martin Hollis, *The Philosophy of Social Science: An Introduction*, revised ed. (Cambridge: Cambridge University Press: 2002), esp. ch. 8 and 9 and Peter T. Manicas, *A Realist Philosophy of Social Science: Explanation and Understanding* (Cambridge: Cambridge University Press, 2006), esp. ch. 3.

3. For a concise overview, see Kenneth N. Waltz, "The Origins of War in Neorealist Theory," *The Journal of Interdisciplinary History*, Vol. 18, No. 4 (Spring 1988), 615–628. For a longer treatment of his mature—and most dyadic—theory, see his *Theory of International Politics* (Boston: McGraw Hill, 1979).

4. Deirdre McCloskey devotes a considerable portion of her *Bourgeois Dignity* to refuting such economic explanations on methodological grounds very similar to Percy's objection to dyadic social science. She argues that innovation rather than material change and its attendant incentives caused the Industrial Revolution, and more pointedly, "that talk and ethics and ideas caused the innovation." See *Bourgeois Dignity: Why Economics Cannot Explain the Modern World* (Chicago: University of Chicago Press, 2010), 6.

5. In terms that also resonate with Percy, Joshua Mitchell argues that social scientists often fail to grasp the central elements of religious experience. See his "Religion is Not a Preference," *The Journal of Politics*, Vol. 69, No. 2 (May 2007), 351–362 and the subsequent debate: Clyde Wilcox, Kenneth D. Wald, and Ted G. Jelen, "Religious Preferences and Social Science: A Second Look" and Joshua Mitchell, "A Reply to My Critics," both in *The Journal of Politics*, Vol. 70, No. 3 (July 2008), 874–883.

6. This would seem also to apply to all products of thought. On this point, Percy assailed the strict behaviorists: Instead of having behaviorists trying to explain language by stimulus-response theory, why not try to account for behaviorists by a larger theory of language (for after all the behavior of behaviorists is notable in that it is not encompassed by behavioral theory: behaviorists not only study responses; they write articles and deliver lectures setting forth what they take to be the truth about responses, and would be offended if anyone suggested that their writings were nothing more than responses and therefore no more true or false than a dog's salivation)? (*MB* 17)

7. In *Lost in the Cosmos*, Percy quickly dismissed the deconstructionists (87n). His account of their notions highlights their bleak picture of the self.

8. For extended discussions of the ways Percy utilized Peirce, see the correspondence between Percy and philosopher Kenneth L. Ketner in *A Thief of Peirce:*

The Letters of Kenneth Laine Ketner and Walker Percy, Patrick H. Samway, S.J., ed. (Jackson: University Press of Mississippi, 1995). On the importance and nature of Peirce's theory more generally see also Norbert Wiley, *The Semiotic Self* (Chicago: University of Chicago Press, 1994).

9. On this point, see also chapter 8, "The Rhetoric of Social Science," in Richard M. Weaver, *The Ethics of Rhetoric* (Davis: Hermagoras Press, 1985), esp. 206–208.

10. Buber's argument focused on the phenomenology of how human beings relate to one another and with their material environment; Percy adapted this notion with particular focus on the nature of how words express this relation or fail to convey respect to the reality of the other person. See Buber, *I and Thou*, Walker Kaufmann, trans. (New York: Touchstone, 1970).

11. For some striking examples of the link between social science and the sort of deprivation I have in mind, see James C. Scott, *Seeing Like A State: How Certain Schemes to Improve the Human Condition Have Failed* (New Haven: Yale University Press, 1999).

12. Alexander George observes that a "passive orientation to action" logically follows from determinism. See his essay, "The 'Operational Code': A Neglected Approach to the Study of Political Leaders and Decision-Making," *International Studies Quarterly* 13 (June 1969): 203.

13. See for example, Deepak Lal, *Poverty and Progress: Realities and Myths about Global Poverty* (Washington, D.C.: Cato Press, 2013), esp. ch. 3, 47–68; and chs. 44–45 in McCloskey, *Bourgeois Dignity*, 420–438.

14. For two examples, see "Is a Theory of Man Possible?" and "The Fateful Rift: The San Andreas Fault in the Modern Mind," in *SSL*, 111–114 and 271–274.

15. McCloskey, *Bourgeois Dignity*, 38.

16. McCloskey, *Bourgeois Dignity*, 31–33.

17. Ceaser describes this form of political analysis as based on "three interrelated parts: (1) an analysis of conditions or place (historical sociology); (2) an analysis of regime types and what maintains or undermines them (general political science); and (3) an analysis of what maintains or undermines regime alternatives in a specific context (American politics, French politics, Iranian politics, etc.)." Ceaser focuses his account of traditional political science on Aristotle, Montesquieu, and Tocqueville, but Smith also nicely fits his account of what qualifies as a traditional approach to the subject matter. See his *Liberal Democracy and Political Science* (Baltimore: Johns Hopkins University Press, 1990), 41–69, quote above at 42.

18. For two accounts of the rise of materialist objectivity in the social sciences, see McCloskey, *The Rhetoric of Economics*, 2nd ed. (Madison: University of Wisconsin Press, 1998) and Peter Novick, *That Noble Dream: The "Objectivity Question" and the American Historical Profession* (Cambridge: Cambridge University Press, 1988).

19. Adam Smith, *An Inquiry into the Nature and Causes of the Wealth of Nations*, R.H. Campbell, A.S. Skinner, and W.B. Todd, eds. (Indianapolis: Liberty Fund, 1981), 25 (I.ii.1).

20. Smith, *Lectures on Jurisprudence*, R.L. Meek, D.D. Raphael, and P.G. Stein, eds. (Indianapolis: Liberty Fund, 1982), 352 (vi.56).

21. Consider in this light McCloskey's arguments about how we cannot view human institutions (that is, institutions produced through language, persuasion, and the like) merely as incentive-generating constraints (read: as a stimulus-response environment). See Ch. 33 in *Bourgeois Dignity*, 296–309.

22. Alexis de Tocqueville, *Memoir on Pauperism*, Seymour Drescher, trans. (Chicago: Ivan R. Dee, 1997), 48–49.

23. Moreover, Percy might criticize Ceaser's account of how to reconstruct a new political science, in part because of its overreliance on regimes as the anchoring point of the argument rather than beginning with human beings. To be fair, Ceaser published *Liberal Democracy and Political Science* in 1990, before the development of a linguistically savvy constructivism and the Perestroika movement in political science. Perhaps a revised edition would read differently?

24. Beginning from Percy's intuitions, Kenneth L. Ketner argues that a hope for prediction would be the first casualty of Percy's new science. See Ketner, "Novel Science: or, How Contemporary Social Science is Not Well and Why Literature and Semeiotic Provide a Cure," in *A Thief of Peirce*, 280–4.

25. Richard Ned Lebow, *A Cultural Theory of International Relations* (Cambridge: Cambridge University Press, 2008), 3.

26. On justifying the turn to the interplay between the "spirited" or reputation-seeking character and other notions of the self and state in international relations, see Lebow, *Cultural Theory*, 14–19. For McCloskey's clearest account for how spreading notions of dignity and liberty shaped modern economic growth, see Ch. 39 in *Bourgeois Dignity*, 366–376.

27. This resonates with C.S. Lewis's argument in *The Abolition of Man* (New York: HarperCollins, 2001), that "controllers" would inevitably diminish liberty as a whole, 57–58.

28. I borrow the notion of "stretching constraints" from another work that challenges dyadic social science. See Richard Samuels, *Machiavelli's Children: Leaders and Their Legacies in Italy and Japan* (Ithaca: Cornell University Press, 2003), 5.

29. Ketner provides a brief, devastating critique of statistically driven social science in his "Novel Science," in *A Thief of Peirce*, 260–263. I would argue that the spirit of much of his analysis applies to formal models, game theory, and the like.

30. For two accounts of this from high-ranking military professionals, see John P. Kiszely, "The Relevance of History to the Military Profession: A British View," and Paul K. Van Riper, "The Relevance of History to the Military Profession: An American Marine's View," in *The Past as Prologue: The Importance of History to the Military Profession*, Williamson Murray and Richard Hart Sinnreich, eds. (Cambridge: Cambridge University Press, 2006), 23–54.

31. For a discussion of this, see Charles Hill, *Grand Strategies: Literature, Statecraft, and World Order* (New Haven: Yale University Press, 2010), 1–8.

Chapter 7

Percy's Vision of Family, Community, and Faith

Any effort at reading Walker Percy's writings for their social and political meaning must at some point account for the way that the majority of Percy's thoughts on these matters were critical, often savagely so. Parts 1 and 2 of this book emphasized the ways that he argued our partially satisfying attempts to fulfill our needs, wants, and dreams all fall short. They tend to actively destroy whatever happiness or repose is available to us in this life, leaving us unable to cope with our alienated state. The mishmash theories of the self and the expert-layman relationship they abet actively undermine our capacity for self-understanding. Neither a life lived in pursuit of honor, nor do various ways of throwing oneself into a community fully satisfy those who undertake these means of navigating our troubled world. For Percy, all of these means—whenever their adherents take them as "solutions" to life's "problems"—lead directly to the love of apocalypse and destruction that colors all his work. Observing the defects of modern political and social life remains an important task, but does not directly lead to a positive political teaching.

Looking to Percy for a positive political teaching requires understanding his various critical accounts in a somewhat unconventional way. As exercises in showing the readers where the most common choices in American life fail to satisfy us, Percy's stories can tell the reader something about the possibilities threatening American political order, or for engaging in renewal. The fact human beings often swing between very flawed means of attenuating their worst tendencies does nothing to undermine the necessity that they eventually find places of rest and support, places that can help alleviate the tendencies that so often lead Americans into political disaster. Percy claimed to write novels as a form of "prophecy in reverse," and he showed through these stories that family, community, and life in the church can help support a decent life (*MB* 101). At the same time, Percy hastened to remind his readers that the principal danger of seeking community and fellowship with others rests in asking too much of any given place of support.

Percy argued that the novel as a form of art in the contemporary world only worked if it strove for both cognitive and diagnostic power, aiming at telling the truth about what it means to live in our world and stimulating the reader into thinking about their life in new ways (*SSL* 139–141). A difficulty appears here in that where he writes to critique, reveal, or mock, his reasoning seems quite clear. By contrast, his social and political message only emerges implicitly in the novels—especially in their concluding pages. This does not make it impossible to draw conclusions about the ways that family, community, politics, and the church each address our needs in partial ways.

In their own way, each of Percy's characters ultimately recognizes the ways their behavior and thoughts denied the need for moderate places of rest. This is not to say that Percy concluded his stories with "happy endings"—far from it in some cases. Indeed, he observed that he never felt obliged to let the "good guys" win in an unambiguous way (*SSL* 369). Percy's characters begin and end their journeys in relation to family, community, and the church, always only partially fulfilled by their circumstances. The combined messages of these stories, however, contribute to showing Percy's political vision in a manner that might guide our thinking today.

FAMILY AND FRIENDSHIP AS ANCHORS FOR THE SELF

By the concluding pages of most of his novels, Percy's characters achieve a partial resolution to their varied searches. In each case, a major component of this resolution emerges in their mending of old family bonds or the creation of new ties of marriage or friendship. The pattern usually involves the protagonist's discovery that their homes and the people near them are more than a burden or source of irony, and the cultivation or renewal of relationships with others. In particular, Percy's characters frequently turn to romantic love as a way of mitigating their malaise—and their stories subsequently resolve themselves in part through an engagement or marriage. But throughout, although Percy utilized the conventional ending where man and woman (re) unite, Percy never implied these bonds "fix" the lovers in any deep sense. The characters remain the same flawed wayfarers throughout, even if they win themselves a place of partial rest at the end.

Percy presents the clearest—if still unorthodox—version of this at the end of *The Second Coming*, when Allison Huger and Will Barrett, widely disparate in age and previously cast adrift without family or a sense of home, find one another through a series of accidents and in a way rescue one another from their physical and mental ailments. They choose to settle on some of Will's land, where Allison has restored an old greenhouse, and Will proceeds to plan both a new life in business with her and a second career for himself in a new law practice. He forms a community that begins with Allison and grows to include a pair of retired builders, "Old men but good," who he sets to making log cabins for sale on her property alongside a few other castoffs (*SC* 344). Having recognized the emptiness of his previous life of searching for authorities to guide him, Will desires a community of those cast off by society, rooted in a new place. He intends to invest his fortune in this new community's work and live with his young second wife with the aim of giving his own life purpose. He rediscovers hope in his ability to restore hope for men who had lost it in their old age and retirement.

Although Percy believed such community was attainable, he recognized that for alienated people, real friendship is a difficult habit to renew. We see this clearly in the *The Moviegoer* where the dramatic tension revolves around Binx Bolling's realization that he might be able to name his predicaments—his boredom, his disaffection with everydayness—in part through his "search." But he undertakes that search alone. He plays out the roles he assumes each person desires him to undertake—roles that are abstract and alienating. Over the span of *The Moviegoer*'s week-long events, lifelong friends Binx and Kate Cutrer recognize their predicament as dislocated and lost souls in need. Their lives have been woven together by complex family relations: with his father's death in World War II, Binx's great aunt Emily offered to take on the responsibility of his education, and he spent much of his youth in her household. Emily embraced Kate as a stepdaughter when she married Jules Cutrer. As I showed earlier, Emily is one of the last representatives of the Southern aristocratic way of life, and judges her wards by that code. Both Kate and Binx know neither of them meets her exacting standards, but moreover, neither of them really fits in to New Orleans's social life, or the rest of their family's conception of a good life.

Both Binx and Kate are beset by their alienation. In their first conversation of the novel, Binx and Kate begin to admit this to one another. Kate asks:

> "And how do you appear so reasonable to Mother?"
> "I feel reasonable with her."
> "She thinks you're one of her kind."
> "What kind is that?"
> "A proper Bolling. Jules thinks you're a go-getter. But you don't fool me."
> "You know."
> "Yes."
> "What kind?"
> "You're like me, but worse. Much worse." (*MG* 43)

Kate recognizes Binx's oddity and his displacement from others. They both understand that their relations with family and friends will always bear the strain of their inability to just accept the predominant ways of being before them: the mishmash theories of the self so prevalent in most of *The Moviegoer*'s characters and Aunt Emily's honor-bound stoicism.

Most of the novel's other characters assume a great deal about where both Kate and Binx stand in relation to the common practices and social life of New Orleans. Binx's former fraternity brother (and Kate's fiancée until late in the novel) Walter tries to draw him into his Mardi Gras carnival krewe, and in their strained conversation, Binx observes:

> To tell the absolute truth, I've always been slightly embarrassed in Walter's company. Whenever I'm with him, I feel the stretch of the old tightrope, the necessity to living up to the friendship of friendships, of cultivating an intimacy beyond words. The fact is we have little to say to each other. There is only this thick sympathetic silence between us. We are comrades, true, but somewhat embarrassed comrades. It is probably my fault. For years now I have had no friends. I spend my entire time working, making money, going to movies and seeking the company of women. (*MG* 41)

These strained relations recur throughout the story; both Binx and Kate exhibit them to others for different reasons. Binx's conviction that the world is filled with spiritual death sets him apart as surely as Kate's depression isolates her from her friends and family. For most of the story, Binx and Kate find it very difficult to relate to anyone but each other. They are anxious and only slowly recognize they might find some respite in one another.

Nothing starts to change for Binx until Kate admits that she cannot marry Walter and falls into a precarious state of depression (*MG* 60–1). At Emily's urging, Binx allows Kate to join his search and travels around the city with her, but refuses to see the possibility they might contemplate marriage, or that being together might actually alleviate some of his restlessness. Ultimately Kate joins Binx on a trip to an investing conference in Chicago. They accept one another's flaws—she Binx's abstracted ways and peculiar need to search, and he her anxiety, which she explained:

> "If I could be sure you knew how frightened I am, it would help a great deal."
> "You can be sure."
> "Not merely of marriage. This afternoon I wanted some cigarettes, but the thought of going to drugstore turned me to jelly."
> I am silent.
> "I am frightened when I am alone and I am frightened when I am with people. The only time I'm not frightened is when I'm with you. You'll have to be with me a great deal."

"I will"
"Do you want to?"
"Yes."
"I will be under treatment for a long time."
"I know that."
"And I'm not sure I'll ever change. Really change."
"You might." (*MG* 234)

The dialogue does not convey much romance; the potential of marriage of this sort seems based less on emotional grounds than practicality mixed with a deep friendship. Both Binx and Kate accept that they need one another, even if Kate in particular refuses the word "love." But neither of them sees the bond as a path to perfection or, as Kate notes, something likely to change her. Percy's realism here about the nature of family serves as another reminder that no single place of rest can keep human beings from falling into abstracted or bestial forms of living. Binx ultimately marries Kate. They live in the Garden District near the Cutrers and he accepts Emily's wishes that he attend medical school—but the novel ends not with a depiction of their happiness in marriage, but rather with Binx pondering the his half-brother Lonnie's death and his recognition of man's position as a wayfarer.

Percy ends *Love in the Ruins* with a similar down-to-earth account of marriage, this time between Dr. Tom More and his former nurse, Ellen Oglethorpe. In it, he depicts the couple five years after the abortive apocalypse at the end of the novel. They stayed in Feliciana Parish for idiosyncratic reasons:

> I stayed because it's home and I like its easygoing ways, its religious confusion, racial hodgepodge, misty green woods, and sleepy bayous. People still stop and help strangers lying in ditches having been set upon by thieves or just plain drunk. Good nature usually prevails, even between enemies. As the saying goes in Louisiana: you may be a son of a bitch but you're my son of a bitch. (*LR* 386)

Though poor, they live well with their two children in a makeshift home, and More knows his life has improved:

> My practice is small. But my health is better. Fewer shakes and depressions and unnatural exaltations. . . . Morning is still not the best of times. As far as morning is concerned, I can't say things have changed much. What has changed is my way of dealing with it. (*LR* 382, 384)

More wakes to a morning run rather than vodka, duck eggs, and orange tang. Ellen—"dour and young and beautiful"—moderates his drinking and orders his days (*LR* 384). Again, the story bears few traces of lofty romance. Ellen is a practical woman and does not expect exultation and constant novelty as he always did. While she curtails Tom's wilder fancies, she does not make any effort to reshape his nature as an erratic dreamer. Tom in return provides her a constant source of amusement, he provides for his family as best as he can, and is a loving husband and father.

Tom still believes in his experiments and the potential of his brain chemistry-altering ontological lapsometer, but notes some differences between his current situation (and the changes he sees around him) and what came before:

> Here's one difference between this age and the last. Now while you work, you also watch and listen and wait. In the last age we planned projects and cast ahead of ourselves. We set out to "reach goals." We listened to the minutes of the previous meeting. Between times we took vacations . . . . I am older, yet there seems to be more time, time for watching and waiting and thinking and working. . . . If you want and work and wait, you can have. Every man a king. What I want is no longer the Nobel, screw prizes, but just to figure out what I've hit on. (*LR* 383–384)

In this story, Tom's departure from restless planning and embrace of patience happens only because he begins to accept the bonds of family and community. The key here, More later notes, is that he no longer pursues his thoughts in solitude, and has stopped seeking the company of young women as distractions.

Having turned away from seeing human beings as amusing abstractions or objects of study, he can find rest in them. Ellen's stability and the place they created together sustain him: "Poor as I am, I feel like God's spoiled child. I am Robinson Crusoe set down on the best possible island with a library, a laboratory, a lusty Presbyterian wife, a cozy tree house, an idea, and all the time in the world" (*LR* 382–384). Without these ties, Tom's arrogance, abstraction, and weaknesses threatened to destroy not just his life, but those of everyone around him. In large part, Ellen brings him back to living as a human being, and not just as an angel or beast.

In *The Second Coming*, *The Moviegoer*, and *Love in the Ruins*, Percy depicted relatively ordinary men and women in moments of distress. These three novels portray relatively short periods in their characters' lives centered on a moral or spiritual crisis. All of these people find a measure of solace, however, in engagement or marriage, and do so without the too-convenient flourish of the sort we see in romantic comedies. They bear the stamp of painful realities—illness, anxiety, and death stand at their center. Without love, these characters could not bear those realities, but those relations alone cannot sustain life, and by the end of these stories, the characters know that. They ask for love and respect but expect neither redemption nor constant rapture from their marriages. The fact that they accept marriage on these terms predisposes them to better accepting their anxieties and alienation in the wider world. On that basis alone, the familial bond serves as a place of rest. But Percy also situated his characters in a wider world, and as such, a chastened sort of politics emerges at the end of several of his stories.

THE NECESSITY OF POLITICAL RESPONSIBILITY

Percy's novels emphasized notions of care and responsibility alongside humor and irony as central elements of a decent political life. To his thinking, the scientific paradigm of problems and solutions did not apply in politics. Instead, Percy suggested we ought to see politics as the messy but necessary business of accepting responsibility for our past, present, and future without disregarding human dignity. In several of his novels, Percy demonstrated the consequences that follow from scientific or technical attempts to control or abolish political controversy.

Percy showed his readers in many ways that the attitude that science can manage our political and social defects poses severe difficulties, in part because the apostles of this approach deny their enemies any means of arguing with them. Percy's implicit message here requires some explanation. In the More novels, Percy borrowed themes from science fiction and dystopian literature to explore the dilemmas this attitude creates. Tom's various struggles center around combating the use of political words that obscure rather than clarify what is actually happening in the world, as his world becomes an Orwellian nightmare.[1] Unwanted children that are candidates for abortion transform into "pre-personhood neonates," a euthanasia facility becomes a "Separation Center," and so on (*LR* 223, 234). In an unpublished letter to the *New York Times*, Percy connected these concerns about where these attitudes might lead:

> I do suggest that once the line is crossed, once the principle gains acceptance—juridically, medically, socially—innocent life can be destroyed for whatever reason, for the most admirable socioeconomic, medical, or social reasons—then it does not take a prophet to predict what will happen next, then sooner or later. At any rate, a warning is in order. Depending upon the disposition of the majority—now in favor of allowing women to get rid of unborn or unwanted babies—it is not difficult to imagine an electorate or a court ten years, fifty years from now, who would favor getting rid of useless old people, retarded children, anti-social blacks, illegal Hispanics, gypsies, Jews.
>
> Why not?—if that is what is wanted by the majority, the polled opinion, the polity of the time. (*SSL* 350–1)

For Percy, technical innovations or legal decisions that define categories of human being out of their formerly guaranteed rights-protections presented severe challenges to justice. But so too did the use of bureaucratic expertise to constrain human choice. The attitudes behind the ubiquitous practice of identifying political and social "problems" and working toward "solutions" increase the severity of the danger. When applied to human life, this model of thinking must always subordinate the choices of human life to one abstraction or another.

Both *Love in the Ruins* and *The Thanatos Syndrome* take place in the shadow of government efforts to reshape human life. In both novels, Percy placed scientific experiments or projects gone wrong in Tom More's path as obstacles to be overcome. Euthanasia figures prominently, justified by appeals to utility and a notion of "death with dignity." Throughout both novels, Percy conveyed his suspicion that legal euthanasia tends to creep inexorably into a settled, authoritarian policy preference, so much so that More finds himself consistently unable to debate his opponents—even after his failures and partial redemption in *Love in the Ruins*, he lacks words with which he might really criticize them.

Near the conclusion of the near-future dystopia *The Thanatos Syndrome*, however, More overcomes this verbal incapacity and confronts Bob Comeaux, the organizer of a dangerous experiment gone wrong. Comeaux and his old friend Max Gottlieb visit More in jail at the end of the novel after More has all the evidence he needs against Comeaux and his co-conspirators. Over the course of the confrontation, More blackmails Comeaux into defunding the euthanasia clinics in Feliciana Parish, but the exchange reveals some dark facets of modern "progress," in particular the tendency for utility rather than morals to more and more govern the decisions of politics:

> "You're talking about violating the law of the land gentleman," he [Comeaux] says quietly. "*Doe vs. Dade*, the landmark case decided by the U.S. Supreme Court which decreed, with solid scientific evidence, that the human infant does not achieve personhood until eighteen months. . . . [More's] talking about shooting down the entire Qualitarian [euthanasia] program in this area. No way."
>
> Max now, dropping group voice: this is serious. "Tom, we don't want to get into a legal hassle. It is, after all, the law of the land."
>
> "Max, the law of the land does not require gereuthanasia of the old of pedeuthanasia of pre-personhood infants. It only permits it under certain circumstances."
>
> "I know, but—" says Max. (*TS* 333–334)

Max, the kind and humanistic psychiatrist who once treated Tom More, is anxious at casting aside the project of euthanasia: only the fact More has incontrovertible proof that Comeaux and others had allowed child abuse to occur as part of their experiment let him win the day. Both Comeaux and Max find it almost inconceivable that anyone would have rational reasons for opposing their preferred policies.

Apart from the devaluation of life itself, this sort of political management of happiness achieves a false solution—it removes the messy realities that flow from accepting man's eventual pain, decay, and death. In *Love in the Ruins* and other stories, Percy suggested that our tendency today to let others care for the permanently disabled and dying betrays a profound incapacity to cope with the reality of death. The relative decline of the funeral in recent decades also suggests this.

At the end of *Lost in the Cosmos*, Percy presented the story of a failed space exploration mission sent to the star Barnard P1 in the near future. This expedition was designed as much as an experiment in living as it was an effort to make contact with alien intelligence whose signals Earth had been receiving for some time. The expedition set out with four adults (Marcus Aurelius Schuyler, the ship's pilot and captain, and three women, Kimberly, Tiffany, and Jane, all scientists with various areas of expertise), who rotated through periods of living together and cryogenic rest with the understanding that a sort of programmed life of sex and companionship would emerge. Since the trip would take several hundred years in real time, but only twenty years or so would pass relativistically on the ship, the planners assumed the crew would create a new kind of extended family. They reach the star, discover that the communications signal that prompted their journey was nothing more than a pulsar, and return to Earth with a dozen children aboard the ship.

The Earth to which they return is not the home they remembered. In the intervening hundreds of years, a final nuclear war destroyed civilization. Only a handful of humans survive in pockets, and virtually all of them suffer from the lingering effects of radiation. Cancer, infertility, and birth defects abound, and humanity teeters on the brink of extinction. Landing at the Bonneville Flats in Utah, the crew and their children meet a strange delegation that had been waiting for their return for some time. The men who awaited them included a local monastery's head, Abbot Liebowitz, and Aristarchus Jones, a scientist who had determined when the ship would return if their mission failed. Jones and Liebowitz each brought a plan for what Schuyler and his extended family might do. Percy presents the reader an account of the implications and future of these mutually exclusive ideas, and then briefly sketches where the reader would find the captain fifteen years later, living with the consequences of each of his alternatives.

As I noted earlier, Aristarchus Jones proposed to abandon the Earth and leave all the deformed, infertile, and unhealthy humans on the planet to their fate. He would have Schuyler use the ship to resettle the crew, their children, and a small number of healthy, free-thinking Californians to Jupiter's moon Europa. Jones chose the moon because it is "planet-size, covered by water ice, [bears] evidence of newly emerging land . . . and, most important of all, an atmosphere of 10 percent oxygen" (*LC* 246). However, Jones intends something more than mere survival and the continuation of the species. Instead, he hopes to found a new world and a new way of life:

> a society based on reason and science, and do so without repeating the mistakes of the past, for example, the Dark Ages, two thousand years of Plato and Judaism and Christianity—a sexually free and peace-loving society where the sciences and arts can flourish freed from superstitions and repressions of religion—no offense to the good monks, who are in fact invited to come along. (*LC* 246)

This only conveys part of Jones's plan, because by advancing a vision driven by scientism rather than the moral authority of arguments based on metaphysical conceptions of the human person, he not only hopes to "solve" the persistent moral conflicts of human history, but in so doing, also abolish the basis for politics itself.

Politics in the fullest sense begins in at least some disagreement about ends. Starting from the premise that science combined with absolute social control can end all the myriad dissatisfactions of human life, Jones's proposal seeks to put an end to the errors of history. Just as Rousseau and his inheritors argued, this requires eliminating the moral and religious grounds for dissent. Without a legitimate and principled basis upon which to differ about the aims of a community, all that remains is *governance*, a sort of technical-managerial process that presupposes all political questions to be settled. In this situation, people would only debate means.

Percy also sketched the future of this experiment on Europa, showing us Schuyler's fate in the New Ionia colony: after the mission succeeds and the ship lands, the group sets to work "on the principles of Skinner's Walden II modified by Jungian self-analysis," and quickly begins to thrive in a material sense (*LC* 257–8).[2] This comes at a cost, however. Fifteen years later, at age sixty-five, the captain has little to do; he reads Shakespeare, listens to Mozart, and enjoys the company of much younger women. He retains his irony and remains reasonably content in stoical solitude, but acutely suffers from his lack of purpose. His role as a leader is done, and the community resolves conflict through intrusive, therapeutic group sessions:

> Group is a daily exercise, in assemblages of ten, of self-criticism and honest appraisal of others. The only rule is honesty, absolute honesty. No more lies,

> no more self-deception, no more secrecy, no more guilt, no more shame. From Aristarchus's own Little Green Book, the aphorism: "The new race will spring from the corpse of the old guilt."
>
> The Captain sighs. He alone of the colonists of the new Ionia is somewhat ironical. Getting rid of guilt is one thing. But he doesn't look forward to the mea culpas and denunciations of the group. It reminds him too much of an AA meeting. (*LC* 257)

As a mechanism for securing unity in a "peace-loving" community, sessions like Percy depicted here carry enormous importance, as they polish the veneer of living in a new mode while stifling departures from the new normal. Free thinking in such a situation would only be as free as the group allowed. By implicitly abolishing moral and political disagreement, real diversity in human life must inevitably suffer—as must our sense of humor.

By contrast with New Ionia's smiling groupthink and the coldly murderous but kindly authoritarianism of Tom More's world, the political communities Percy developed as alternatives to them can only be described as disorderly and imperfect. At the same time, they provide something for their members that New Ionia's attempt at perfection lacks—a sense of home. At the end of *Love in the Ruins*, Tom More highlights his hometown's ability to deal with conflict in good humor (*LR* 386). After all, the very willingness to live and appreciate one's neighbors—even the unlovable ones—virtually requires a capacity to live with persistent differences of opinion and challenges to one's preferred way of life.

In his biting 1977 *Esquire* magazine self-interview, Percy explained the attitudes that he thought a decent political community needed. In this discussion, he suggested that the thorniest political dilemmas of American life cannot be managed or educated away. In the case of race relations in particular, Percy wondered whether the situation might find a partial remedy in the peculiar dynamics of Southern community. This setting was important, because small Southern towns hold out the possibility of providing a context where "blacks and whites may learn the best of each other rather than the worst" (*SSL* 414). The best-case scenario that might flow from the strange relations of a decent (which is to say, all too flawed) political order:

> All I can say is that it has something to do with Southern good nature, good manners, kidding around, with music, with irony, with being able to be pissed off without killing other people or yourself, maybe with Jewish humor, with passing the time, with small, unpretentious civic-minded meetings. Some whites and blacks are sitting around a table in Louisiana, eating crawfish and drinking beer at a PTA fund-raiser. The table is somewhat polarized, whites at one end, blacks at the other, segregated not ill-naturedly but from social unease, like men and women at a party. The talk is somewhat stiff and conversation-making

> and highfalutin—about reincarnation, in fact. Says a white to a white who has only had a beer or two: "I think I'd rather come back as an English gentleman in the eighteenth century than in this miserable century of war, alienation, and pollution," Says a black to a black who has had quite a few beers: "I'd rather come back as this damn crawfish than as a nigger in Louisiana." All four laugh and have another beer. I don't know why I'm telling you this. You wouldn't understand it. You wouldn't understand what is bad about it, what is good about it, what is unusual about it, or what there is about it that might be the hundred-to-one shot that holds the solution. (*SSL* 415)

This might be an unsatisfying solution. Given today's racial tensions, it may even appear to be entirely impractical one that fails to recognize the deeper claims of African-Americans. After his writings on segregation in the 1950s and 1960s, Percy's other writings on race appear entirely in his novels. Yet throughout Percy's work, long-term political and moral injustices only find resolution through patient conversation. Percy's short anecdote provides little more than a starting point and a clue to how racial reconciliation might proceed.

Percy does not directly give voice to this point, but the key elements that emerge here and in his novels revolve around the indirectness and the willingness to accept one another's flaws and limitations: the whites and blacks do not presume they can force tolerance or a sense of perfect equality and ease; instead, they relate to one another as human beings in humor, not in direct conflict over the matters that certainly divide them. This work is unforced. Toleration emerges here in a manner not mandated by law but through face-to-face engagement. This is the sort of remedy that can help attenuate not only racial distrust, but also our more general sense of alienation.

An equally flawed sort of community also appears at the end of *Lost in the Cosmos*, where Percy briefly sketched Marcus Schuyler's other possible future, the one that would result from Abbot Liebowitz's plan to settle his family and the refugees to Lost Cove, Tennessee. After fifteen years, Percy explained that the colony would have grown through a mixture of new children and "locals, strays, wanderers, refugees from the old Northeast" (*LC* 258). Every Sunday, while his wife Jane Smith and his children celebrate Mass with the elderly Abbot, he gathers with assorted misfits on a hilltop, and drinks whisky:

> The "heathen," as they call themselves, begin their usual good-natured bickering, mostly about political and agricultural subjects—whether to start a corn co-op, what to do about a rumored Celtic enclave across the old Carolina line, a growing community with a reputation for violence and snake-handling. (*LC* 260)

The old conflicts remain, and Schuyler handles them in good humor. The political conversations have to do with day to day responsibilities and moderate the temptation to ideology. Confronted with an outsider from Carolina proposing an alliance of white "Americans" against Jews, blacks, and Catholics, he drinks more whisky, and can only laugh:

> The others look at him in astonishment. When he catches sight of their faces, he laughs all the harder.
>
> Presently Jason McBee asks him: What you laughing at, Captain?
>
> Nothing much, says the Captain. I was just thinking: Jesus Christ, here we go again. (*LC* 261)

Of course, the potential for ideologies that thrive on distrust and hate will remain. Being small enough and separated enough to exile deviants poses certain dangers. Perhaps man would be even more tempted toward such views in a future like that Percy describes. No community can eliminate these temptations without destroying the liberty and dignity of their citizens. Schuyler accepts that this is the price of a real political community—conflict and human foibles remain. Despite Lost Cove's flaws, Percy depicted him as happier amid the toil and unresolvable difficulties of life in post-apocalyptic times.

Lost Cove serves as an analogy for why the endings of Percy's stories all implicitly favor a kind of federalism and subsidiarity. One of the central features of scientific schemes of politics is their uniformity and abstractness: they flow from a center and presume to dictate the terms of life to all equally. In opposing Lost Cove to New Ionia, Percy suggested that a wayfaring sensibility is best protected by local self-government. If we wish to defend that value now—before some catastrophe allows us to imagine new institutions—the only route open to us is through the mechanisms of local government and the civic associations that can flourish under laws that encourage them.

Throughout these examples and others in his novels and essays, Percy suggested that a decent form of human community can neither abolish politics nor eliminate real differences by educating or nudging them away. The attempt to do so provokes dangers just as great as those we face when people invest too much in politics. The mean state here relies on irony, humor, and real respect for difference, a balance difficult to achieve but one that Percy argued is vital for a decent life together. One other possible source of moral moderation and rest Percy described remains with the churches and orthodox religious belief.

THE PERSISTENT APPEAL OF THE CHURCH

As alienated creatures lost in a complex world, human beings require multiple places of rest. Interestingly for a committed Catholic, Percy rarely wrote in direct support of the orthodox Christian doctrine that men can only truly find certainty and rest in the church. Instead, he indirectly focused attention on all the ways that faith completes his characters' varied searches for meaning and truth in life. At the same time, he never hesitated to show all the ways that Christian faith can fall prey to extremes that reflect the broken, deranged nature of human communities.

Percy presented his readers with a few stark examples of how churches can lose their way. Perhaps the most plausible future he articulates for American churches comes in the Tom More novels, where even the Catholic Church has fallen on extremely hard times. Percy imagined a Catholicism split into three sects: "(1) The American Catholic Church whose new Rome is Cicero, Illinois; (2) the Dutch schismatics who believe in relevance but not God; (3) the Roman Catholic remnant, a tiny scattered flock with no place to go" (*LR* 5–6). Percy spared neither conservatives nor radicals in this account, as the divisions in the church bear more political and cultural than strictly theological importance:

> The American Catholic Church, which emphasizes property rights and the integrity of neighborhoods, retained the Latin mass and plays *The Star-Spangled Banner* at the elevation.
>
> The Dutch schismatics in this area comprise several priests and nuns who left Rome to get married. They threw in with the Dutch schismatic Catholics. Now several divorced priests and nuns are importuning the Dutch cardinal to allow them to remarry.
>
> The Roman Catholics hereabouts are scattered and demoralized. The one priest, an obscure curate, who remained faithful to Rome [Fr. Rinaldo Smith], could not support himself and had to hire out as a fire-watcher. (*LR* 6)

The prophecy in reverse here seems telling: Percy implied in this tale that other than a small remnant hewing to orthodoxy, most churches will turn to contemporary relevance rather than focusing their ministries on the doctrines of the faith. Both the American and Dutch Catholic churches pursue projects in the here and now at the expense of maintaining a focus on the theological hope that formed the center of orthodoxy in earlier generations. In the American church of Percy's imagination, "Property Rights Sunday is a major feast day," where a "blue banner beside the crucifix shows Christ holding the American home, which has a picket fence, in his two hands" (*LR* 181). The Dutch Church as he described it centered its attention on liberation and social justice. Percy implied that while churches of those sorts can certainly provide a sense of community, the Dutch and American churches cannot really serve as sources of theological hope, or for that matter, provide believers any great reason to remember their status as wayfarers with another home.

Percy was as unstinting in his criticism of Protestants as he was of Catholics. In *The Thanatos Syndrome*, More's wife Ellen abandons her stoical and formal Presbyterianism (which in *Love in the Ruins* seems to amount solely to her knowing right and doing it, but offered her no consolation of faith) for one different denomination after another. She eventually settles on a Pentecostal church, but her new faith, focused entirely as it is on the Holy Spirit, brought with it some of the same dangers secular mishmash theories of the self:

> She is herself a little holy spirit hooked up to a lusty body. In her case spirit has nothing to do with body. Each goes its own way. Even when she was a Presbyterian and I was a Catholic, I remember she was horrified by the Eucharist: *Eating* the body of Christ. That's pagan and barbaric, she said. What she meant and what horrified her was the mixing up of body and spirit, Catholic trafficking in break, wine, oil, salt, water, body, blood, spit—things. What does the Holy Spirit need with things? Body does body things. Spirit does sprit things. (*TS* 353)

The idea that body and soul could be united in one faith and one understanding of the human person remains as alien to some Protestants as it is to those who desire a more objective-material view of human being. The difficulty Ellen's faith presents is that it provides her no coherent way to think about the whole human person. If body and spirit go their separate ways—as happened in Ellen's story—the human being can much more easily fall prey to alternating extremes of abstract, inhuman transcendence or immanent beastliness.

This unstinting criticism of this-worldly churches is important, as Percy heaped scorn on deviations from the Christian orthodoxy. While he insists in his *Esquire* self-interview that the only possible answer to the question, "why are you a Catholic?" is "what else is there?," he framed this in peculiarly ecumenical terms:

> *What do you mean, what else is there? There is humanism, atheism, agnosticism, Marxism, behaviorism, materialism, Buddhism, Muhammadanism, Sufism, astrology, occultism, theosophy.*
>
> That's what I mean.
>
> *To say nothing of Judaism and Protestantism.*
>
> Well, I would include them along with the Catholic Church in the whole peculiar Jewish-Christian thing. (*SSL* 416)

Within the span of the "Jewish-Christian thing," Percy suggested, human beings can find an explanation of the self—preposterous as it is to the objective-material sensibility—that explains the peculiarities of being a self in our world: the alienation, the incapacity to really articulate a story about oneself, and so on (*SSL* 416–7). The theology of the Judeo-Christian tradition helps ultimately ground our sense of wayfaring.

As we have seen, for Percy, people cannot live well without an adequate theory of the self. Without a conceptual language and a self-understanding adequate to the task of explaining our world short of reducing life to its constituent environment, our alienation and confusion become impossible to bear. This alienation is why we are so drawn to the many methods of negating the tensions within the self: sex, drugs, alcohol, causes, or suicide. While Christian or Jewish faith by itself is insufficient as a means for living well, human beings stand in profound need of its comforts and the understanding it brings to life, to say nothing of the hope that comes from a belief in one's salvation.

One clue into Percy's attitudes about religion emerges in *Lancelot*, where Lance Lamar proclaims his creed to Father Percival. Proclaiming his intolerance for the present age, Lance observes:

> I might have tolerated you and your Catholic Church, and even joined it, if you had remained true to yourself. Now you're part of the age. You've the same fleas as the dogs you've lain down with. I would have felt at home at Mont-Saint-Michel, the Mount of the Archangel with the flaming sword, or with Richard Coeur de Lion at Acre. They believed in a God who said he came not to bring peace but the sword. Make love not war? I'll take war rather than what this age calls love. (*L* 157–8)

Lance's condemnation of the church here has more to do with his deranged love of honor than his acceptance of its creeds, for Lance's way such as it is owes more to Nietzsche than Jesus. In the closing pages of the novel, when Percival makes his series of one-word replies—his affirmations—Lance comes to the heart of the matter. Knowing Percival remains unmoved by his nihilistic appeal to honor, he ends his harangue with a concession:

> Very well. But you know this! One of us is wrong. It will be your way or it will be my way.
> *Yes.*
> All we can agree on is that it will not be their way. Out there.
> *Yes.*
> There is no other way than yours or mine, true?
> *Yes.* (*L* 257)

This passage cuts to the heart of Percy's convictions about the real moral alternatives available to us in life. The difficulty is a largely unrecognized one. Committed as ordinary denizens of our world are to mishmash theories of the self, they do not quite notice how little these theories explain. Fewer still recognize the ways that position empties their life of moral guidance. For a man who despairs of mishmash liberalism, there remains only a faithfully Nietzschean affirmation of great men making an honorable creed by which they wish to live and following it, or the church and its dogma. For Percy, no middle ground could survive a searching inquiry into this dilemma of life. Yet as an account of the necessity of faith, this remains primarily a negative one—an argument by subtraction that only asserts the emptiness of all other creeds. Percy did not attempt to establish the truth or falsehood of the statement that human beings *need* faith. But they do need *something* they cannot name, and he offered his readers the possibility a church can provide it.

Perhaps the indirectness of Percy's approach in the novels reflects the impossibility of proving the necessity of religious belief to a skeptical audience. But these stories allowed Percy to disclose to the reader what encountering faith in the most difficult of circumstances might do to a typically materialist but alert denizen of our age. Both *The Moviegoer* and *The Last Gentleman* end with a young man's lingering death—and in each, he depicted these men as convinced in their faith despite their circumstances. Other examples abound, but in every case, Percy implied that coming to faith reflects not so much an intellectual experience as a relational one—that is, faith often finds its way through love, through a couple's discovery of mutual need in each other and a recognition that even love cannot satisfy all their needs.

An example from *The Second Coming* helps demonstrate this. After planning his community of misfits and having become engaged to Allie, Will Barrett meets an old, grizzled priest, Father Weatherbee. Unlike the novel's more worldly (and less-faithful) curate Jack Curl, Weatherbee holds firmly to the dogmas of the church. The priest is perplexed by his demand that despite Will's claim not to believe in the Christian teaching, that he allow the couple to be married in the church. Having secured the priest's help Will turned inward:

> Will Barrett thought about Allie in her greenhouse, her wide gray eyes, her lean muscled boy's arms, her strong quick hands. His heart leapt with a secret joy. What is it I want from her and him [Weatherbee], he wondered, not only want have but must have? It she a gift and therefore a sign of a giver? Could it be that the face of the Lord is here, masquerading behind this simple silly holy face? Am I crazy to want both, her and Him? No, not want, must have. And will have. (*SC* 359)

Will ultimately interprets his love for Allie as a clue to the truth of our existence. He sees others, finally, as something more than abstractions. The gateway to both the reestablishment of a community and his potential love for God was finding a place of rest in a particular person.

Will Barrett's desire at the end of *Second Coming* comports nicely with Percy's own description of the insufficiency of the other alternatives:

> This life is much too much trouble, far too strange, to arrive at the end of it and then be asked what you make of it and have to answer, "Scientific humanism." That won't do. A poor show. Life is a mystery, love is a delight. Therefore, I take it as axiomatic that one should settle for nothing less than the infinite mystery and the infinite delight; i.e., God. In fact, I demand it. I refuse to settle for anything less. I don't see why anyone should settle for less than Jacob, who actually grabbed aholt [*sic*] of God and wouldn't let go until God identified himself and blessed him. (*SSL* 417)

Life's mysteries demand a response that operates at a level commensurate with life's complexities.[3] A creature responding to an environment would not invent something as peculiar as the Christian faith, but a symbol-using being that makes a world with its language and culture, might accept that mystery as the only explanation that makes sense of that world. In this sense, then, Percy showed that faith and a church form an irreplaceable resource for the self in an otherwise hostile, meaningless world.

THE SIDEWAYS ACCOUNT OF POLITICS AND SOCIETY

Some general lessons flow from Percy's peculiar way of explaining the limits of family, community, and church life. Each of these bonds is insufficient for living well by itself. Worse still, each set of relationships poses dangers when pursued in isolation, and this bears particular importance for politics. Percy argued that modern Americans tend toward immoderate responses to their alienation and despair. This is partly because of our faulty scientistic "problem-solution" orientation and partly because we yearn for a completion and fullness this world never can quite provide.

A person who lives entirely for their family and eschews other forms of relational bonding or a faith that tethers their hope faces peculiar dangers. Lance Lamar exemplifies some of the worst possibilities here: as a disillusioned liberal with few friends and honor-loving spirit, his immoderate attachment to family led to death and destruction. But many other characters in Percy's universe betray similar tendencies, placing too much weight on the bonds with their family, and falling to pieces when this bond does not suffice as a way of escaping their alienation. Throwing oneself into a community and hoping for it to grant succor of one's alienation results in some similar problems, as Will Barrett discovered in *The Last Gentleman*. Filling one's day with purposeful endeavors as a means of escape only heightens the moments of solitude and devalues the simple pleasures of family time. Faith, too, can lead to immoderacy at the expense of one's finding a place of rest in the world—consider here Ellen More's flight into "spirit things," at the expense of her family life.

The conclusions to Percy's stories depict characters on their way to making a temporary home in the world. Lance Lamar appears as the least successful. Yet he also begins in the worst position, having recalled his wickedness and pledging to start a new community with his neighbor in the mental asylum. His quest for evil took him to the realization he needed a new order, and a place to call home, but the story ends more ambiguously than any of his other works, with Lance expressing his willingness to listen for the first time to Father Percival. There the monologue ends, and, one imagines, the possibility of Lance recognizing the potential to be a wayfarer begins. Binx Bolling and Will Barrett's stories end on a similarly ambiguous note, with a marriage, a sense of having joined or made a community, and with them embarking on the tentative steps toward accepting the Christian faith. With all three of these characters, the reader is left with a definitive sense that something has changed in their lives. The extremes by which they had guided their lives no longer sufficed, and this opens the door to the life of the wayfarer. These and Percy's other stories suggest the limitations of all human means of happiness and perfection. None of our communities or churches or relationships can provide a complete source of stability; all of them together can only occasionally allow the human person a sense of fullness and rest that we might believe a glimpse of where we really belong.

NOTES

1. On this, see George Orwell, *Politics and the English Language* (New York: Penguin, 2013).

2. On Schuyler's options and their meaning, see Elizabeth Amato, "Walker Percy's Critique of the Pursuit of Happiness," in *A Political Companion to Walker Percy*, ed. Peter Augustine Lawler and Brian A. Smith (Lexington: University Press of Kentucky, 2013), 53–54.

3. Compare to Aldous Huxley's John Savage's plea to the World Controller Mustapha Mond: "But I don't want comfort. I want God, I want poetry, I want real danger, I want freedom, I want goodness. I want sin," in Huxley, *Brave New World* (Garden City, New York: Doubleday, 1974), 187.

Conclusion

A Defense of Moderate Politics and Human Dignity

At the end of *Lost in the Cosmos*, Marcus Schuyler is forced to make a choice: settle a humanist colony on Europa that attempts to transcend all the old limits of human society, or take the chance that Lost Cove, Tennessee could shelter his family and preserve something of humanity's old life. In a purely material and hedonistic sense, Percy sketched out the future on Europa as quite good for Schuyler. He reads Shakespeare and listens to Mozart, regularly has sex with a pair of lovely young women, and yet, his life seems quite diminished, lacking in both family and real friendship. He is denied an outlet for his irony and humor. In Lost Cove, life remains difficult but Schuyler retains a sense of purpose and authority. He engages in politics and farming and he lives well as a husband, father, and wayfarer. Confronted with a stranger's political paranoia, he can only say, "here we go again" (*LC* 261). This is a fitting reminder that human beings can never transcend the perennial troubles that come with living together.

In Lost Cove and on Europa some human longings never change—the desire for love and stability, the perennial allure of political enthusiasm and hate, and mankind's anxiety that nothing is ever fully in its proper place. Percy's account of these yearnings takes shape across various genres of writing and serves as a mirror for our own society and politics. His essays and stories together form a coherent teaching about the persistence of alienation and the partial remedies we can find in our life together. Where his essays illuminate aspects of American social life, Percy's fiction dramatizes the consequences that flow from our choices, and it also shows some of the limitations of turning to stories for politics.

Novels that easily lend themselves to a clear political teaching tend to lose the reader's attention because they subordinate the art to the mission. The thesis overawes the characters and sense of life the author might aim at suggesting. However, articulating a fully formed political philosophy out of serious literature alone remains a tenuous and probably fruitless endeavor. Stories alone paint pictures of individual human lives, experiences from which it is often difficult to generalize. While Percy grew more direct in his novels over time, none of them amount to a complete political education by themselves. The combination of Percy's fiction and philosophical essays allows for some conclusions about the sort of political thinking he believed we needed in times as deranged as ours. Each of these kinds of writing does different cognitive work. A scholar might advance his claims through dense, abstract argument. This might persuade some and likely confuses others; the rest yawn and move on. The detached rhetorical mode such writing takes on usually cannot move people in an existential sense the way stories can. Moreover, there are elements of human life these more erudite scribblings probably cannot grasp at all. In a 1968 interview with Carlton Cremeens, Percy asked:

> How is the historian or sociologist or social scientist of any kind going to deal with the subject of personal alienation? Take the situation of a young man, a college student, a graduate student, or a young man in business. . . . He has fulfilled his needs. He has a wife and children, his house and car and plenty to eat, his art, television, everything. Now suppose in spite of all that this man experiences deep unrest, feels a deep sense of estrangement. . . . You can't measure it with a psychological device, with a physical device, but it's something that's there, it's part of reality, and so the novelist is concerned with it. (*CWP* 27–28)

By giving voice to a feeling or sensibility, novels potentially alert their readers to little-recognized fault lines in their beliefs, or elements in their lives that an argument cannot quite capture. By doing both of these things, Percy's work acquires uncommon breadth and depth.[1] By way of conclusion, I want to return to five of the most important political themes that Percy draws out in his writings.

First, Percy's critique of scientism and the reliance on an objective-material approach to culture bears importance for politics. Percy reminds us that while scientists *can* attempt to study the products of human choice and speech using assumptions and methods analogous to the physical and natural sciences, these efforts come at a significant cost to our self-understanding. The truth or falsehood of beliefs in such an analysis becomes irrelevant; the questions science asks of what we think or do have to do with utility. When social scientists study human action, it is not usually the rationally explainable personal motives that they count as "valid" explanations of our conduct, but rather our environment and context that "count." Consider analyses of voting behavior: political scientists obsess over the role of race, class, and gender as a predictor, but rarely take voters' avowed beliefs as an important piece of evidence for why they act as they do at election time. But what does this deprivation mean for politics?

For Percy, treating human beings as the preformed results of their environment is to deprive them of their sovereignty and place them under the auspices of various forms of expertise. If political science could honestly claim a degree of wisdom about how we *should* order our politics (as opposed to telling us about *efficiency*), perhaps Percy would have accepted this authority. For alienated wayfarers struggling to find places of temporary rest, politics cannot be so clean and neat. The act of reducing human beliefs and culture to secondary causes cannot help but create a kind of passivity in the hearts of the citizenry, which Percy suggested is one of the causes of increasing anxiety and distress in our culture. If human beings believe they are incapable of rebuilding communities on their own without the need for various forms of expertise, one of the surest ways of finding a place of rest becomes unattainable.

Just as Percy argued psychiatry and linguistics need to reformulate their analysis to account for the triadic nature of language, so too does politics need to treat human life in something very different from an objective-materialist manner. This requires rethinking the aims and goals political science, but it would also demand a change in the way we approach politics as a whole. The wayfaring citizens of a republic deserve to be treated not as need- and want-satisfying consumers, but as creatures with dignity and purposes the state cannot fully comprehend.

Taking language and choice as important objects of study might lead politics back to treating reason with more seriousness as well. This is a second major lesson we might draw from Percy's work, one that builds on taking culture itself seriously. If we treat culture as more than just a measurable product of our lived environment, and instead view it as a product of human reason, choice, and action, language takes on renewed meaning. Percy argued that part of the reason language itself seems less important—part of the reason we treat words as meaningless—is that scientism assumes it can be traced to some more fundamental cause. But if we invert this hypothesis and view human reason as a creative cause of events in the world, we should also restore our belief in the importance of words.

This will not lead to some new paradise of reason or full restoration of natural law as a basis for politics. Human beings are too flawed and fallen for that to be the case. What Percy's reasoning does suggest, though, is that taking words and culture seriously mean we cannot attempt to shut down public debate of various topics by appealing to egalitarian theories of public reason. Political authorities should not ban religious faith or other metaphysical claims from debate. Moreover, assuming the meaningfulness of language allows interlocutors to take one another's reasons as important in themselves and avoid assumptions of bad faith. After all, if a politician believes in principle that their opponent's morality or faith actually motivates their actions rather than their material interests, assuming they act in bad faith no longer seems necessary. Real debate could become possible again in a way that hardly seems likely given the ways our political culture has been shaped by failed theories of the self.

This change in outlook might help restore some lost assumptions about human dignity as well, which leads to a third lesson. Percy's imagined restoration of respect for culture and language also implies a path toward respecting persons more fully as well. Throughout his writings, he placed great emphasis on the dangers of functional or utilitarian definitions of law, since any reasoning that correlates personhood with the maintenance of either objective criteria (the capacity for speech) or subjective criteria ("quality of life"), directly leads to arguments *denying* respect to those who do not measure up. Although Percy was by no means an authority on constitutionalism, he did have an eye for the logical consequences of this devaluation. He argued that the logical problems American and European societies now face concerning how to draw limitations on euthanasia and abortion would creep in the moment we accepted the first premise that life only holds contingent value.

Percy's restoration of meaning in language opens the possibility that the sorts of stable moral and legal categories upon which earlier natural rights doctrines rely might find wider acceptance. Unless our sense of what regimes can and cannot do respects that dignity in their constitutions and lower forms of legislation, the state will contribute to the devaluation of human life. Moving politics out of the realm of materialist-objectivity would carry a benefit here as well. Without the assumption that political "reality" always centers on who gets what, when, and how, the logic of the American Founding might grow more plausible again. Citizens no longer corrupted by scientism and the passivity caused by experts might more easily accept that laws, rather than men hold sway over politics. Moreover, those same citizens might not so easily accept political doctrines and policies that treat adults like children, or that impugn the citizens' judgment in various ways.

If we cannot explain politics or culture in reductionist ways, this directly suggests a fourth lesson: for Percy, any decent politics requires a respect for local distinctness and history, and a healthy political respect for federalism, localism, and subsidiarity. As I noted above, for Percy, local distinctiveness makes it possible for people to not see their communities as interchangeable, and for them to develop deep ties of responsibility toward their neighbors. Arguably, the only way liberal regimes have successfully defended local cultures is through granting them a strong basis for local particularity in and through the law. Percy's essays on the South in particular convey the idea that to govern well, one must understand a wide range of issues that the federal government refused to acknowledge and Percy argued that this failure came at a significant cost in race relations and respect for the American regime.

More generally, abstract knowledge about a people cannot say very much about how they live or the reasons their community operates. Percy dramatized many ways that without a concrete, relational awareness of what people need, legal and social scientific experts can very easily destroy the basis for local communities to flourish. By making policy around abstract assumptions about the human person with little or no regard for how people actually live, it is very easy for experts to erode folkways and economies around which small towns thrive.

The conclusions to Percy's stories vary in their details, but one consistent element in each of these stories is an emphasis on a decentralized scale and scope to human ambition, particularly in politics. This is particularly true in *Love in the Ruins* and *The Thanatos Syndrome*, where large-scale government designs collapse, and the characters find themselves returning to the necessity of engaging in politics on a very small scale. Percy suggested throughout his work that only face-to-face confrontations with one's neighbors can overcome the looming sense of alienation that politics so often brings at the abstract level of party platforms and ideologies.

This brings me to my final observation. Percy rejected "isms" in general and political ideology in particular as modes of managing our life together. His stance was anti-ideological in part because ideology just as much as social science requires its adherents accept an excessively shorthand vision of human beings, a reduction of their personhood to social types, environmental inputs, and the needs of the movement. As Will Barrett affirms to himself in *The Second Coming*, these modes are little more than paths to destruction, and forces that the wayfarer must reject:

> Death in the guise of belief is not going to prevail over me, for believers now believe anything and everything and do not love the truth, are in fact in despair of the truth, and that is death.
>
> Death in the guise of unbelief is not going to prevail over me, for unbelievers believe nothing, not because truth does not exist but because they have already chosen not to believe, and would not believe, cannot believe, even if the living truth stood before them, and that is death.
>
> Death in the form of isms and asms shall not prevail over me, orgasm, enthusiasm, liberalism, conservatism, Communism, Buddhism, Americanism, for an ism is only another way of despairing of the truth. (*SC* 272–3)

Despairing about the truths of the human condition—in particular, our dependence upon one another, on our communities, and in faith—comes in many forms. Speaking through Barrett, Percy's denunciation of them starkly challenges conventional ways of understanding the world, as he suggested that alternatives to the truth mire human beings in the death-in-life that so often haunts them. Political moderation can be found in despairing of "isms" because this choice draws us out of abstract political organizing and into personal encounters on a local level. But we must always remember the limited aims of wayfaring politics—if we cannot make the world fully our home, all politics can do is keep the peace and pursue what limited forms of justice mankind's flaws allow.

Not politics then, but only family, faith, and community can lead men out of the despair of alienation to any degree. Our alienation will persist no matter what remedies we attempt to use to escape it. This should chasten our expectations from politics, and lead us to restore what we are so often tempted to ignore. Many of the projects of contemporary politics destroy what temporal happiness we might achieve, fraying the bonds between men that keep alienation at bay. Percy's written legacy reminds us to constantly reknit what the world tears asunder. As wayfarers without a home, we can aspire to no more, and justice demands we do no less.

NOTES

1. On the general ways that storytelling serves as a kind of political teaching, see Susan McWilliams, "Moral Education and the Art of Storytelling," in *First Things: A Case for Conservative Politics. The Hadley Arkes Festschrift*. Eds. Francis J. Beckwith, Robert P. George, and Susan McWilliams. (South Bend, IN: St. Augustine's Press, 2013).

Bibliography

WORKS BY WALKER PERCY

Lancelot. New York: Farrar, Straus, and Giroux, 1977.
The Last Gentleman. New York: Farrar, Straus, and Giroux, 1966.
Lost in the Cosmos. New York: Farrar, Straus, and Giroux, 1983.
Love in the Ruins. New York: Farrar, Straus, and Giroux, 1971.
The Message in the Bottle. New York: Farrar, Straus, and Giroux, 1975.
The Moviegoer. New York: Alfred A. Knopf, 1961.
The Second Coming. New York: Farrar, Straus, and Giroux, 1980.
Signposts in a Strange Land. Edited with an introduction by Patrick Samway, S. J. New York: Farrar, Straus, and Giroux, 1991.
The Thanatos Syndrome. New York: Farrar, Straus, and Giroux, 1987.

OTHER SOURCES

Amato, Elizabeth. "The Pursuit of Happiness in the American Regime." Ph.D. Dissertation, Department of Political Science, Baylor University, 2011.
Appiah, Kwame Anthony. *The Honor Code: How Moral Revolutions Happen*. New York: W.W. Norton, 2010.
Aristotle. *Nicomachean Ethics*. Trans. Martin Ostwald. Upper Saddle River: Prentice Hall, 1999.
Arkes, Hadley. *First Things: An Inquiry into the First Principles of Morals and Justice*. Princeton: Princeton University Press, 1986.
Armstrong, Karen. *A Short History of Myth*. New York: Canongate, 2005.
Arnhart, Larry. *Darwinian Natural Right*. Albany: SUNY Press, 1998.
Augustine. *The Confessions*. Trans. Henry Chadwick. Oxford: Oxford University Press. 1998.
Baym, Nancy K. *Personal Connections in the Digital Age*. New York: Polity, 2010.

Beckwith, Francis J., Robert P. George, and Susan McWilliams (eds). *First Things: A Case for Conservative Politics; The Hadley Arkes Festschrift*. South Bend, IN: St. Augustine's Press, 2013.

Bowman, James. *Honor: A History*. New York: Encounter Books, 2006.

Bradford, M.E. *The Reactionary Imperative: Essays Literary and Political*. New York: Open Court, 1999.

Brooks, Cleanth. "Walker Percy and Modern Gnosticism." *Southern Review*. Vol. 13 (1977).

Broughton, Panthea Reid (ed.) *The Art of Walker Percy: Stratagems for Being*. Baton Rouge: Louisiana State University Press, 1979.

Buber, Martin. *I and Thou*. Trans. Walker Kaufmann. New York: Touchstone, 1970.

Budziszewski, J. *The Revenge of Conscience: Politics and the Fall of Man*. Eugene, OR: Wipf and Stock, 2010.

Camus, Albert. *The Rebel: An Essay on Man in Revolt*. Trans. Anthony Bower. New York: Vintage, 1991.

Ceaser, James W. *Liberal Democracy and Political Science*. Baltimore and London: Johns Hopkins University Press, 1990.

Ciuba, Gary M. *Walker Percy: Books of Revelations*. Athens and London: University of Georgia Press, 1991.

Dalrymple, Theodore. *Life at the Bottom: The Worldview of the Underclass*. Chicago: Ivan R. Dee, 2001.

Dawson, Doyne. *The Origins of Western Warfare: Militarism and Morality in the Ancient World*. Boulder: Westview Press, 1996.

Delbanco, Andrew. *The Real American Dream: A Meditation on Hope*. Cambridge: Harvard University Press, 1999.

Desmond, John F. *Walker Percy's Search for Community*. Athens and London: University of Georgia Press, 2004.

———. "Walker Percy and Suicide." *Modern Age*. Vol. 47, No. 1 (Winter 2005).

Dewey, John. *Freedom and Culture*. Amherst, New York: Prometheus Books, 1989.

DiLorenzo, Thomas. *The Real Lincoln: A New Look at Abraham Lincoln, His Agenda, and an Unnecessary War*. New York: Crown Forum, 2003.

Donovan, Jack. *The Way of Men*. Cascadia, OR: Dissonant Hum. 2013.

———. *Becoming a Barbarian*. Cascadia, OR: Dissonant Hum. 2016.

Dunkelheim, Marc J. *The Vanishing Neighbor: The Transformation of American Community*. New York: W.W. Norton, 2014.

Dupuy, Edward J. *Autobiography in Walker Percy: Repetition, Recovery, and Redemption*. Baton Rouge: Louisiana State University Press, 1996.

Ellickson, Robert C. *Order without Law: How Neighbors Settle Disputes*. Cambridge: Harvard University Press, 1991.

Edmonson, Henry T., III. *John Dewey and the Decline of American Education*. Wilmington: ISI Books, 2006.

Etizoni, Amitai. *The Spirit of Community: The Reinvention of American Society*. New York: Touchstone, 1994.

Frankl, Victor. *Man's Search for Meaning*. New York: Beacon Press, 2006.

———. *The Feeling of Meaninglessness: A Challenge to Psychotherapy and Philosophy*. Milwaukee: Marquette University Press, 2010.

George, Alexander. "The 'Operational Code': A Neglected Approach to the Study of Political Leaders and Decision-Making." *International Studies Quarterly*. Vol. 13 (June 1969).

Gray, J. Glenn. *The Warriors: Reflections on Men in Battle*. Lincoln: University of Nebraska Press, 1998.

Hankins, Peter S. *The Language of Grace: Flannery O'Connor, Walker Percy, and Iris Murdoch*. New York: Seabury Classics, 2004.

Harwell, David Horace. *Walker Percy Remembered: A Portrait in the Words of Those Who Knew Him*. Chapel Hill: University of North Carolina Press, 2006.

Hayek, Friedrich A. *The Constitution of Liberty*. Ed. Ronald Hamowy. Chicago: University of Chicago Press, 2011.

———. *The Counter-Revolution of Science: Studies on the Abuse of Reason*. Indianapolis: Liberty Fund, 1979.

Herf, Jeffrey. *Reactionary Modernism: Technology, Culture, and Politics in Weimar and the Third Reich*. Cambridge: Cambridge University Press, 1984.

Herman, Arthur. *The Idea of Decline in Western History*. New York: The Free Press, 1997.

Hill, Charles. *Grand Strategies: Literature, Statecraft, and World Order*. New Haven: Yale University Press, 2010.

Hillman, James. *A Terrible Love of War*. New York: Penguin, 2004.

Hobson, Linda Whitney. *Understanding Walker Percy*. Columbia: University of South Carolina Press, 1988.

Hollis, Martin. *The Philosophy of Social Science: An Introduction*. Revised edition. Cambridge: Cambridge University Press: 2002.

Howland, Mary Deems. *The Gift of the Other: Gabriel Marcel's Concept of Intersubjectivity in Walker Percy's Novels*. Pittsburgh: Dusquene University Press, 1990.

Huxley, Aldous. *Brave New World*. Garden City, New York: Doubleday. 1974.

James, William. *Writings, 1902–1910*. New York: Literary Classics of the United States, 1988.

Jones, George Fenwick. *Honor in German Literature*. Chapel Hill: University of North Carolina Press, 1959.

Jünger, Ernst. *Storm of Steel*. Trans. Michael Hofmann. New York: Penguin, 2004.

Kerouac, Jack. *On the Road*. New York: Penguin, 1999.

Krause, Sharon. *Liberalism with Honor*. Cambridge: Harvard University Press, 2002.

Lal, Deepak. *Poverty and Progress: Realities and Myths about Global Poverty*. Washington, DC: Cato Press, 2013.

Lampert, Lawrence. *Nietzsche's Teaching: An Interpretation of Thus Spoke Zarathustra*. New Haven: Yale University Press, 1986.

———. *Nietzsche's Task: An Interpretation of Beyond Good and Evil*. New Haven: Yale University Press, 2001.

Lawler, Peter Augustine. *Postmodernism Rightly Understood: The Return to Realism in American Thought*. Lanham, MD: Rowman and Littlefield, 1999.

———. *Aliens in America: The Strange Truth about Our Souls*. Wilmington: ISI Books, 2002.

———. *Stuck with Virtue: The American Individual and Our Biotechnological Future*. Wilmington: ISI Books, 2005.

Lawler, Peter Augustine, and Brian A. Smith (eds.) *A Political Companion to Walker Percy*. Lexington: University Press of Kentucky, 2013.

Lawson, Lewis A., and Victor A. Kramer. *Conversations with Walker Percy*. Jackson: University Press of Mississippi, 1985.

———. *More Conversations with Walker Percy*. Jackson: University Press of Mississippi. 1993.

Lebow, Richard Ned. *A Cultural Theory of International Relations*. Cambridge: Cambridge University Press, 2008.

———. *The Tragic Vision of Politics: Ethics, Interests and Orders*. Cambridge: Cambridge University Press, 2003.

Lewis, C.S. *Surprised by Joy: The Shape of My Early Life*. New York: Harcourt Brace, 1955.

———. *The Abolition of Man*. New York: HarperCollins, 2001.

Luschei, Martin. *The Sovereign Wayfarer: Walker Percy's Diagnosis of the Malaise*. Baton Rouge: Louisiana State University Press, 1972.

Manicas, Peter T. *A Realist Philosophy of Social Science: Explanation and Understanding*. Cambridge: Cambridge University Press, 2006.

Mansfield, Harvey C. *Manliness*. New Haven: Yale University Press, 2006.

Martin, Jay. *The Education of John Dewey*. New York: Columbia University Press, 2002.

McClay, Wilfred. *The Masterless: Self and Society in America*. Chapel Hill: University of North Carolina Press, 1994.

———. "The Moral Equivalent of War?" *National Affairs*, No. 5 (Fall 2010).

McCloskey, Deirdre. *Bourgeois Dignity: Why Economics Can't Explain the Modern World*. Chicago: University of Chicago Press, 2010.

Minogue, Kenneth. *The Servile Mind: How Democracy Erodes the Moral Life*. New York: Encounter Books, 2010.

Mitchell, Joshua. *The Fragility of Freedom: Tocqueville on Religion, Democracy, and the Human Future*. Chicago: University of Chicago Press, 1995.

———. "Religion is Not a Preference." *The Journal of Politics*, Vol. 69, No. 2 (May 2007).

———. "A Reply to My Critics." *The Journal of Politics*. Vol. 70, No. 3 (July 2008).

Montgomery, Marion. *Eudora Welty & Walker Percy: The Concept of Home in their Lives and Literature*. Jefferson, NC: McFarland & Company, 2004.

Mosse, George L. *Fallen Soldiers: Reshaping the Memory of the World Wars*. Oxford: Oxford University Press, 1990.

Murray, Williamson and Richard Hart Sinnreich (eds.) *The Past as Prologue: The Importance of History to the Military Profession*. Cambridge: Cambridge University Press, 2006.

Nietzsche, Friedrich. *Thus Spoke Zarathurstra*. Trans. Walter Kaufmann. New York: Penguin, 1978.

Nisbet, Robert. *The Quest for Community: A Study in the Ethics of Order and Freedom*. Wilmington: ISI Books, 2010.

Oldenburg, Ray. *The Great Good Place: Cafes, Coffee Shops, Bookstores, Bars, Hair Salons, and Other Hangouts at the Heart of a Community*. Emeryville, CA: Avalon Publishing Group, 1999.

Orwell, George. *1984*. New York: Penguin, 2013.

———. *Politics and the English Language*. New York: Penguin, 2013.

Peirce, Charles Sanders. *Selected Writings (Values in a Universe of Chance)*. Ed. Philip P. Wiener. New York: Dover, 1958.

Percy, William Alexander. *Lanterns on the Levee: Recollections of a Planter's Son*. Baton Rouge: Louisiana State University Press, 1973.

Petigny, Alan C. *The Permissive Society: America, 1941–1965*. Cambridge: Cambridge University Press, 2009.

Poteat, Patricia Lewis. *Walker Percy and the Old Modern Age: Reflections on Language, Argument, and the Telling of Stories*. Baton Rouge: Louisiana State University Press, 1985.

Prigden, Allen. *Walker Percy's Sacramental Landscapes: The Search in the Desert*. Selinsgrove, PA: Susquehanna University Press, 2000.

Putnam, Robert. *Bowling Alone: The Collapse and Revival of American Community*. New York: Simon and Schuster, 2000.

Rousseau, Jean-Jacques. *Basic Political Writings*. Trans. Donald A. Cress. Indianapolis: Hackett Publishing, 1987.

Ryn, Claes G. *America the Virtuous: The Crisis of Democracy and the Quest for Empire*. New Brunswick: Transaction Publishing, 2003.

Samuels, Richard. *Machiavelli's Children: Leaders and Their Legacies in Italy and Japan*. Ithaca: Cornell University Press, 2003.

Samway, Patrick, S.J. (ed.) *A Thief of Peirce: The Letters of Kenneth Laine Ketner and Walker Percy*. Jackson: University Press of Mississippi, 1995.

———. *Walker Percy: A Life*. Chicago: Loyola Press, 1997.

Scheureman, William E. *Carl Schmitt: The End of Law*. Lanham: Rowman and Littlefield, 1999.

Schmitt, Carl. *The Concept of the Political*. Expanded edition. Translated with an Introduction by George Schwab. Chicago: University of Chicago Press, 2007.

Scott, James C. *Seeing Like A State: How Certain Schemes to Improve the Human Condition Have Failed*. New Haven: Yale University Press, 1999.

Singer, Peter. *Rethinking Life and Death: The Collapse of Our Traditional Ethics*. New York: St. Martin's, 1994.

Sitman, Matthew, and Brian A. Smith. "The Rift in the Modern Mind: Tocqueville and Percy on the Rise of the Cartesian Self." *Perspectives on Political Science*. Vol. 36, No. 1. (Winter 2007).

Skinner, Quentin (ed.) *The Return of Grand Theory in the Human Sciences*. Cambridge: Cambridge University Press, 1985.

Smith, Adam. *An Inquiry into the Nature and Causes of the Wealth of Nations*. 2 volumes. Eds. R.H. Campbell, A.S. Skinner, W.B. Todd. Indianapolis: Liberty Fund, 1981.

———. *Lectures on Jurisprudence*. Eds. R.L. Meek, D.D. Raphael, and P.G. Stein. Indianapolis: Liberty Fund, 1982.

Smith, Brian A. "Losing Sight of Man: Percy and Tocqueville on the Fate of the Human Sciences." *Perspectives on Political Science,* Vol. 40, No. 3 (July-September 2011).

Stewart, Frank Henderson. *Honor*. Chicago: University of Chicago Press, 1994.

Strauss, Leo. *Natural Right and History*. Chicago: University of Chicago Press, 1953.
Stromberg, Roland N. *Redemption by War: The Intellectuals and 1914*. Lawrence: The Regent's Press of Kansas, 1982.
Sweeny, Mary K. *Walker Percy and the Postmodern World*. Chicago: Loyola University Press, 1987.
Taylor, Charles. *A Secular Age*. Cambridge, MA: Belknap/Harvard University Press, 2007.
Taylor, Jerome. *In Search of the Self: Life, Death and Walker Percy*. Cambridge, MA: Cowley Publications, 1986.
Tharpe, Jac. *Walker Percy*. Boston: Twayne Publishers, 1983.
Thompson, Norma. *Unreasonable Doubt: Circumstantial Evidence and the Art of Judgment*. Philadelphia: Paul Dry Books, 2011.
de Tocqueville, Alexis. *Democracy in America*. Trans. George Lawrence. Ed. J. P. Mayer. New York: Harper, 1969.
———. *Memoir on Pauperism*. Trans. Seymour Drescher. Chicago: Ivan R. Dee, 1997.
Tolson, Jay. *Pilgrim in the Ruins: A Life of Walker Percy*. Chapel Hill: University of North Carolina Press, 1994.
Turkle, Sherry. *Alone Together: Why We Expect More from Technology and Less from Each Other*. New York: Basic Books, 2012.
Voegelin, Eric. *Science, Politics & Gnosticism*. Wilmington: ISI Books, 2004.
Waller, Bruce N. *Against Moral Responsibility*. Cambridge: MIT Press, 2011.
Waltz, Kenneth N. "The Origins of War in Neorealist Theory." *The Journal of Interdisciplinary History*, Vol. 18, No. 4 (Spring 1988).
———. *Theory of International Politics*. Bosston: McGraw Hill, 1979.
Weaver, Richard M. *The Ethics of Rhetoric*. Davis, CA: Hermagoras Press, 1985.
Westbrook, Robert B. *John Dewey and American Democracy*. Ithaca: Cornell University Press, 1991.
Wilcox, Clyde, Kenneth D. Wald, and Ted G. Jelen. "Religious Preferences and Social Science: A Second Look." *The Journal of Politics*, Vol. 70, No. 3 (July 2008).
Wiley, Norbert. *The Semiotic Self*. Chicago: University of Chicago Press, 1994.
Wise, Benjamin E. *William Alexander Percy: The Curious Life of a Mississippi Planter and Sexual Freethinker*. Chapel Hill: University of North Carolina Press, 2012.
Wyatt-Brown, Bertram. *The House of Percy: Honor, Melancholy, and Imagination in a Southern Family*. New York and Oxford: Oxford University Press, 1994.
———. *Southern Honor: Ethics & Behavior in the Old South*. Oxford and New York: Oxford University Press, 2007.
Zerubavel, Eviatar. *Social Mindscapes: An Invitation to Cognitive Sociology*. Cambridge: Harvard University Press, 1997.

Index

About the Author

Brian A. Smith is associate professor and deputy chair in the Department of Political Science and Law at Montclair State University, where he has taught since 2009. In addition to his work on politics and literature, he has published extensively on Adam Smith, Edmund Burke, and Alexis de Tocqueville. He was educated at Moorpark College, UCLA, and Georgetown University.